An Essential Guide to Music in the 1970s

JOHNNY ZERO

PARKBENCH PUBLICATIONS

Published in Great Britain by Parkbench Publications,
PO Box 1081, Belfast BT1 9EP

ISBN 978-0-9555756-5-5

Designed and typeset by Bookcraft Ltd,
Stroud, Gloucestershire
Printed and bound in Great Britain by
CPI Antony Rowe, Eastbourne

PROLOGUE

This "brilliant compendium" (author's own words) is a sharp reminder to any silly people out there in book-reading land who erroneously feel that popular music ended on the 31st of December 1969. Equally, it is a "stunning riposte" (author's own words again) to any silly souls who mistakenly suggest that popular music was born on the 1st of January 1980. Mind you, if one were to assume that popular music did indeed emerge from its mother's womb in January 1980, then the sounds that preceded this date would presumably constitute pre-history. Given that some of the artists of the 1970s have been described even by their own contemporaries as "dinosaurs", perhaps there is a grain of truth in this statement.

Meanwhile back at the ranch, this "worthwhile volume" (quoting the author) is neither intended to bury nor praise the sounds of the 'seventies. The author accepts that this turbulent decade possessed both its fair share of quality songs as well as forgettable stuff, some of which made cringeworthy progress towards the top of various hit parades. Record buyers of yesteryear, what indeed were you thinking of? Instead, this "essential guide" (quoting the author again) is merely a factual reminder of the good, the bad, and the ugly of the music scene in the 1970s.

Those who lived through the highs and lows of the 'seventies will have experienced a range of emotions, conditioned by their own personal experiences, as well as by the unfolding world events. The musical contents contained within thus form a soundtrack that will evoke a variety of memories, as well as being a curious museum piece for those post–70s children who fortunately or unfortunately missed out on this tumultuous decade.

Aside from the "huge and impressive welter of statistics" (according to the author), I have assembled what I consider to be the best songs and albums of the 'seventies, whilst also throwing in a plethora of news headlines and sporting highlights which collectively contribute to the fabric of a decade that included the end of the Vietnam War, Nixon and Watergate, troubles in Ulster, the Munich massacre, the raid on Entebbe, oil crisis, industrial unrest, economic recessions, international terrorism, the Cold War, and such sporting greats as Muhammad Ali, Bjorn Borg, and Jack Nicklaus, as well as such musical legends as Abba, Marc Bolan, David Bowie, Elton John, and Queen, not forgetting the deaths of Jimi Hendrix, Elvis Presley, and John Wayne. The 'seventies were nothing, if not dull. I trust that this mini-encyclopedia does justice to the sounds that dominated the airwaves whilst the world kept turning for better ... or for worse.

Johnny Zero, August 2008

ABOUT THE AUTHOR
(Plus Credit Where Credit is Due)

The author's own sad story can be traced back to 1969 when he began life imprisoned inside his mummy's tummy. The writer then daringly escaped this nine month captivity in September of that year, though his attempts to run away hopelessly failed. To cut a long story short, the author evolved from a little baby in the 1970s into a big baby in the 21st century. He would at this point in the proceedings like to take the opportunity to thank the following: Gary Watton (he was an enormous help to me, bless him); Sean Walshe (with an E!); Christine "burr with me" Traversari; John 'Old Shep' Sheppard; Tommy Dangerous; and not forgetting the 150 staff employed 24 hours per day, seven days a week at my fan club who are constantly mailing pin-up posters, badges, and other souvenirs to my thousands of readers. Credit ought to be apportioned to the following sources that I exploited as part of my 'fact-finding mission': the BBC Charts; www.polyhex.com <http://.www.polyhex.com/>; www.yearsofgold.org.uk <http://www.yearsof-gold.org.uk/>; and www.popreport.co.uk <http://www.popreport.co.uk/> as well as to google and wikipedia too!

The UK Top 10 singles for the week ending January the 3rd

1   Rolf Harris   Two Little Boys
2   Kenny Rogers And The First Edition Ruby Don't Take Your Love To Town
3   The Archies   Sugar Sugar
4   Elvis Presley   Suspicious Minds
5   Blue Mink   Melting Pot
6   Stevie Wonder   Yester Me Yester You
7   Bobbie Gentry And Glen Campbell All I Have To Do Is Dream
8   Engelbert Humperdinck   Winter World Of Love
9   The Cufflinks   Tracy
10 Tom Jones   Without Love

The US Number One single: B.J. Thomas – Raindrops Keep Fallin' On My Head
The US Number One album: Beatles – Abbey Road
The UK Number One album: Beatles – Abbey Road
Also this week: The age of consent in Britain is reduced to eighteen. (1st)

The UK Top 10 singles for the week ending January the 10th

1   Rolf Harris   Two Little Boys
2   Kenny Rogers And The First Edition Ruby Don't Take Your Love To Town
3   Blue Mink   Melting Pot
4   The Cufflinks   Tracy
5   Bobbie Gentry And Glen Campbell All I Have To Do Is Dream
6   The Archies   Sugar Sugar
7   Elvis Presley   Suspicious Minds
8   Dave Clark Five   Good Old Rock And Roll
9   Stevie Wonder   Yester Me Yester You
10 Harry J. And The All Stars   The Liquidator

The US Number One single: B.J. Thomas – Raindrops Keep Fallin' On My Head
The US Number One album: Beatles – Abbey Road
The UK Number One album: Beatles – Abbey Road
Also this week: Three thousand British people have died from flu this year. (9th)

The UK Top 10 singles for the week ending January the 17th

1 Rolf Harris   Two Little Boys
2 Elvis Presley   Suspicious Minds
3 Bobbie Gentry And Glen Campbell   All I Have To Do Is Dream
4 Kenny Rogers And The First Edition   Ruby Don't Take Your Love To Town
5 The Cufflinks   Tracy
6 The Archies   Sugar Sugar
7 Blue Mink   Melting Pot
8 Dave Clark Five   Good Old Rock And Roll
9 Marmalade   Reflections Of My Life
10 Badfinger   Come And Get It

The US Number One single: B.J. Thomas – Raindrops Keep Fallin' On My Head
The US Number One album: Led Zeppelin – Led Zeppelin II
The UK Number One album: Beatles – Abbey Road
Also this week: Conflict in Nigeria ends with the surrender of Biafra. (12th)

The UK Top 10 singles for the week ending January the 24th

1 Rolf Harris   Two Little Boys
2 Kenny Rogers And The First Edition   Ruby Don't Take Your Love To Town
3 Marmalade   Reflections Of My Life
4 Bobbie Gentry And Glen Campbell   All I Have To Do Is Dream
5 The Cufflinks   Tracy
6 Elvis Presley   Suspicious Minds
7 Dave Clark Five   Good Old Rock And Roll
8 Badfinger   Come And Get It
9 The Archies   Sugar Sugar
10 Blue Mink   Melting Pot

The US Number One single: B.J. Thomas – Raindrops Keep Fallin' On My Head
The US Number One album: Beatles – Abbey Road
The UK Number One album: Beatles – Abbey Road
Also this week: The first 'Jumbo' jet arrives in London from New York. (23rd)

The UK Top 10 singles for the week ending January the 31st

1 Edison Lighthouse   Love Grows (Where My Rosemary Goes)
2 Rolf Harris   Two Little Boys
3 Marmalade   Reflections Of My Life
4 Badfinger   Come And Get It
5 Bobbie Gentry And Glen Campbell   All I Have To Do Is Dream
6 Elvis Presley   Suspicious Minds
7 Kenny Rogers And The First Edition   Ruby Don't Take Your Love To Town
8 Arrival   Friends
9 Peter, Paul & Mary   Leaving On A Jet Plane
10 Jethro Tull   The Witch's Promise/Teacher

The US Number One single: Jackson 5 – I Want You Back
The US Number One album: Led Zeppelin – Led Zeppelin II
The UK Number One album: Beatles – Abbey Road
Also this week: Three British diplomats are expelled from Warsaw. (27th)

Song of the month for January 1970

The Only Living Boy In New York by Simon And Garfunkel (album track)

The 1970s could hardly have made a more impressive start with the release of Simon and Garfunkel's farewell project, 'Bridge Over Troubled Water'. The album not surprisingly climbed to the summit of the American and British charts, assisted in no small way by the success of the title track in the singles listings. In truth, there are at least half a dozen songs which could have coped more than adequately in the hit parade. Chief among them is perhaps 'The Only Living Boy In New York'. This item was decorated by spectacular harmonies as Paul Simon takes centre stage on a composition that is quite breath-taking. The tune is undoubtedly a strong contender for the best album track of the 'seventies.

The UK Top 10 singles for the week ending February the 7th

1	Edison Lighthouse	Love Grows (Where My Rosemary Goes)
2	Rolf Harris	Two Little Boys
3	Marmalade	Reflections Of My Life
4	Peter, Paul & Mary	Leaving On A Jet Plane
5	Badfinger	Come And Get It
6	Jethro Tull	The Witch's Promise/Teacher
7	Kenny Rogers And The First Edition	Ruby Don't Take Your Love To Town
8	Chicago	I'm A Man
9	Arrival	Friends
10	Mary Hopkin	Temma Harbour

The US Number One single: Shocking Blue – Venus
The US Number One album: Led Zeppelin – Led Zeppelin II
The UK Number One album: Led Zeppelin – Led Zeppelin II
Also this week: The first nerve transplant is performed in Munich. (2nd)

The UK Top 10 singles for the week ending February the 14th

1	Edison Lighthouse	Love Grows (Where My Rosemary Goes)
2	Peter, Paul & Mary	Leaving On A Jet Plane
3	Canned Heat	Let's Work Together
4	Jethro Tull	The Witch's Promise/Teacher
5	Badfinger	Come And Get It
6	Marmalade	Reflections Of My Life
7	Rolf Harris	Two Little Boys
8	Mary Hopkin	Temma Harbour
9	Chicago	I'm A Man
10	Shocking Blue	Venus

The US Number One single: Sly & The Family Stone – Thank You/Everybody Is A Star
The US Number One album: Led Zeppelin – Led Zeppelin II
The UK Number One album: Various Artist Compilation – Motown Chartbusters, Volume 3
Also this week: A bomb wrecks the Saigon National Press Centre. (8th)

The UK Top 10 singles for the week ending February the 21st

1	Edison Lighthouse	Love Grows (Where My Rosemary Goes)
2	Canned Heat	Let's Work Together
3	Peter, Paul & Mary	Leaving On A Jet Plane
4	Jackson 5	I Want You Back
5	Lee Marvin	Wand'rin' Star
6	Mary Hopkin	Temma Harbour
7	John Lennon	Instant Karma
8	Jethro Tull	The Witch's Promise/Teacher
9	Shocking Blue	Venus
10	Rolf Harris	Two Little Boys

The US Number One single: Sly & The Family Stone – Thank You/Everybody Is A Star
The US Number One album: Led Zeppelin – Led Zeppelin II
The UK Number One album: Simon And Garfunkel – Bridge Over Troubled Water
Also this week: Joe Frazier becomes the world heavyweight boxing champion. (16th)

The UK Top 10 singles for the week ending February the 28th

1	Edison Lighthouse	Love Grows (Where My Rosemary Goes)
2	Lee Marvin	Wand'rin' Star
3	Canned Heat	Let's Work Together
4	Jackson 5	I Want You Back
5	John Lennon	Instant Karma
6	Peter, Paul & Mary	Leaving On A Jet Plane
7	Mary Hopkin	Temma Harbour
8	Shocking Blue	Venus
9	White Plains	My Baby Loves Loving
10	Brotherhood Of Man	United We Stand

The US Number One single: Simon And Garfunkel – Bridge Over Troubled Water
The US Number One album: Led Zeppelin – Led Zeppelin II
The UK Number One album: Simon And Garfunkel – Bridge Over Troubled Water
Also this week: Rupert Murdoch sacks the News Of The World's editor. (26th)

Song of the month for February 1970

Instant Karma by John Lennon (peak chart position: No.5)

'Instant Karma' was instant by name and instant by nature as it was recorded and released in a mere three weeks. Remarkably, whilst this marvellous single proceeded into a lofty position in the Transatlantic charts, many folk still harboured the illusion that John Lennon was simply taking a little sabbatical from the Beatles. However, the success of Lennon's third solo single would have fortified his desire to obtain his 'divorce' from the Fab Four. The bespectacled one even appeared on 'Top Of The Pops' with his previously long hair cropped off – further signs of a soul desperately keen to break from his past and plot new territory. As for 'Instant Karma', it was another of those sing-along anthems that John Lennon turned into an art form.

The UK Top 10 singles for the week ending March the 7th

1	Lee Marvin	Wand'rin' Star
2	Jackson 5	I Want You Back
3	Canned Heat	Let's Work Together
4	Edison Lighthouse	Love Grows (Where My Rosemary Goes)
5	John Lennon	Instant Karma
6	Peter, Paul & Mary	Leaving On A Jet Plane
7	Simon And Garfunkel	Bridge Over Troubled Water
8	Herman's Hermits	Years May Come
9	White Plains	My Baby Loves Loving
10	Mary Hopkin	Temma Harbour

The US Number One single: Simon And Garfunkel – Bridge Over Troubled Water
The US Number One album: Simon And Garfunkel – Bridge Over Troubled Water
The UK Number One album: Simon And Garfunkel – Bridge Over Troubled Water
Also this week: The rebel colony of Rhodesia becomes a republic. (2nd)

The UK Top 10 singles for the week ending March the 14th

1	Lee Marvin	Wand'rin' Star
2	Beatles	Let It Be
3	Simon And Garfunkel	Bridge Over Troubled Water
4	Jackson 5	I Want You Back
5	Edison Lighthouse	Love Grows (Where My Rosemary Goes)
6	John Lennon	Instant Karma
7	Canned Heat	Let's Work Together
8	Pickettywitch	That Same Old Feeling
9	Herman's Hermits	Years May Come
10	Sacha Distel	Raindrops Keep Falling On My Head

The US Number One single: Simon And Garfunkel – Bridge Over Troubled Water
The US Number One album: Simon And Garfunkel – Bridge Over Troubled Water
The UK Number One album: Simon And Garfunkel – Bridge Over Troubled Water
Also this week: Archbishop Makarios survives an assassination attempt in Cyprus. (8th)

The UK Top 10 singles for the week ending March the 21st

1	Lee Marvin	Wand'rin' Star
2	Simon And Garfunkel	Bridge Over Troubled Water
3	Beatles	Let It Be
4	Jackson 5	I Want You Back
5	Pickettywitch	That Same Old Feeling
6	Andy Williams	Can't Help Falling In Love
7	Herman's Hermits	Years May Come
8	Elvis Presley	Don't Cry Daddy
9	Steam	Na Na Hey Hey Kiss Him Goodbye
10	John Lennon	Instant Karma

The US Number One single: Simon And Garfunkel – Bridge Over Troubled Water
The US Number One album: Simon And Garfunkel – Bridge Over Troubled Water
The UK Number One album: Simon And Garfunkel – Bridge Over Troubled Water
Also this week: Cambodia's Prince Sihanouk is ousted in a right-wing coup. (18th)

The UK Top 10 singles for the week ending March the 28th

1	Simon And Garfunkel	Bridge Over Troubled Water
2	Lee Marvin	Wand'rin' Star
3	Andy Williams	Can't Help Falling In Love
4	Beatles	Let It Be
5	Pickettywitch	That Same Old Feeling
6	Bob And Marcia	Young Gifted And Black
7	Mary Hopkin	Knock Knock Who's There
8	Dave Clark Five	Everybody Get Together
9	Elvis Presley	Don't Cry Daddy
10	Steam	Na Na Hey Hey Kiss Him Goodbye

The US Number One single: Simon And Garfunkel – Bridge Over Troubled Water

The US Number One album: Simon And Garfunkel – Bridge Over Troubled Water

The UK Number One album: Simon And Garfunkel – Bridge Over Troubled Water

Also this week: Eighteen British thalidomide children are awarded compensation. (23rd)

Song of the month for March 1970

Young Gifted And Black by Bob And Marcia
(peak chart position:No.5)

'Young Gifted And Black' was the latest success story for Jamaica's Trojan Records. One half of the performing duo was Marcia Griffiths who would later provide harmonies as a member of Bob Marley's backing band, the I-Threes. She was assisted in this duet by the American, Bob Andy. The song's subject matter was unashamedly an anthem of black consciousness, exhorting young black people to step forth and embrace the changing world with pride and confidence. Whatever the worthy sentiments, the single was sufficiently enjoyable to attract record buyers of all races and colours, hence its lofty chart position.

The UK Top 10 singles for the week ending April the 4th

1	Simon And Garfunkel	Bridge Over Troubled Water
2	Mary Hopkin	Knock Knock Who's There
3	Andy Williams	Can't Help Falling In Love
4	Lee Marvin	Wand'rin' Star
5	Bob And Marcia	Young Gifted And Black
6	Pickettywitch	That Same Old Feeling
7	Beatles	Let It Be
8	Kenny Rogers	Something's Burning
9	Dave Clark Five	Everybody Get Together
10	Elvis Presley	Don't Cry Daddy

The US Number One single: Simon And Garfunkel – Bridge Over Troubled Water
The US Number One album: Simon And Garfunkel – Bridge Over Troubled Water
The UK Number One album: Simon And Garfunkel – Bridge Over Troubled Water
Also this week: Cambodia complains to the US about Viet Cong incursions. (30th)

The UK Top 10 singles for the week ending April the 11th

1	Simon And Garfunkel	Bridge Over Troubled Water
2	Dana	All Kinds Of Everything
3	Andy Williams	Can't Help Falling In Love
4	Mary Hopkin	Knock Knock Who's There
5	Lee Marvin	Wand'rin' Star
6	Norman Greenbaum	Spirit In The Sky
7	Pickettywitch	That Same Old Feeling
8	Bob And Marcia	Young Gifted And Black
9	Kenny Rogers	Something's Burning
10	The Pipkins	Gimme Dat Ding

The US Number One single: Beatles – Let It Be
The US Number One album: Simon And Garfunkel – Bridge Over Troubled Water
The UK Number One album: Simon And Garfunkel – Bridge Over Troubled Water
Also this week: Paul McCartney announces that the Beatles are splitting up. (9th)

The UK Top 10 singles for the week ending April the 18th

1	Dana	All Kinds Of Everything
2	Simon And Garfunkel	Bridge Over Troubled Water
3	Andy Williams	Can't Help Falling In Love
4	Mary Hopkin	Knock Knock Who's There
5	Norman Greenbaum	Spirit In The Sky
6	The Pipkins	Gimme Dat Ding
7	Bob And Marcia	Young Gifted And Black
8	Lee Marvin	Wand'rin' Star
9	Jimmy Ruffin	Farewell Is A Lonely Sound
10	The Four Tops	I Can't Help Myself

The US Number One single: Beatles – Let It Be
The US Number One album: Simon And Garfunkel – Bridge Over Troubled Water
The UK Number One album: Simon And Garfunkel – Bridge Over Troubled Water
Also this week: Apollo Thirteen returns safely to planet earth. (17th)

The UK Top 10 singles for the week ending April the 25th

1	Dana	All Kinds Of Everything
2	Norman Greenbaum	Spirit In The Sky
3	Simon And Garfunkel	Bridge Over Troubled Water
4	Andy Williams	Can't Help Falling In Love
5	Mary Hopkin	Knock Knock Who's There
6	The Pipkins	Gimme Dat Ding
7	Bob And Marcia	Young Gifted And Black
8	Stevie Wonder	Never Had A Dream Come True
9	Jimmy Ruffin	Farewell Is A Lonely Sound
10	Blue Mink	Good Morning Freedom

The US Number One single: Jackson 5 – ABC
The US Number One album: Simon And Garfunkel – Bridge Over Troubled Water
The UK Number One album: Simon And Garfunkel – Bridge Over Troubled Water
Also this week: Bernice Rubens wins the Booker Prize for 'The Elected Member'. (21st)

Song of the month for April 1970

Back Home by The England World Cup Squad
(peak chart position:No.1)

It is peculiar to think that the England football team's World Cup 1970 rallying call should have been composed by a Scotsman (Bill Martin) and a Northern Irishman (Phil Coulter). Although the current world football champions were agonisingly evicted at the quarter-finals by West Germany, Bobby Moore and the rest of the squad found themselves reaching the summit of the singles chart. The trouble was that the success of this record prompted other football teams to subsequently cash in on their cup final appearances and irritatingly release their own signature tunes. Meanwhile, the celtic songwriting duo of Coulter and Martin would find further chart success when their material was performed by the likes of Elvis Presley and Slik.

The UK Top 10 singles for the week ending May the 2nd

1	Norman Greenbaum	Spirit In The Sky
2	Dana	All Kinds Of Everything
3	England World Cup Squad	Back Home
4	Simon And Garfunkel	Bridge Over Troubled Water
5	Andy Williams	Can't Help Falling In Love
6	Stevie Wonder	Never Had A Dream Come True
7	The Pipkins	Gimme Dat Ding
8	Jimmy Ruffin	Farewell Is A Lonely Sound
9	Frijid Pink	House Of The Rising Sun
10	The Cufflinks	When Julie Comes Around

The US Number One single: Jackson 5 – ABC
The US Number One album: Simon And Garfunkel – Bridge Over Troubled Water
The UK Number One album: Simon And Garfunkel – Bridge Over Troubled Water
Also this week: US troops attack Communist bases in Cambodia. (30th)

The UK Top 10 singles for the week ending May the 9th

1	Norman Greenbaum	Spirit In The Sky
2	England World Cup Squad	Back Home
3	Dana	All Kinds Of Everything
4	Simon And Garfunkel	Bridge Over Troubled Water
5	Tom Jones	Daughter Of Darkness
6	Frijid Pink	House Of The Rising Sun
7	Andy Williams	Can't Help Falling In Love
8	Creedence Clearwater Revival	Travelling Band
9	Stevie Wonder	Never Had A Dream Come True
10	Hollies	I Can't Tell The Bottom

The US Number One single: The Guess Who – American Woman/No Sugar Tonight
The US Number One album: Simon And Garfunkel – Bridge Over Troubled Water
The UK Number One album: Simon And Garfunkel – Bridge Over Troubled Water
Also this week: Four protesters are shot dead at Kent State University,Ohio. (4th)

The UK Top 10 singles for the week ending May the 16th

1	England World Cup Squad	Back Home
2	Norman Greenbaum	Spirit In The Sky
3	Moody Blues	Question
4	Frijid Pink	House Of The Rising Sun
5	Dana	All Kinds Of Everything
6	Christie	Yellow River
7	Hollies	I Can't Tell The Bottom
8	Tom Jones	Daughter Of Darkness
9	Creedence Clearwater Revival	Travelling Band
10	The Move	Brontosaurus

The US Number One single: The Guess Who – American Woman/No Sugar Tonight
The US Number One album: Crosby, Stills, Nash & Young – Deja Vu
The UK Number One album: Simon And Garfunkel – Bridge Over Troubled Water
Also this week: South Africa is banned from competing in the next Olympics. (15th)

The UK Top 10 singles for the week ending May the 23rd

1 England World Cup Squad | Back Home
2 Norman Greenbaum | Spirit In The Sky
3 Christie | Yellow River
4 Moody Blues | Question
5 Tom Jones | Daughter Of Darkness
6 Frijid Pink | House Of The Rising Sun
7 The Move | Brontosaurus
8 Roger Whittaker | I Don't Believe In If
9 Hollies | I Can't Tell The Bottom
10 Dana | All Kinds Of Everything

The US Number One single: The Guess Who – American Woman/No Sugar Tonight
The US Number One album: Paul McCartney – McCartney
The UK Number One album: Beatles – Let It Be
Also this week: Harold Wilson calls a general election for June the 18th. (18th)

The UK Top 10 singles for the week ending May the 30th

1 England World Cup Squad | Back Home
2 Moody Blues | Question
3 Christie | Yellow River
4 Norman Greenbaum | Spirit In The Sky
5 Glen Campbell | Honey Come Back
6 The Supremes | Up The Ladder To The Roof
7 Frijid Pink | House Of The Rising Sun
8 Roger Whittaker | I Don't Believe In If
9 Tom Jones | Daughter Of Darkness
10 The Move | Brontosaurus

The US Number One single: Ray Stevens – Everything Is Beautiful
The US Number One album: Paul McCartney – McCartney
The UK Number One album: Beatles – Let It Be
Also this week: Charles Haughey appears in court, suspected of arms smuggling. (28th)

Song of the month for May 1970

The Long And Winding Road by The Beatles (album track)

It is remarkable to think that Paul McCartney did not actually approve of the final released version of his own composition. Originally conceived as an acoustic piece, Macca's ballad was then given the 'Spector treatment', as North America's ace producer applied his trademark 'wall of sound', assisted by a 'heavenly choir'. The result was a monumental recording that climbed to the top of the American Billboard chart. Although amazingly not released in the United Kingdom as a single, this item was clearly one of the highlights of the Beatles' 'Let It Be' album which saw the light of day at the beginning of May.

The UK Top 10 singles for the week ending June the 6th

1	Christie	Yellow River
2	England World Cup Squad	Back Home
3	Moody Blues	Question
4	Glen Campbell	Honey Come Back
5	Tom Jones	Daughter Of Darkness
6	Ray Stevens	Everything Is Beautiful
7	Mr Bloe	Groovin With Mr Bloe
8	Jackson 5	ABC
9	Norman Greenbaum	Spirit In The Sky
10	The Supremes	Up The Ladder To The Roof

The US Number One single: Ray Stevens – Everything Is Beautiful
The US Number One album: Paul McCartney – McCartney
The UK Number One album: Beatles – Let It Be
Also this week: Tonga becomes independent of Britain. (4th)

The UK Top 10 singles for the week ending June the 13th

1	Mungo Jerry	In The Summertime
2	Christie	Yellow River
3	England World Cup Squad	Back Home
4	Mr Bloe	Groovin With Mr Bloe
5	Glen Campbell	Honey Come Back
6	Moody Blues	Question
7	Beach Boys	Cottonfields
8	The Supremes	Up The Ladder To The Roof
9	Ray Stevens	Everything Is Beautiful
10	Jackson 5	ABC

The US Number One single: Beatles – The Long And Winding Road/For You Blue
The US Number One album: Beatles – Let It Be
The UK Number One album: Simon And Garfunkel – Bridge Over Troubled Water
Also this week: The Who perform their rock opera, 'Tommy', in New York. (7th)

The UK Top 10 singles for the week ending June the 20th

1	Mungo Jerry	In The Summertime
2	Christie	Yellow River
3	Mr Bloe	Groovin With Mr Bloe
4	Free	All Right Now
5	Beach Boys	Cottonfields
6	Glen Campbell	Honey Come Back
7	Gerry Monroe	Sally
8	Ray Stevens	Everything Is Beautiful
9	England World Cup Squad	Back Home
10	Fleetwood Mac	The Green Manalishi

The US Number One single: Beatles – The Long And Winding Road/For You Blue
The US Number One album: Beatles – Let It Be
The UK Number One album: Simon And Garfunkel – Bridge Over Troubled Water
Also this week: West Germany defeat England 3–2 in soccer's World Cup. (14th)

The UK Top 10 singles for the week ending June the 27th

1	Mungo Jerry	In The Summertime
2	Mr Bloe	Groovin With Mr Bloe
3	Free	All Right Now
4	Christie	Yellow River
5	Gerry Monroe	Sally
6	Beach Boys	Cottonfields
7	Cliff Richard	Goodbye Sam Hello Samantha
8	Glen Campbell	Honey Come Back
9	Marvin Gaye	Abraham Martin And John
10	Fleetwood Mac	The Green Manalishi

The US Number One single: Jackson 5 – The Love You Save
The US Number One album: Beatles – Let It Be
The UK Number One album: Simon And Garfunkel – Bridge Over Troubled Water
Also this week: New Prime Minister, Edward Heath, announces his new cabinet. (21st

Song of the month for June 1970
All Right Now by Free (peak chart position:No.2)

Free's first hit single has stood the test of time as one of the most enduring of all rock anthems. The music is of the highest quality, notably the guitar work of the tragic Paul Kossoff. This monster hit also benefits from amusing lyrics delivered by the throaty singing of Paul Rodgers. Unfortunately for Free, the fabulous foursome were very young and consequently their immaturity ruined any possibility of stability and durability. As a result, the group peaked with their debut hit, even if some of their subsequent recordings were equally impressive.

The UK Top 10 singles for the week ending July the 4th

1	Mungo Jerry	In The Summertime
2	Free	All Right Now
3	Mr Bloe	Groovin With Mr Bloe
4	Gerry Monroe	Sally
5	Beach Boys	Cottonfields
6	Cliff Richard	Goodbye Sam Hello Samantha
7	Christie	Yellow River
8	The Four Tops	It's All In The Game
9	Creedence Clearwater Revival	Up Around The Bend
10	Fleetwood Mac	The Green Manalishi

The US Number One single: Jackson 5 – The Love You Save
The US Number One album: Beatles – Let It Be
The UK Number One album: Simon And Garfunkel – Bridge Over Troubled Water
Also this week: A British Comet airliner crashes in Spain,killing 112. (3rd)

The UK Top 10 singles for the week ending July the 11th

1	Mungo Jerry	In The Summertime
2	Free	All Right Now
3	Mr Bloe	Groovin With Mr Bloe
4	Creedence Clearwater Revival	Up Around The Bend
5	The Four Tops	It's All In The Game
6	Beach Boys	Cottonfields
7	Gerry Monroe	Sally
8	Cliff Richard	Goodbye Sam Hello Samantha
9	Nicky Thomas	Love Of The Common People
10	Fleetwood Mac	The Green Manalishi

The US Number One single: Three Dog Night – (Mama Told Me) Not To Come
The US Number One album: Soundtrack – Woodstock: Music From The Original Soundtrack
The UK Number One album: Bob Dylan – Self Portrait
Also this week: The British Labour Party elects Roy Jenkins as deputy leader. (8th)

The UK Top 10 singles for the week ending July the 18th

1	Mungo Jerry	In The Summertime
2	Free	All Right Now
3	Creedence Clearwater Revival	Up Around The Bend
4	The Kinks	Lola
5	The Four Tops	It's All In The Game
6	Gerry Monroe	Sally
7	Beach Boys	Cottonfields
8	Mr Bloe	Groovin With Mr Bloe
9	Cliff Richard	Goodbye Sam Hello Samantha
10	Shirley Bassey	Something

The US Number One single: Three Dog Night – (Mama Told Me) Not To Come

The US Number One album: Soundtrack – Woodstock: Music From The Original Soundtrack

The UK Number One album: Simon And Garfunkel – Bridge Over Troubled Water

Also this week: Britain's first national dockers' strike since 1926 takes place. (16th)

The UK Top 10 singles for the week ending July the 25th

1	Mungo Jerry	In The Summertime
2	Free	All Right Now
3	Elvis Presley	The Wonder Of You
4	The Kinks	Lola
5	Creedence Clearwater Revival	Up Around The Bend
6	The Four Tops	It's All In The Game
7	Shirley Bassey	Something
8	Hotlegs	Neanderthal Man
9	Nicky Thomas	Love Of The Common People
10	Beach Boys	Cottonfields

The US Number One single: Carpenters – (They Long To Be) Close To You

The US Number One album: Soundtrack – Woodstock: Music From The Original Soundtrack

The UK Number One album: Simon And Garfunkel – Bridge Over Troubled Water

Also this week: Construction of the Aswan Dam is completed. (21st)

Song of the month for July 1970

The Wonder Of You by Elvis Presley (peak chart position:No.1)

In 1968 the King of rock and roll mercifully turned his back on his mediocre movie career and went back to basics, to do what he did best – performing. Over the next few years, the result was a spectacular return to form for Elvis which culminated in the American Number One, 'Suspicious Minds', and the United Kingdom chart-topper, 'The Wonder Of You'. Regrettably each hit would be the King's last chart-topper in his lifetime as personal excess and self abuse destroyed the promise that had flowed from the wondrous 'The Wonder Of You' live recording.

The UK Top 10 singles for the week ending August the 1st

1	Elvis Presley	The Wonder Of You
2	Free	All Right Now
3	The Kinks	Lola
4	Mungo Jerry	In The Summertime
5	Shirley Bassey	Something
6	Hotlegs	Neanderthal Man
7	The Four Tops	It's All In The Game
8	Creedence Clearwater Revival	Up Around The Bend
9	Jimmy Ruffin	I'll Say Forever My Love
10	Cat Stevens	Lady D'Arbanville

The US Number One single: Carpenters – (They Long To Be) Close To You
The US Number One album: Soundtrack – Woodstock: Music From The Original Soundtrack
The UK Number One album: Simon And Garfunkel – Bridge Over Troubled Water
Also this week: 28 British thalidomide children are awarded compensation. (30th)

The UK Top 10 singles for the week ending August the 8th

1	Elvis Presley	The Wonder Of You
2	The Kinks	Lola
3	Hotlegs	Neanderthal Man
4	Free	All Right Now
5	Shirley Bassey	Something
6	Mungo Jerry	In The Summertime
7	Jimmy Ruffin	I'll Say Forever My Love
8	Cat Stevens	Lady D'Arbanville
9	The Four Tops	It's All In The Game
10	Ten Years After	Love Like A Man

The US Number One single: Carpenters – (They Long To Be) Close To You
The US Number One album: Blood, Sweat & Tears – Blood, Sweat & Tears 3
The UK Number One album: Simon And Garfunkel – Bridge Over Troubled Water
Also this week: The Soviets sign a non-aggression treaty with West Germany. (7th)

The UK Top 10 singles for the week ending August the 15th

1	Elvis Presley	The Wonder Of You
2	Hotlegs	Neanderthal Man
3	The Kinks	Lola
4	Shirley Bassey	Something
5	Free	All Right Now
6	Fair Weather	Natural Sinner
7	Marmalade	Rainbow
8	Mungo Jerry	In The Summertime
9	Jimmy Ruffin	I'll Say Forever My Love
10	Ten Years After	Love Like A Man

The US Number One single: Carpenters – (They Long To Be) Close To You
The US Number One album: Blood, Sweat & Tears – Blood, Sweat & Tears 3
The UK Number One album: Simon And Garfunkel – Bridge Over Troubled Water
Also this week: Troops fire rubber bullets at rioters in Derry's Bogside. (12th)

The UK Top 10 singles for the week ending August the 22nd

1	Elvis Presley	The Wonder Of You
2	Hotlegs	Neanderthal Man
3	Marmalade	Rainbow
4	The Kinks	Lola
5	Smokey Robinson & The Miracles	Tears Of A Clown
6	Shirley Bassey	Something
7	Fair Weather	Natural Sinner
8	Jackson 5	The Love You Save
9	Mungo Jerry	In The Summertime
10	Jimmy Ruffin	I'll Say Forever My Love

The US Number One single: Bread – Make It With You
The US Number One album: Creedence Clearwater Revival – Cosmo's Factory
The UK Number One album: Moody Blues – A Question Of Balance
Also this week: Bobby Moore is cleared of theft by three Colombian judges. (20th)

The UK Top 10 singles for the week ending August the 29th

1	Elvis Presley	The Wonder Of You
2	Smokey Robinson & The Miracles	Tears Of A Clown
3	Hotlegs	Neanderthal Man
4	Marmalade	Rainbow
5	The Kinks	Lola
6	Fair Weather	Natural Sinner
7	Chicago	25 Or 6 To 4
8	Shirley Bassey	Something
9	Three Dog Night	Mama Told Me Not To Come
10	Jackson 5	The Love You Save

The US Number One single: Edwin Starr – War
The US Number One album: Creedence Clearwater Revival – Cosmo's Factory
The UK Number One album: Moody Blues – A Question Of Balance
Also this week: The second Isle of Wight Pop Festival begins. (26th)

Song of the month for August 1970
Wild World by Jimmy Cliff (peak chart position:No.8)

Sandwiched between the emergence of Desmond Dekker and the arrival of Bob Marley, Jimmy Cliff was Jamaica's latest singing sensation. 'Wild World' would propel Cliff into the British Top Ten, which he had previously visited a year earlier with the more positive 'Wonderful World, Beautiful People'. Just what led Cliff to travel from a 'wonderful world' to a 'wild world' in less than a year is open to question, although a clue may lie in an intervening hit, the majestic 'Vietnam'. Anyhow, 'Wild World' (written by Cat Stevens) was not so much a global critique as words of caution uttered to a former sweetheart.

The UK Top 10 singles for the week ending September the 5th

1	Elvis Presley	The Wonder Of You
2	Smokey Robinson & The Miracles	Tears Of A Clown
3	Three Dog Night	Mama Told Me Not To Come
4	Marmalade	Rainbow
5	Chairmen Of The Board	Give Me Just A Little More Time
6	Hotlegs	Neanderthal Man
7	Bread	Make It With You
8	Chicago	25 Or 6 To 4
9	Shirley Bassey	Something
10	Johnny Johnson	Sweet Inspiration

The US Number One single: Edwin Starr – War
The US Number One album: Creedence Clearwater Revival – Cosmo's Factory
The UK Number One album: Moody Blues – A Question Of Balance
Also this week: Salvador Allende is elected Chile's President. (4th)

The UK Top 10 singles for the week ending September the 12th

1 Smokey Robinson & The Miracles — Tears Of A Clown
2 Elvis Presley — The Wonder Of You
3 Three Dog Night — Mama Told Me Not To Come
4 Chairmen Of The Board — Give Me Just A Little More Time
5 Bread — Make It With You
6 Freda Payne — Band Of Gold
7 Chicago — 25 Or 6 To 4
8 Jimmy Cliff — Wild World
9 Marmalade — Rainbow
10 Hot Chocolate — Love Is Life

The US Number One single: Edwin Starr – War
The US Number One album: Creedence Clearwater Revival – Cosmo's Factory
The UK Number One album: Creedence Clearwater Revival – Cosmo's Factory
Also this week: Concorde lands for the first time at Heathrow Airport. (12th)

The UK Top 10 singles for the week ending September the 19th

1 Freda Payne — Band Of Gold
2 Smokey Robinson & The Miracles — Tears Of A Clown
3 Chairmen Of The Board — Give Me Just A Little More Time
4 Elvis Presley — The Wonder Of You
5 Three Dog Night — Mama Told Me Not To Come
6 Hot Chocolate — Love Is Life
7 Bread — Make It With You
8 Desmond Dekker & The Aces — You Can Get It If You Really Want It
9 Jimmy Cliff — Wild World
10 The Poppy Family — Which Way You Going Billy?

The US Number One single: Diana Ross – Ain't No Mountain High Enough
The US Number One album: Creedence Clearwater Revival – Cosmo's Factory
The UK Number One album: Rolling Stones – Get Yer Ya-Yas Out
Also this week: Australia's Margaret Court seals the coveted tennis Grand Slam. (13th)

The UK Top 10 singles for the week ending September the 26th

1 Freda Payne   Band Of Gold
2 Smokey Robinson & The Miracles   Tears Of A Clown
3 Chairmen Of The Board   Give Me Just A Little More Time
4 Desmond Dekker & The Aces   You Can Get It If You Really Want It
5 Elvis Presley   The Wonder Of You
6 Three Dog Night   Mama Told Me Not To Come
7 The Poppy Family   Which Way You Going Billy?
8 Bobby Bloom   MontegoBay
9 Deep Purple   Black Night
10 Bread   Make It With You

The US Number One single: Diana Ross – Ain't No Mountain High Enough
The US Number One album: Creedence Clearwater Revival – Cosmo's Factory
The UK Number One album: Rolling Stones – Get Yer Ya-Yas Out
Also this week: Abdul Razak succeeds Abdul Rahman as Malaysia's Premier. (22nd)

Song of the month for September 1970

Ain't No Mountain High Enough by Diana Ross
(peak chart position:No.6)

Diana Ross took the bold step of casting off the umbilical cord of her supremely successful Supremes career in favour of a solo journey. This decision paid handsome dividends with the marvellous American Number One, 'Ain't No Mountain High Enough'. The British record-buying public however let themselves down by only helping this disco and love song crossover to a brief stay in the Top Ten. This romantic recording had previously surfaced on princess Diana's debut solo album which also contained the equally beautiful 'Reach Out And Touch (Somebody's Hand)'.

The UK Top 10 singles for the week ending October the 3rd

1	Freda Payne	Band Of Gold
2	Desmond Dekker & The Aces	You Can Get It If You Really Want It
3	Bobby Bloom	Montego Bay
4	Smokey Robinson & The Miracles	Tears Of A Clown
5	Deep Purple	Black Night
6	Chairmen Of The Board	Give Me Just A Little More Time
7	The Poppy Family	Which Way You Going Billy?
8	Black Sabbath	Paranoid
9	Elvis Presley	The Wonder Of You
10	Hot Chocolate	Love Is Life

The US Number One single: Diana Ross – Ain't No Mountain High Enough
The US Number One album: Creedence Clearwater Revival – Cosmo's Factory
The UK Number One album: Simon And Garfunkel – Bridge Over Troubled Water
Also this week: The Jordanian army and the PLO end hostilities. (27th)

The UK Top 10 singles for the week ending October the 10th

1	Freda Payne	Band Of Gold
2	Desmond Dekker & The Aces	You Can Get It If You Really Want It
3	Deep Purple	Black Night
4	Black Sabbath	Paranoid
5	Bobby Bloom	Montego Bay
6	Carpenters	(They Long To Be) Close To You
7	Diana Ross	Ain't No Mountain High Enough
8	The Tremeloes	Me And My Life
9	Chairmen Of The Board	Give Me Just A Little More Time
10	The Poppy Family	Which Way You Going Billy?

The US Number One single: Neil Diamond – Cracklin' Rosie
The US Number One album: Creedence Clearwater Revival – Cosmo's Factory
The UK Number One album: Black Sabbath – Paranoid
Also this week: Fiji gains independence from Britain. (10th)

The UK Top 10 singles for the week ending October the 17th

1	Freda Payne	Band Of Gold
2	Deep Purple	Black Night
3	Desmond Dekker & The Aces	You Can Get It If You Really Want It
4	The Tremeloes	Me And My Life
5	Black Sabbath	Paranoid
6	Diana Ross	Ain't No Mountain High Enough
7	Bobby Bloom	Montego Bay
8	Carpenters	(They Long To Be) Close To You
9	The Poppy Family	Which Way You Going Billy?
10	Temptations	Ball Of Confusion

The US Number One single: Jackson 5 – I'll Be There
The US Number One album: Creedence Clearwater Revival – Cosmo's Factory
The UK Number One album: Simon And Garfunkel – Bridge Over Troubled Water
Also this week: 33 die when Melbourne's West Gate Bridge collapses. (15th)

The UK Top 10 singles for the week ending October the 24th

1	Freda Payne	Band Of Gold
2	Deep Purple	Black Night
3	Clarence Carter	Patches
4	The Tremeloes	Me And My Life
5	Black Sabbath	Paranoid
6	Carpenters	(They Long To Be) Close To You
7	Diana Ross	Ain't No Mountain High Enough
8	Desmond Dekker & The Aces	You Can Get It If You Really Want It
9	Temptations	Ball Of Confusion
10	Matthews Southern Comfort	Woodstock

The US Number One single: Jackson 5 – I'll Be There
The US Number One album: Santana – Abraxas
The UK Number One album: Pink Floyd – Atom Heart Mother
Also this week: The Irish High Court acquits Charles Haughey of arms smuggling. (23rd)

The UK Top 10 singles for the week ending October the 31st

1 Matthews Southern Comfort   Woodstock
2 Clarence Carter   Patches
3 Freda Payne   Band Of Gold
4 The Tremeloes   Me And My Life
5 Deep Purple   Black Night
6 Black Sabbath   Paranoid
7 Temptations   Ball Of Confusion
8 Bobby Bloom   Montego Bay
9 Diana Ross   Ain't No Mountain High Enough
10 The Four Tops   Still Waters

The US Number One single: Jackson 5 – I'll Be There
The US Number One album: Led Zeppelin – Led Zeppelin III
The UK Number One album: Various Artist Compilation – Motown Chartbusters,
Volume 4
Also this week: Formula One driver Jack Brabham announces his retirement. (25th)

Song of the month for October 1970

Ride A White Swan by T.Rex (peak chart position: No.2)

Although Tyrannosaurus Rex had been in existence for a few years, Marc Bolan was a virtual stranger to the singles chart. However, 'Ride A White Swan' would prove to be his 'road to Damascus moment' as he made the transition from cult hippy hero to glam rock star. The excellent 'Ride A White Swan' lingered in the British Top Ten for many weeks at the end of 1970 and the beginning of the following year. This smash hit was the first example of T. Rex's fusion of pop and rock. It worked like a charm, even if the likes of his former champion John Peel were less amused.

The UK Top 10 singles for the week ending November the 7th

1 Matthews Southern Comfort   Woodstock
2 Clarence Carter   Patches
3 Deep Purple   Black Night
4 Freda Payne   Band Of Gold
5 Edwin Starr   War
6 The Tremeloes   Me And My Life
7 Temptations   Ball Of Confusion
8 The Rattles   The Witch
9 Melanie   Ruby Tuesday
10 Black Sabbath   Paranoid

The US Number One single: Jackson 5 – I'll Be There
The US Number One album: Led Zeppelin – Led Zeppelin III
The UK Number One album: Led Zeppelin – Led Zeppelin III
Also this week: Salvador Allende is sworn in as Chile's socialist President. (3rd)

The UK Top 10 singles for the week ending November the 14th

1 Matthews Southern Comfort   Woodstock
2 Clarence Carter   Patches
3 Edwin Starr   War
4 Don Fardon   Indian Reservation
5 The Jimi Hendrix Experience   Voodoo Chile
6 The Tremeloes   Me And My Life
7 Christie   San Bernadino
8 The Rattles   The Witch
9 Melanie   Ruby Tuesday
10 Freda Payne   Band Of Gold

The US Number One single: Jackson 5 – I'll Be There
The US Number One album: Led Zeppelin – Led Zeppelin III
The UK Number One album: Led Zeppelin – Led Zeppelin III
Also this week: General Assad seizes power in a coup in Syria. (13th)

The UK Top 10 singles for the week ending November the 21st

1 The Jimi Hendrix Experience   Voodoo Chile
2 Matthews Southern Comfort   Woodstock
3 Don Fardon   Indian Reservation
4 Clarence Carter   Patches
5 Edwin Starr   War
6 Jimmy Ruffin   It's Wonderful
7 Christie   San Bernadino
8 The Rattles   The Witch
9 Melanie   Ruby Tuesday
10 Neil Diamond   Cracklin' Rosie

The US Number One single: Partridge Family – I Think I Love You
The US Number One album: Led Zeppelin – Led Zeppelin III
The UK Number One album: Led Zeppelin – Led Zeppelin III
Also this week: Poland and West Germany sign a treaty of reconciliation. (18th)

The UK Top 10 singles for the week ending November the 28th

1 Dave Edmunds   I Hear You Knocking
2 The Jimi Hendrix Experience   Voodoo Chile
3 Don Fardon   Indian Reservation
4 Matthews Southern Comfort   Woodstock
5 Neil Diamond   Cracklin' Rosie
6 Edwin Starr   War
7 T. Rex   Ride A White Swan
8 Clarence Carter   Patches
9 Elvis Presley   I've Lost You
10 White Plains   Julie Do Ya Love Me?

The US Number One single: Partridge Family – I Think I Love You
The US Number One album: Santana – Abraxas
The UK Number One album: Bob Dylan – New Morning
Also this week: Pope Paul VI escapes unhurt from a knife attack. (27th)

Song of the month for November 1970

Voodoo Chile by The Jimi Hendrix Experience
(peak chart position: No.1)

Two months after the premature death of arguably popular music's greatest guitarist, 'Voodoo Chile' (alternatively known as 'Slight Return') would provide Jimi Hendrix with a slight and hugely successful return to the British singles chart. This five-minute closing track to the 1968 'Electric Ladyland' double album must surely rate as one of the most unlikely of chart-toppers. It certainly showcased the guitar prowess of Hendrix. Incidentally, this rock song has absolutely nothing whatsover to do with Chile!

The UK Top 10 singles for the week ending December the 5th

1	Dave Edmunds	I Hear You Knocking
2	The Jimi Hendrix Experience	Voodoo Chile
3	Neil Diamond	Cracklin' Rosie
4	Don Fardon	Indian Reservation
5	Chairmen Of The Board	You've Got Me Dangling
6	McGuinness Flint	When I'm Dead And Gone
7	T. Rex	Ride A White Swan
8	White Plains	Julie Do Ya Love Me?
9	Elvis Presley	I've Lost You
10	Jimmy Ruffin	It's Wonderful

The US Number One single: Partridge Family – I Think I Love You

The US Number One album: Santana – Abraxas

The UK Number One album: Andy Williams – Andy Williams Greatest Hits

Also this week: The Heath Government's Industrial Relations Bill is published. (3rd)

The UK Top 10 singles for the week ending December the 12th

1	Dave Edmunds	I Hear You Knocking
2	McGuinness Flint	When I'm Dead And Gone
3	Neil Diamond	Cracklin' Rosie
4	Glen Campbell	It's Only Make Believe
5	The Jimi Hendrix Experience	Voodoo Chile
6	T. Rex	Ride A White Swan
7	Andy Williams	Home Loving Man
8	Chairmen Of The Board	You've Got Me Dangling
9	Don Fardon	Indian Reservation
10	Elvis Presley	I've Lost You

The US Number One single: Smokey Robinson & The Miracles – Tears Of A Clown
The US Number One album: Santana – Abraxas
The UK Number One album: Led Zeppelin – Led Zeppelin III
Also this week: Alexander Solzhenitsyn claims the Nobel Prize for literature. (10th)

The UK Top 10 singles for the week ending December the 19th

1	Dave Edmunds	I Hear You Knocking
2	McGuinness Flint	When I'm Dead And Gone
3	Neil Diamond	Cracklin' Rosie
4	Glen Campbell	It's Only Make Believe
5	Jackson 5	I'll Be There
6	Clive Dunn	Grandad
7	Andy Williams	Home Loving Man
8	Gilbert O'Sullivan	Nothing Rhymed
9	Gerry Monroe	My Prayer
10	Chairmen Of The Board	You've Got Me Dangling

The US Number One single: Smokey Robinson & The Miracles – Tears Of A Clown
The US Number One album: Santana – Abraxas
The UK Number One album: Andy Williams – Andy Williams Greatest Hits
Also this week: The Pravda newspaper denounces Solzhenitsyn as "alien". (17th)

The UK Top 10 singles for the week ending December the 26th

1	Dave Edmunds	I Hear You Knocking
2	Clive Dunn	Grandad
3	McGuinness Flint	When I'm Dead And Gone
4	Glen Campbell	It's Only Make Believe
5	Jackson 5	I'll Be There
6	Neil Diamond	Cracklin' Rosie
7	Andy Williams	Home Loving Man
8	Gilbert O'Sullivan	Nothing Rhymed
9	Gerry Monroe	My Prayer
10	T. Rex	Ride A White Swan

The US Number One single: George Harrison – My Sweet Lord/Isn't It A Pity
The US Number One album: Santana – Abraxas
The UK Number One album: Andy Williams – Andy Williams Greatest Hits
Also this week: Edward Gierek replaces Wladyslaw Gomulka as Poland's leader. (20th)

Song of the month for December 1970

Layla by Derek And The Dominos (peak chart position: No.4 in 1982)

After the relative failure of his Blind Faith venture, Eric Clapton 'disguised' himself in Derek And The Dominos. This new combo's debut offering was entitled 'Layla And Other Assorted Love Songs', which was released in December, whereupon it failed mysteriously to make much of a splash in the album charts. Whilst 'Bell Bottom Blues' has a credible claim for being the best item on the album, pride of place must surely go to 'Layla'. With the considerable assistance of Duane Allman's guitar, Clapton reveals his intense yearning for 'Layla' (or his future wife Pattie Harrison, to be precise). If the track's first part is a perennial rock favourite, then part two's instrumental interplay between guitar, piano, and drums is simply out of this world.

Listed Below are the Top 10 Best Selling UK Singles of 1970

1	The Wonder Of You	Elvis Presley
2	Yellow River	Christie
3	In The Summertime	Mungo Jerry
4	Band Of Gold	Freda Payne
5	Something	Shirley Bassey
6	Wanderin' Star	Lee Marvin
7	Spirit In The Sky	Norman Greenbaum
8	Bridge Over Troubled Water	Simon and Garfunkel
9	Back Home	England World Cup Squad
10	All Right Now	Free

1970's CONCERTS OF THE YEAR

Perhaps the first historic concert of the new decade was the farewell outing for Diana Ross and The Supremes, during which the audience were introduced to Miss Ross's replacement, Jean Terrell. Meanwhile on St.Valentine's Day, the Who cemented their reputation as a formidable live act with their performance at Leeds University, which would be thereafter immortalised on the 'Live At Leeds' album. The Rolling Stones too avoided a studio album, in favour of the live recordings of 'Get Yer Ya-Yas Out'. Gig of the year was arguably the Isle of Wight festival at the end of August. This now annual shindig featured the likes of the Doors and the Jimi Hendrix Experience (or 'Band of Gypsies'). However, within three weeks, the virtuoso guitarist would be dead, whilst Jim Morrison of the Doors would be going through life's departure lounge a mere ten months later.

1970's ALBUM OF THE YEAR

Led Zeppelin III by Led Zeppelin; released in October; reached No.1 in the UK

SIDE ONE:

1. Immigrant Song; 2:25
2. Friends; 3:54
3. Celebration Day; 3:29
4. Since I've Been Loving You; 7:23
5. Out on the Tiles; 4:08

SIDE TWO:

1. Gallows Pole; 4:58
2. Tangerine; 3:12
3. That's the Way; 5:39
4. Bron-Y-Aur Stomp; 4:18
5. Hats Off to (Roy) Harper; 3:42

The mighty Zep took the most peculiar step of retreating from their fearsome onslaught upon Californian five-star hotels in favour of some quality time in the depths of rural, north-west Wales. The fab four's self-imposed exile in the rustic setting of the hamlet of Bron-Y-Aur, in Snowdonia would be commemorated in the jaunty track 'Bron-Y-Aur stomp' which would surface in the group's third album. Yet again choosing to avoid an album title, Led Zeppelin proceeded to confuse fans and critics further still with several tracks which were a far cry from the heavy rock that had stamped its considerable presence upon the band's first two projects. The acoustic guitar was very much to the fore as Robert Plant and Jimmy Page indulged in their passion for folk music. 'Gallows Pole' is a case in point, whilst the item, 'Friends' showcased the group's desire to extend into eastern music. The LP still possessed its moments of sonic mayhem, courtesy of 'Out On The Tiles' and the stirring curtain-raiser, 'Immigrant Song'. Pride of place perhaps goes to the epic blues of 'Since I've Been Loving You' which represents seven and a half minutes of a combo at the very peak of their artistic development. Sandwiched in between the towering giants of Led Zeppelin II and IV, the third offering has never quite received its due recognition, but it can make a strong case for being the outstanding album of 1970, even ahead of Simon And Garfunkel's 'Bridge Over Troubled Water'.

SPORT IN 1970

English Division One football champions: Everton; runners-up: Leeds United

English FA Cup final: Chelsea 2 Leeds United 1 (after extra time, in a replay)

English League Cup Final: Manchester City 2 West Bromwich Albion 1

Scottish Division One football champions: Glasgow Celtic; runners-up: Glasgow Rangers

Scottish FA Cup final: Aberdeen 3 Glasgow Celtic 1

Scottish League Cup final: Glasgow Celtic 1 St Johnstone 0

Irish League football champions: Glentoran; Irish Cup final: Linfield 2 Ballymena United 1

League Of Ireland football champions: Waterford; cup winners: Bohemians

European Cup final: Feyenoord 2 Glasgow Celtic 1

European Cup-Winners' Cup final: Manchester City 2 Gornik Zabrze 1

European Fairs Cup final: Arsenal beat Anderlecht 4–3 on aggregate

English county cricket champions: Kent

Five Nations' rugby union champions: France and Wales (both 6 points)

Formula One world drivers' champion: Jochen Rindt (Austria) in a Lotus car

Gaelic football All-Ireland champions: Kerry; runners-up: Meath

British Open golf champion: Jack Nicklaus (at St. Andrews)

US Masters golf champion: Billy Casper

US Open golf champion: Tony Jacklin

USPGA golf champion: Dave Stockton

Rugby league Challenge Cup final: Castleford 7 Wigan 2

Wimbledon men's singles tennis final: J Newcombe beat K Rosewall 5–7, 6–3, 6–2, 3–6, 6–1

Wimbledon ladies' singles tennis final: M Court beat B-J King 14–12, 11–9

World snooker final: Ray Reardon (Wales) beat John Pulman (England) 37–33

The Aintree Grand National steeplechase winner: Gay Trip; price 15–1

The Epsom Derby winner: Nijinsky; jockey – Lester Piggott; price 11–8F

Football World Cup final: Brazil 4 Italy 1

1970's DEATHS

January 29th: Sir Basil Henry Liddell Hart (British historian), aged 74

February 2nd: Bertrand Arthur William Russell (British philosopher), aged 97

February 11th: Henry Mayo Bateman (British cartoonist), aged 82

February 15th: Air Chief Marshal Dowding (of the RAF), aged 87

February 25th: Mark Rothko (US artist), aged 66

June 7th: Edward Morgan Forster (British author), aged 91

June 11th: Alexander Kerensky (ex-Russian leader), aged 89

June 21st: Ahmed Sukarno (ex-Indonesian President), aged 69

July 8th: Sir Allen Lane (British publisher), aged 67

July 8th: Dame Laura Knight (British artist), aged 92

July 20th: Iain Macleod (British politician), aged 56

July 27th: Antonio de Oliveira Salazar (Portugal's dictator), aged 81

July 29th: Sir John Barbirolli (British conductor), aged 70

September 5th: Jochen Rindt (Austrian Formula 1 driver), aged 28

September 18th: Jimi Hendrix (US musician), aged 27

September 25th: Erich Maria Remarque (German author), aged 72

September 28th: Colonel Gamal Abdel Nasser (Egypt's President), aged 81

September 28th: John Dos Passos (US author), aged 74

October 4th: Janis Joplin (US singer), aged 27

October 10th: Edouard Daladier (French statesman), aged 86

November 9th: General Charles de Gaulle (ex-French President), aged 79

November 25th: Yukio Mishima (Japanese author), aged 45

December 14th: Field Marshal William Slim (British soldier), aged 79

December 26th: Lillian Board (British athlete), aged 22

The UK Top 10 singles for the week ending January the 2nd

1	Dave Edmunds	I Hear You Knocking
2	Clive Dunn	Grandad
3	McGuinness Flint	When I'm Dead And Gone
4	Glen Campbell	It's Only Make Believe
5	Jackson 5	I'll Be There
6	Neil Diamond	Cracklin' Rosie
7	Andy Williams	Home Loving Man
8	Gilbert O'Sullivan	Nothing Rhymed
9	Gerry Monroe	My Prayer
10	T. Rex	Ride A White Swan

The US Number One single: George Harrison – My Sweet Lord/Isn't It A Pity
The US Number One album: George Harrison – All Things Must Pass
The UK Number One album: Andy Williams – Andy Williams Greatest Hits
Also this week: 66 die as Ibrox Park's football barriers collapse. (2nd)

The UK Top 10 singles for the week ending January the 9th

1	Clive Dunn	Grandad
2	Dave Edmunds	I Hear You Knocking
3	McGuinness Flint	When I'm Dead And Gone
4	T. Rex	Ride A White Swan
5	Jackson 5	I'll Be There
6	Neil Diamond	Cracklin' Rosie
7	Johnny Johnson	Blame It On The Pony Express
8	Gilbert O'Sullivan	Nothing Rhymed
9	Glen Campbell	It's Only Make Believe
10	Andy Williams	Home Loving Man

The US Number One single: George Harrison – My Sweet Lord/Isn't It A Pity
The US Number One album: George Harrison – All Things Must Pass
The UK Number One album: Andy Williams – Andy Williams Greatest Hits
Also this week: Britain's ambassador to Uruguay is kidnapped by left-wing guerrillas. (8th)

The UK Top 10 singles for the week ending January the 16th

1	Clive Dunn	Grandad
2	Dave Edmunds	I Hear You Knocking
3	McGuinness Flint	When I'm Dead And Gone
4	T. Rex	Ride A White Swan
5	Jackson 5	I'll Be There
6	Glen Campbell	It's Only Make Believe
7	Neil Diamond	Cracklin' Rosie
8	Johnny Johnson	Blame It On The Pony Express
9	Andy Williams	Home Loving Man
10	Gilbert O'Sullivan	Nothing Rhymed

The US Number One single: George Harrison – My Sweet Lord/Isn't It A Pity
The US Number One album: George Harrison – All Things Must Pass
The UK Number One album: Simon And Garfunkel – Bridge Over Troubled Water
Also this week: The Jordanian army deports 384 Palestinian guerrillas. (10th)

The UK Top 10 singles for the week ending January the 23rd

1	Clive Dunn	Grandad
2	T. Rex	Ride A White Swan
3	McGuinness Flint	When I'm Dead And Gone
4	Jackson 5	I'll Be There
5	The Kinks	Apeman
6	Dave Edmunds	I Hear You Knocking
7	George Harrison	My Sweet Lord
8	Judy Collins	Amazing Grace
9	Elvis Presley	You Don't Have To Say You Love Me
10	The Equals	Black Skin Blue Eyed Boys

The US Number One single: Dawn – Knock Three Times
The US Number One album: George Harrison – All Things Must Pass
The UK Number One album: Simon And Garfunkel – Bridge Over Troubled Water
Also this week: Britain's postmen take strike action. (20th)

The UK Top 10 singles for the week ending January the 30th

1	George Harrison	My Sweet Lord
2	Clive Dunn	Grandad
3	The Mixtures	Pushbike Song
4	T. Rex	Ride A White Swan
5	The Kinks	Apeman
6	Jackson 5	I'll Be There
7	Dave Edmunds	I Hear You Knocking
8	Judy Collins	Amazing Grace
9	The Equals	Black Skin Blue Eyed Boys
10	Neil Diamond	Cracklin' Rosie

The US Number One single: Dawn – Knock Three Times
The US Number One album: George Harrison – All Things Must Pass
The UK Number One album: Simon And Garfunkel – Bridge Over Troubled Water
Also this week: General Idi Amin ousts Milton Obote in a coup. (25th)

Song of the month for January 1971

My Sweet Lord by George Harrison (peak chart position:No.1)

He may have described himself as an economy-class Beatle, but the quiet one surpassed his former musical associates with the huge-selling 'My Sweet Lord'. This beautiful Hare Krishna anthem was a statement of George's own religious state of mind. It certainly struck a chord with many record-buyers who ensured that Harrison would land himself a Transatlantic chart-topper long before either Lennon or McCartney could even begin to emulate this accomplishment. The trouble was that the self-described 'dark horse' peaked with this single and its accompanying album, 'All Things Must Pass'. He never reached these heights again.

The UK Top 10 singles for the week ending February the 6th

1	George Harrison	My Sweet Lord
2	The Mixtures	Pushbike Song
3	Supremes	Stoned Love
4	Clive Dunn	Grandad
5	Badfinger	No Matter What
6	Judy Collins	Amazing Grace
7	T. Rex	Ride A White Swan
8	The Kinks	Apeman
9	Ashton, Gardner And Dyke	Resurrection Shuffle
10	Jackson 5	I'll Be There

The US Number One single: Dawn – Knock Three Times
The US Number One album: George Harrison – All Things Must Pass
The UK Number One album: George Harrison – All Things Must Pass
Also this week: Rolls-Royce declares itself to be bankrupt. (4th)

The UK Top 10 singles for the week ending February the 13th

1	George Harrison	My Sweet Lord
2	The Mixtures	Pushbike Song
3	Supremes	Stoned Love
4	Ashton, Gardner And Dyke	Resurrection Shuffle
5	Judy Collins	Amazing Grace
6	Badfinger	No Matter What
7	Elton John	Your Song
8	The Kinks	Apeman
9	Clive Dunn	Grandad
10	Dawn	Candida

The US Number One single: Osmonds – One Bad Apple
The US Number One album: George Harrison – All Things Must Pass
The UK Number One album: George Harrison – All Things Must Pass
Also this week: A Swiss referendum awards women the vote in national elections. (7th)

The UK Top 10 singles for the week ending February the 20th

1 George Harrison   My Sweet Lord
2 The Mixtures   Pushbike Song
3 Ashton, Gardner And Dyke   Resurrection Shuffle
4 Supremes   Stoned Love
5 Judy Collins   Amazing Grace
6 Badfinger   No Matter What
7 Perry Como   It's Impossible
8 Elton John   Your Song
9 Clive Dunn   Grandad
10 Dawn   Candida

The US Number One single: Osmonds – One Bad Apple
The US Number One album: Various Artist Compilation – Jesus Christ Superstar
The UK Number One album: George Harrison – All Things Must Pass
Also this week: General Idi Amin declares himself to be President of Uganda. (20th)

The UK Top 10 singles for the week ending February the 27th

1 George Harrison   My Sweet Lord
2 The Mixtures   Pushbike Song
3 Ashton, Gardner And Dyke   Resurrection Shuffle
4 Perry Como   It's Impossible
5 Supremes   Stoned Love
6 Judy Collins   Amazing Grace
7 Mungo Jerry   Baby Jump
8 Elton John   Your Song
9 Dawn   Candida
10 Badfinger   No Matter What

The US Number One single: Osmonds – One Bad Apple
The US Number One album: Janis Joplin – Pearl
The UK Number One album: George Harrison – All Things Must Pass
Also this week: Two policemen are shot dead in Belfast. (26th)

Song of the month for February 1971

Hot Love by T. Rex (peak chart position:No.1)

Following fast behind the huge success of 'Ride A White Swan', T. Rex scored the first of their four British chart-toppers with 'Hot Love'. This song appears to live in the shadow of its successor, 'Get It On', which is quite strange given that it originally sold more copies and spent longer at Number One (six weeks to be precise). Meanwhile Marc Bolan's previous followers were dismayed that he had swapped trippy lyrics in favour of "la la la la la la la", but his new teenage fanbase were not complaining.

The UK Top 10 singles for the week ending March the 6th

1	Mungo Jerry	Baby Jump
2	George Harrison	My Sweet Lord
3	The Mixtures	Pushbike Song
4	Paul McCartney	Another Day
5	Perry Como	It's Impossible
6	Ashton, Gardner And Dyke	Resurrection Shuffle
7	Judy Collins	Amazing Grace
8	Supremes	Stoned Love
9	Neil Diamond	Sweet Caroline
10	Lynn Anderson	Rose Garden

The US Number One single: Osmonds – One Bad Apple
The US Number One album: Janis Joplin – Pearl
The UK Number One album: George Harrison – All Things Must Pass
Also this week: Liechtenstein's male electorate refuse to give the vote to women. (28th)

The UK Top 10 singles for the week ending March the 13th

1	Mungo Jerry	Baby Jump
2	Paul McCartney	Another Day
3	George Harrison	My Sweet Lord
4	Lynn Anderson	Rose Garden
5	Perry Como	It's Impossible
6	The Mixtures	Pushbike Song
7	T. Rex	Hot Love
8	Neil Diamond	Sweet Caroline
9	Judy Collins	Amazing Grace
10	Supremes	Stoned Love

The US Number One single: Osmonds – One Bad Apple
The US Number One album: Janis Joplin – Pearl
The UK Number One album: George Harrison – All Things Must Pass
Also this week: Associated Newspapers announce the closure of the *Daily Sketch*. (8th)

The UK Top 10 singles for the week ending March the 20th

1	T. Rex	Hot Love
2	Mungo Jerry	Baby Jump
3	Paul McCartney	Another Day
4	Lynn Anderson	Rose Garden
5	Perry Como	It's Impossible
6	George Harrison	My Sweet Lord
7	The Mixtures	Pushbike Song
8	Deep Purple	Strange Kind Of Woman
9	Neil Diamond	Sweet Caroline
10	Ashton, Gardner And Dyke	Resurrection Shuffle

The US Number One single: Janis Joplin – Me And Bobby McGee
The US Number One album: Janis Joplin – Pearl
The UK Number One album: George Harrison – All Things Must Pass
Also this week: James Chichester-Clark resigns as Northern Ireland's Prime Minister. (20th)

The UK Top 10 singles for the week ending March the 27th

1 T. Rex   Hot Love
2 Paul McCartney   Another Day
3 Lynn Anderson   Rose Garden
4 Mungo Jerry   Baby Jump
5 Perry Como   It's Impossible
6 Judy Collins   Amazing Grace
7 George Harrison   My Sweet Lord
8 Neil Diamond   Sweet Caroline
9 Ray Stevens   Bridget The Midget
10 Clodagh Rodgers   Jack In The Box

The US Number One single: Janis Joplin – Me And Bobby McGee
The US Number One album: Janis Joplin – Pearl
The UK Number One album: George Harrison – All Things Must Pass
Also this week: Brian Faulkner becomes the new Prime Minister of Northern Ireland. (23rd)

Song of the month for March 1971

Double Barrel by Dave And Ansil Collins (peak chart position:No.1)

'Double Barrel' was effectively an instrumental and not exactly the most likely song to reach the pop summit. It was yet another outpouring from Jamaica's very own hit factory, Trojan Records. This tune was expected to be another novelty hit from the Carribbean, but Dave and Ansil Collins demolished the likelihood of being one-hit wonders when they followed up with another Top Ten hit, the slightly similar, 'Monkey Spanner', which featured "the heavy heavy monster sound", which was later re-visited by Madness on 'One Step Beyond'.

The UK Top 10 singles for the week ending April the 3rd

1   T. Rex   Hot Love
2   Ray Stevens   Bridget The Midget
3   Lynn Anderson   Rose Garden
4   Paul McCartney   Another Day
5   Mungo Jerry   Baby Jump
6   Clodagh Rodgers   Jack In The Box
7   John Lennon   Power To The People
8   Elvis Presley   There Goes My Everything
9   Perry Como   It's Impossible
10 C.C.S.   Walkin'

The US Number One single: Temptations – (Just My Imagination) Running Away With Me
The US Number One album: Janis Joplin – Pearl
The UK Number One album: Andy Williams – Home Lovin' Man
Also this week: Anthony Barber reveals the first Conservative budget since 1964. (30th)

The UK Top 10 singles for the week ending April the 10th

1   T. Rex   Hot Love
2   Ray Stevens   Bridget The Midget
3   Lynn Anderson   Rose Garden
4   Clodagh Rodgers   Jack In The Box
5   Paul McCartney   Another Day
6   Elvis Presley   There Goes My Everything
7   C.C.S.   Walkin'
8   John Lennon   Power To The People
9   Perry Como   It's Impossible
10 Mungo Jerry   Baby Jump

The US Number One single: Temptations – (Just My Imagination) Running Away With Me
The US Number One album: Janis Joplin – Pearl
The UK Number One album: Andy Williams – Home Lovin' Man
Also this week: Thousands are reported dead in East Pakistan's disturbances. (5th)

The UK Top 10 singles for the week ending April the 17th

1 T. Rex   Hot Love
2 Ray Stevens   Bridget The Midget
3 Lynn Anderson   Rose Garden
4 Dave And Ansil Collins   Double Barrel
5 Clodagh Rodgers   Jack In The Box
6 Andy Williams   Where Do I Begin?
7 Elvis Presley   There Goes My Everything
8 Olivia Newton-John   If Not For You
9 C.C.S.   Walkin'
10 John Lennon   Power To The People

The US Number One single: Three Dog Night – Joy To The World
The US Number One album: Janis Joplin – Pearl
The UK Number One album: Various Artist Compilation – Motown Chartbusters, Vol 5
Also this week: President Nixon relaxes the trade sanctions against China. (14th)

The UK Top 10 singles for the week ending April the 24th

1 T. Rex   Hot Love
2 Dave And Ansil Collins   Double Barrel
3 Ray Stevens   Bridget The Midget
4 Andy Williams   Where Do I Begin?
5 Lynn Anderson   Rose Garden
6 Waldo De Los Rios   Mozart Symphony Number 40
7 Olivia Newton-John   If Not For You
8 C.C.S.   Walkin'
9 The Fantastics   Something Old, Something New
10 Clodagh Rodgers   Jack In The Box

The US Number One single: Three Dog Night – Joy To The World
The US Number One album: Janis Joplin – Pearl
The UK Number One album: Various Artist Compilation – Motown Chartbusters, Vol 5
Also this week: Figures show that unemployment in Britain is 800,000. (19th)

Song of the month for April 1971

Can't You Hear Me Knocking by The Rolling Stones (album track)

'Can't You Hear Me Knocking' was far too long to be released as a single, but it was a key track on the 'Sticky Fingers' album, released in April 1971. Opinion is divided on the merits of this extended jam. Some Stones' 'purists' complain that the lads were getting much too self-indulgent. I however am firmly in the camp which hails this item as a delightful jazz-rock fusion which sets it apart from many other more typical Stones' recordings. Quite simply, the instrumental second half is a joy to behold, helped by the keyboards input of Billy Preston and the saxophonist Bobby Keyes.

The UK Top 10 singles for the week ending May the 1st

1	Dave And Ansil Collins	Double Barrel
2	T. Rex	Hot Love
3	Dawn	Knock Three Times
4	Rolling Stones	Brown Sugar/Bitch/Let It Rock
5	Waldo De Los Rios	Mozart Symphony Number 40
6	Ray Stevens	Bridget The Midget
7	Ringo Starr	It Don't Come Easy
8	Andy Williams	Where Do I Begin?
9	Diana Ross	Remember Me
10	C.C.S.	Walkin'

The US Number One single: Three Dog Night – Joy To The World
The US Number One album: Various Artist Compilation – Jesus Christ Superstar
The UK Number One album: Various Artist Compilation – Motown Chartbusters, Vol 5
Also this week: The Times receives a letter bomb from the Angry Brigade. (28th)

The UK Top 10 singles for the week ending May the 8th

1	Dave And Ansil Collins	Double Barrel
2	Dawn	Knock Three Times
3	Rolling Stones	Brown Sugar/Bitch/Let It Rock
4	Ringo Starr	It Don't Come Easy
5	Waldo De Los Rios	Mozart Symphony Number 40
6	T. Rex	Hot Love
7	Diana Ross	Remember Me
8	Andy Williams	Where Do I Begin?
9	The Fantastics	Something Old, Something New
10	Ray Stevens	Bridget The Midget

The US Number One single: Three Dog Night – Joy To The World
The US Number One album: Various Artist Compilation – Jesus Christ Superstar
The UK Number One album: Rolling Stones – Sticky Fingers
Also this week: Erich Honecker becomes East Germany's new head of state. (3rd)

The UK Top 10 singles for the week ending May the 15th

1	Dawn	Knock Three Times
2	Rolling Stones	Brown Sugar/Bitch/Let It Rock
3	Dave And Ansil Collins	Double Barrel
4	Ringo Starr	It Don't Come Easy
5	Waldo De Los Rios	Mozart Symphony Number 40
6	R Dean Taylor	Indiana Wants Me
7	Diana Ross	Remember Me
8	East Of Eden	Jig A Jig
9	T. Rex	Hot Love
10	Andy Williams	Where Do I Begin?

The US Number One single: Three Dog Night – Joy To The World
The US Number One album: Crosby, Stills, Nash & Young – 4 Way Street
The UK Number One album: Rolling Stones – Sticky Fingers
Also this week: Mick Jagger marries Bianca de Macias in Saint Tropez. (12th)

The UK Top 10 singles for the week ending May the 22nd

1	Dawn	Knock Three Times
2	Rolling Stones	Brown Sugar/Bitch/Let It Rock
3	R Dean Taylor	Indiana Wants Me
4	Ringo Starr	It Don't Come Easy
5	Dave And Ansil Collins	Double Barrel
6	Waldo De Los Rios	Mozart Symphony Number 40
7	East Of Eden	Jig A Jig
8	The Elgins	Heaven Must Have Sent You
9	McGuinness Flint	Malt And Barley Blues
10	Diana Ross	Remember Me

The US Number One single: Three Dog Night – Joy To The World
The US Number One album: Rolling Stones – Sticky Fingers
The UK Number One album: Rolling Stones – Sticky Fingers
Also this week: Egyptians celebrate the defeat of a coup to overthrow Sadat. (16th)

The UK Top 10 singles for the week ending May the 29th

1	Dawn	Knock Three Times
2	Rolling Stones	Brown Sugar/Bitch/Let It Rock
3	R Dean Taylor	Indiana Wants Me
4	Free	My Brother Jake
5	McGuinness Flint	Malt And Barley Blues
6	The Elgins	Heaven Must Have Sent You
7	East Of Eden	Jig A Jig
8	Ringo Starr	It Don't Come Easy
9	Severine	Un Banc, Un Arbre, Une Rue
10	Dave And Ansil Collins	Double Barrel

The US Number One single: Rolling Stones – Brown Sugar
The US Number One album: Rolling Stones – Sticky Fingers
The UK Number One album: Rolling Stones – Sticky Fingers
Also this week: President Sadat signs a friendship treaty with the Soviet Union. (28th)

Song of the month for May 1971

My Brother Jake by Free (peak chart position:No.4)

The consensus of opinion may be that their best single was 'All Right Now', but I have a slight preference for the Top Five hit, 'My Brother Jake', which was released in May of 1971. This tune is a far cry from the tongue-in-cheek humour of their biggest smash, as the subject matter is darker. Here Paul Rodgers is pleading to Jake to clean up his act and pull his life around. The song's message ought to have been heeded by young guitarist, Paul Kossoff, who died of a heart attack in 1976, another victim of rock and roll excess.

The UK Top 10 singles for the week ending June the 5th

1	Dawn	Knock Three Times
2	R Dean Taylor	Indiana Wants Me
3	The Elgins	Heaven Must Have Sent You
4	Free	My Brother Jake
5	Rolling Stones	Brown Sugar/Bitch/Let It Rock
6	Neil Diamond	I Am ... I Said
7	McGuinness Flint	Malt And Barley Blues
8	Tony Christie	I Did What I Did For Maria
9	Elvis Presley	Rags To Riches
10	East Of Eden	Jig A Jig

The US Number One single: Rolling Stones – Brown Sugar
The US Number One album: Rolling Stones – Sticky Fingers
The UK Number One album: Paul & Linda McCartney – Ram
Also this week: Pakistan's Zaheer Abbas hits 274 in an Edgbaston test match. (4th)

The UK Top 10 singles for the week ending June the 12th

1 Dawn   Knock Three Times
2 Tony Christie   I Did What I Did For Maria
3 R Dean Taylor   Indiana Wants Me
4 Neil Diamond   I Am ... I Said
5 The Elgins   Heaven Must Have Sent You
6 Free   My Brother Jake
7 Mungo Jerry   Lady Rose
8 Tammi Lynn   I'm Gonna Run Away From You
9 Blue Mink   Banner Man
10 Rolling Stones   Brown Sugar/Bitch/Let It Rock

The US Number One single: The Honey Cone – Want Ads
The US Number One album: Rolling Stones – Sticky Fingers
The UK Number One album: Paul & Linda McCartney – Ram
Also this week: Joe Gormley becomes president of the National Union of
Mineworkers. (10th)

The UK Top 10 singles for the week ending June the 19th

1 Middle Of The Road   Chirpy Chirpy Cheep Cheep
2 Dawn   Knock Three Times
3 Tony Christie   I Did What I Did For Maria
4 Blue Mink   Banner Man
5 Tammi Lynn   I'm Gonna Run Away From You
6 Mungo Jerry   Lady Rose
7 John Kongos   He's Gonna Step On You Again
8 The Elgins   Heaven Must Have Sent You
9 Neil Diamond   I Am ... I Said
10 R Dean Taylor   Indiana Wants Me

The US Number One single: Carole King – It's Too Late/I Feel The Earth Move
The US Number One album: Carole King – Tapestry
The UK Number One album: Rolling Stones – Sticky Fingers
Also this week: Dom Mintoff's socialists win the Malta general election. (17th)

The UK Top 10 singles for the week ending June the 26th

1	Middle Of The Road	Chirpy Chirpy Cheep Cheep
2	Tony Christie	I Did What I Did For Maria
3	Blue Mink	Banner Man
4	Tammi Lynn	I'm Gonna Run Away From You
5	Mungo Jerry	Lady Rose
6	John Kongos	He's Gonna Step On You Again
7	Dawn	Knock Three Times
8	Hurricane Smith	Don't Let It Die
9	Sweet	Co-Co
10	Neil Diamond	I Am ... I Said

The US Number One single: Carole King – It's Too Late/I Feel The Earth Move
The US Number One album: Carole King – Tapestry
The UK Number One album: Emerson, Lake & Palmer – Tarkus
Also this week: Britain grants asylum to Russian space expert Anatol Fedoseyev. (20th)

Song of the month for June 1971
Black And White by Greyhound (peak chart position:No.6)

Jamiaca's Greyhound helped themselves to a Top Ten hit, courtesy of the standard 'Black And White', which was a well-intentioned appeal for inter-racial harmony. Not content with this hugely listenable tune, the act found further success with their own decent interpretation of 'Moon River' and the commendable 'I Am What I Am'. Here was another surprise triumph for the Caribbean's very own 'Motown' – Trojan Records.

The UK Top 10 singles for the week ending July the 3rd

1	Middle Of The Road	Chirpy Chirpy Cheep Cheep
2	Hurricane Smith	Don't Let It Die
3	Blue Mink	Banner Man
4	John Kongos	He's Gonna Step On You Again
5	Sweet	Co-Co
6	Tony Christie	I Did What I Did For Maria
7	Tammi Lynn	I'm Gonna Run Away From You
8	Mungo Jerry	Lady Rose
9	Dawn	Knock Three Times
10	Temptations	Just My Imagination

The US Number One single: Carole King – It's Too Late/I Feel The Earth Move
The US Number One album: Carole King – Tapestry
The UK Number One album: Simon And Garfunkel – Bridge Over Troubled Water
Also this week: The Supreme Court clears Muhammed Ali of draft-dodging. (28th)

The UK Top 10 singles for the week ending July the 10th

1	Middle Of The Road	Chirpy Chirpy Cheep Cheep
2	Sweet	Co-Co
3	Hurricane Smith	Don't Let It Die
4	Blue Mink	Banner Man
5	John Kongos	He's Gonna Step On You Again
6	Tammi Lynn	I'm Gonna Run Away From You
7	Tony Christie	I Did What I Did For Maria
8	Temptations	Just My Imagination
9	Greyhound	Black And White
10	Mungo Jerry	Lady Rose

The US Number One single: Carole King – It's Too Late/I Feel The Earth Move
The US Number One album: Carole King – Tapestry
The UK Number One album: Simon And Garfunkel – Bridge Over Troubled Water
Also this week: King Hassan of Morocco crushes a coup attempt. (10th)

The UK Top 10 singles for the week ending July the 17th

1	Middle Of The Road	Chirpy Chirpy Cheep Cheep
2	Sweet	Co-Co
3	Hurricane Smith	Don't Let It Die
4	T. Rex	Get It On
5	Lobo	Me And You And A Dog Named Boo
6	Greyhound	Black And White
7	Dave And Ansil Collins	Monkey Spanner
8	Blue Mink	Banner Man
9	John Kongos	He's Gonna Step On You Again
10	Tammi Lynn	I'm Gonna Run Away From You

The US Number One single: Carole King – It's Too Late/I Feel The Earth Move
The US Number One album: Carole King – Tapestry
The UK Number One album: Simon And Garfunkel – Bridge Over Troubled Water
Also this week: Jordan's army launches an all-out attack on Palestinian guerrillas. (14th)

The UK Top 10 singles for the week ending July the 24th

1	T. Rex	Get It On
2	Middle Of The Road	Chirpy Chirpy Cheep Cheep
3	Sweet	Co-Co
4	Lobo	Me And You And A Dog Named Boo
5	Hurricane Smith	Don't Let It Die
6	Greyhound	Black And White
7	Dave And Ansil Collins	Monkey Spanner
8	New World	Tom Tom Turnaround
9	Blue Mink	Banner Man
10	Temptations	Just My Imagination

The US Number One single: The Raiders – Indian Reservation
The US Number One album: Carole King – Tapestry
The UK Number One album: Simon And Garfunkel – Bridge Over Troubled Water
Also this week: General Gaafar al-Numeiry is restored to power in Sudan. (22nd)

The UK Top 10 singles for the week ending July the 31st

1   T. Rex   Get It On
2   Middle Of The Road   Chirpy Chirpy Cheep Cheep
3   Sweet   Co-Co
4   Lobo   Me And You And A Dog Named Boo
5   New Seekers   Never Ending Song Of Love
6   New World   Tom Tom Turnaround
7   Dave And Ansil Collins   Monkey Spanner
8   Greyhound   Black And White
9   Hurricane Smith   Don't Let It Die
10 Atomic Rooster   Devil's Answer

The US Number One single: James Taylor – You've Got A Friend
The US Number One album: Carole King – Tapestry
The UK Number One album: Simon And Garfunkel – Bridge Over Troubled Water
Also this week: Two American astronauts go for a drive on the moon. (31st)

Song of the month for July 1971

Let Your Yeah Be Yeah by The Pioneers (peak chart position:No.5)

Although the Pioneers are regarded as something of a reggae group, this marvellous single was more akin to Motown or soul. Written by new Jamaican superstar Jimmy Cliff, 'Let Your Yeah Be Yeah' deserves to be credited as one of the great pop songs of all time, with its excellent vocal harmonies and brass accompaniment. It certainly sounds much different from the group's previous hit single, 'Long Shot Kick De Bucket'!

The UK Top 10 singles for the week ending August the 7th

1	T. Rex	Get It On
2	New Seekers	Never Ending Song Of Love
3	Middle Of The Road	Chirpy Chirpy Cheep Cheep
4	Atomic Rooster	Devil's Answer
5	Sweet	Co-Co
6	Lobo	Me And You And A Dog Named Boo
7	New World	Tom Tom Turnaround
8	Diana Ross	I'm Still Waiting
9	Dave And Ansil Collins	Monkey Spanner
10	The Who	Won't Get Fooled Again

The US Number One single: Bee Gees – How Can You Mend A Broken Heart?
The US Number One album: Carole King – Tapestry
The UK Number One album: No Artist(s) Credited – Hot Hits 6
Also this week: The American Apollo Fifteen splashes down safely on earth. (7th)

The UK Top 10 singles for the week ending August the 14th

1	T. Rex	Get It On
2	New Seekers	Never Ending Song Of Love
3	Diana Ross	I'm Still Waiting
4	Atomic Rooster	Devil's Answer
5	Family	In My Own Time
6	Lobo	Me And You And A Dog Named Boo
7	New World	Tom Tom Turnaround
8	Middle Of The Road	Chirpy Chirpy Cheep Cheep
9	The Who	Won't Get Fooled Again
10	Sweet	Co-Co

The US Number One single: Bee Gees – How Can You Mend A Broken Heart?
The US Number One album: Carole King – Tapestry
The UK Number One album: Moody Blues – Every Good Boy Deserves Favour
Also this week: Internment without trial is introduced in Northern Ireland. (9th)

The UK Top 10 singles for the week ending August the 21st

1	Diana Ross	I'm Still Waiting
2	New Seekers	Never Ending Song Of Love
3	T. Rex	Get It On
4	Atomic Rooster	Devil's Answer
5	Family	In My Own Time
6	Dawn	What Are You Doing Sunday?
7	New World	Tom Tom Turnaround
8	Middle Of The Road	Chirpy Chirpy Cheep Cheep
9	The Who	Won't Get Fooled Again
10	Elvis Presley	Heartbreak Hotel

The US Number One single: Bee Gees – How Can You Mend A Broken Heart?
The US Number One album: Carole King – Tapestry
The UK Number One album: No Artist(s) Credited – Top Of The Pops, Volume 18
Also this week: The emirate of Bahrain becomes independent. (15th)

The UK Top 10 singles for the week ending August the 28th

1	Diana Ross	I'm Still Waiting
2	New Seekers	Never Ending Song Of Love
3	Dawn	What Are You Doing Sunday?
4	T. Rex	Get It On
5	Family	In My Own Time
6	The Pioneers	Let Your Yeah Be Yeah
7	Atomic Rooster	Devil's Answer
8	Buffy Sainte-Marie	Soldier Blue
9	The Tams	Hey Girl Don't Bother Me
10	George Harrison	Bangla Desh

The US Number One single: Bee Gees – How Can You Mend A Broken Heart?
The US Number One album: Carole King – Tapestry
The UK Number One album: No Artist(s) Credited – Top Of The Pops, Volume 18
Also this week: An IRA bomb destroys the gates of Crumlin Road prison. (22nd)

Song of the month for August 1971

It's Too Late by Carole King (peak chart position:No.6)

Taken from an album, 'Tapestry', which had already surfaced successfully back in the spring, this 'new release' made predictable progress into the British Top Ten, though Carole King's radio-friendly double A-side failed to match the chart-topping success it achieved in the United States. This sad song was further evidence of Carole King's songwriting gifts and it was a key ingredient on a massive-selling long player that took up a mere 300 weeks' residency in the American album charts.

The UK Top 10 singles for the week ending September the 4th

1	Diana Ross	I'm Still Waiting
2	New Seekers	Never Ending Song Of Love
3	The Tams	Hey Girl Don't Bother Me
4	Family	In My Own Time
5	Dawn	What Are You Doing Sunday?
6	The Pioneers	Let Your Yeah Be Yeah
7	Buffy Sainte-Marie	Soldier Blue
8	Carole King	It's Too Late/I Feel The Earth Move
9	Atomic Rooster	Devil's Answer
10	T. Rex	Get It On

The US Number One single: Paul & Linda McCartney – Uncle Albert/Admiral Halsey
The US Number One album: Carole King – Tapestry
The UK Number One album: No Artist(s) Credited – Top Of The Pops, Volume 18
Also this week: 1d. and 3d. cease to be legal tender. (1st)

The UK Top 10 singles for the week ending September the 11th

1	Diana Ross	I'm Still Waiting
2	The Tams	Hey Girl Don't Bother Me
3	Dawn	What Are You Doing Sunday?
4	New Seekers	Never Ending Song Of Love
5	The Pioneers	Let Your Yeah Be Yeah
6	Nancy Sinatra And Lee Hazlewood	Did You Ever
7	Buffy Sainte-Marie	Soldier Blue
8	Supremes	Nathan Jones
9	Curved Air	Back Street Luv
10	Carole King	It's Too Late/I Feel The Earth Move

The US Number One single: Donny Osmond – Go Away Little Girl
The US Number One album: Carole King – Tapestry
The UK Number One album: Simon And Garfunkel – Bridge Over Troubled Water
Also this week: A riot erupts in New York state's Attica prison. (9th)

The UK Top 10 singles for the week ending September the 18th

1	The Tams	Hey Girl Don't Bother Me
2	Diana Ross	I'm Still Waiting
3	Nancy Sinatra And Lee Hazlewood	Did You Ever
4	Curved Air	Back Street Luv
5	Supremes	Nathan Jones
6	Carole King	It's Too Late/I Feel The Earth Move
7	New Seekers	Never Ending Song Of Love
8	Hot Chocolate	I Believe In Love
9	Buffy Sainte-Marie	Soldier Blue
10	Dawn	What Are You Doing Sunday?

The US Number One single: Donny Osmond – Go Away Little Girl
The US Number One album: Carole King – Tapestry
The UK Number One album: Who – Who's Next
Also this week: Duke Ellington performs a concert in the Soviet Union. (14th)

The UK Top 10 singles for the week ending September the 25th

1	The Tams	Hey Girl Don't Bother Me
2	Nancy Sinatra And Lee Hazlewood	Did You Ever
3	Rod Stewart	Maggie May/Reason To Believe
4	Middle Of The Road	Tweedledee Tweedledum
5	Supremes	Nathan Jones
6	C.C.S.	Tap Turns On the Water
7	Marmalade	Cousin Norman
8	Hot Chocolate	I Believe In Love
9	James Taylor	You've Got A Friend
10	Diana Ross	I'm Still Waiting

The US Number One single: Donny Osmond – Go Away Little Girl
The US Number One album: Carole King – Tapestry
The UK Number One album: Deep Purple – Fireball
Also this week: Ninety Russian diplomats and officials are expelled from Britain. (24th)

Song of the month for September 1971
Maggie May by Rod Stewart (peak chart position: No.1)

The new release, 'Maggie May' announced the arrival of one of the 1970s' great institutions, Mr. Rod Stewart. Abandoning his footballing ambitions in favour of delivering from the mike stand, 'Rod The Mod' sang "it's late September and I really should be back at school". Instead of which he was located at the top of the British hit parade. Scotland's finest was joined on stage for a memorable 'Top Of The Pops' cameo by John Peel on mandolin, while the Brentford FC reject dribbled a football. Credit must also go to the Faces for their musical contribution. For three glorious October weeks, Rod and the Faces were Number One in British and American singles and album charts simultaneously, emulating Simon And Garfunkel's 'Bridge Over Troubled Water'.

The UK Top 10 singles for the week ending October the 2nd

1	The Tams	Hey Girl Don't Bother Me
2	Rod Stewart	Maggie May/Reason To Believe
3	Nancy Sinatra And Lee Hazlewood	Did You Ever
4	Middle Of The Road	Tweedledee Tweedledum
5	C.C.S.	Tap Turns On the Water
6	Marmalade	Cousin Norman
7	Supremes	Nathan Jones
8	James Taylor	You've Got A Friend
9	Hot Chocolate	I Believe In Love
10	Shirley Bassey	For All We Know

The US Number One single: Rod Stewart – Maggie May/Reason To Believe
The US Number One album: Rod Stewart – Every Picture Tells A Story
The UK Number One album: Rod Stewart – Every Picture Tells A Story
Also this week: Chelsea beat Juenesse Hautcharage 13–0 in a European tie. (29th)

The UK Top 10 singles for the week ending October the 9th

1	Rod Stewart	Maggie May/Reason To Believe
2	The Tams	Hey Girl Don't Bother Me
3	Nancy Sinatra And Lee Hazlewood	Did You Ever
4	Middle Of The Road	Tweedledee Tweedledum
5	James Taylor	You've Got A Friend
6	C.C.S.	Tap Turns On the Water
7	Shirley Bassey	For All We Know
8	Marmalade	Cousin Norman
9	The Fortunes	Freedom Come, Freedom Go
10	Hot Chocolate	I Believe In Love

The US Number One single: Rod Stewart – Maggie May/Reason To Believe
The US Number One album: Rod Stewart – Every Picture Tells A Story
The UK Number One album: Rod Stewart – Every Picture Tells A Story
Also this week: Japan's Emperor Hirohito makes a controversial state visit to Britain. (9th)

The UK Top 10 singles for the week ending October the 16th

1	Rod Stewart	Maggie May/Reason To Believe
2	Middle Of The Road	Tweedledee Tweedledum
3	The Tams	Hey Girl Don't Bother Me
4	James Taylor	You've Got A Friend
5	Nancy Sinatra And Lee Hazlewood	Did You Ever
6	Shirley Bassey	For All We Know
7	Marmalade	Cousin Norman
8	C.C.S.	Tap Turns On the Water
9	Redbone	The Witch Queen Of New Orleans
10	The Fortunes	Freedom Come, Freedom Go

The US Number One single: Rod Stewart – Maggie May/Reason To Believe
The US Number One album: Rod Stewart – Every Picture Tells A Story
The UK Number One album: Rod Stewart – Every Picture Tells A Story
Also this week: The French secret service is implicated in alleged drug-trafficking. (16th)

The UK Top 10 singles for the week ending October the 23rd

1	Rod Stewart	Maggie May/Reason To Believe
2	Redbone	The Witch Queen Of New Orleans
3	Middle Of The Road	Tweedledee Tweedledum
4	James Taylor	You've Got A Friend
5	The Four Tops	Simple Game
6	The Fortunes	Freedom Come, Freedom Go
7	Shirley Bassey	For All We Know
8	Nancy Sinatra And Lee Hazlewood	Did You Ever
9	The Tams	Hey Girl Don't Bother Me
10	Titanic	Sultana

The US Number One single: Rod Stewart – Maggie May/Reason To Believe
The US Number One album: Rod Stewart – Every Picture Tells A Story
The UK Number One album: Rod Stewart – Every Picture Tells A Story
Also this week: Exiled Hungarian primate Cardinal Mindszenty moves to Vienna. (23rd)

The UK Top 10 singles for the week ending October the 30rd

1	Rod Stewart	Maggie May/Reason To Believe
2	Redbone	The Witch Queen Of New Orleans
3	Middle Of The Road	Tweedledee Tweedledum
4	The Four Tops	Simple Game
5	Titanic	Sultana
6	Shirley Bassey	For All We Know
7	The Fortunes	Freedom Come, Freedom Go
8	James Taylor	You've Got A Friend
9	Bay City Rollers	Keep On Dancing
10	Al Green	Tired Of Being Alone

The US Number One single: Rod Stewart – Maggie May/Reason To Believe
The US Number One album: John Lennon & The Plastic Ono Band – Imagine
The UK Number One album: John Lennon & The Plastic Ono Band – Imagine
Also this week: Congo changes its name to Zaire. (27th)

Song of the month for October 1971
How Do You Sleep? by John Lennon (album track)

John Lennon's 'Imagine' album was first released in September in the United States before seeing the light of day in the United Kingdom in October, by which time the ex-Beatle was now a citizen of New York. 'How Do You Sleep' is not necessarily the long player's best song, but it is certainly the most noteworthy. After divorcing Cynthia, John found himself embroiled in another bitter divorce situation as he and Paul McCartney embarked on a war of words amidst legal proceedings. 'How Do You Sleep?' was a savage put-down of his songwriting partner and (former) friend, suggesting that "the only thing you've done was 'Yesterday'". Fortunately sanity eventually prevailed and diplomatic relations were restored between the two legends.

The UK Top 10 singles for the week ending November the 6th

1	Rod Stewart	Maggie May/Reason To Believe
2	Redbone	The Witch Queen Of New Orleans
3	The Four Tops	Simple Game
4	Al Green	Tired Of Being Alone
5	Tom Jones	Till
6	Joan Baez	The Night They Drove Old Dixie Down
7	Titanic	Sultana
8	Slade	Coz I Luv You
9	Shirley Bassey	For All We Know
10	Middle Of The Road	Tweedledee Tweedledum

The US Number One single: Cher – Gypsys, Tramps & Thieves
The US Number One album: Isaac Hayes/Soundtrack – Shaft
The UK Number One album: John Lennon & The Plastic Ono Band – Imagine
Also this week: India's Premier, Mrs Gandhi, arrives in Washington for talks. (3rd)

The UK Top 10 singles for the week ending November the 13th

1	Slade	Coz I Luv You
2	Rod Stewart	Maggie May/Reason To Believe
3	Redbone	The Witch Queen Of New Orleans
4	Tom Jones	Till
5	The Four Tops	Simple Game
6	Al Green	Tired Of Being Alone
7	The Piglets	Johnny Reggae
8	Springwater	I Will Return
9	Joan Baez	The Night They Drove Old Dixie Down
10	Titanic	Sultana

The US Number One single: Cher – Gypsys, Tramps & Thieves
The US Number One album: Santana – Santana III
The UK Number One album: Rod Stewart – Every Picture Tells A Story
Also this week: President Nixon announces further troop withdrawals from
Vietnam. (12th)

The UK Top 10 singles for the week ending November the 20th

1	Slade	Coz I Luv You
2	Tom Jones	Till
3	The Piglets	Johnny Reggae
4	Rod Stewart	Maggie May/Reason To Believe
5	Springwater	I Will Return
6	Olivia Newton-John	Banks Of The Ohio
7	Cher	Gypsys, Tramps & Thieves
8	T. Rex	Jeepster
9	Al Green	Tired Of Being Alone
10	Joan Baez	The Night They Drove Old Dixie Down

The US Number One single: Isaac Hayes – Theme From Shaft
The US Number One album: Santana – Santana III
The UK Number One album: Rod Stewart – Every Picture Tells A Story
Also this week: Roy Jenkins defeats Michael Foot to remain Labour's deputy leader. (17th)

The UK Top 10 singles for the week ending November the 27th

1	Slade	Coz I Luv You
2	T. Rex	Jeepster
3	Benny Hill	Ernie (The Fastest Milkman In The West)
4	Cher	Gypsys, Tramps & Thieves
5	The Piglets	Johnny Reggae
6	Tom Jones	Till
7	Springwater	I Will Return
8	Olivia Newton-John	Banks Of The Ohio
9	Rod Stewart	Maggie May/Reason To Believe
10	Diana Ross	Surrender

The US Number One single: Isaac Hayes – Theme From Shaft
The US Number One album: Santana – Santana III
The UK Number One album: No Artist(s) Credited – Top Of The Pops, Volume 20
Also this week: Ninety Indian troops die in border clashes with Pakistan. (21st)

Song of the month for November 1971
Echoes by Pink Floyd (album track)

Arch-purveyors of progressive rock, the Floyd were always keen to stretch themselves by fleeing from the conventional format of three-minute songs in favour of something more daring. 'Echoes' followed 'Atom Heart Mother' as a track which lasted for a whole album side. It was risky, but it worked. Starting with a plucked piano, the song is a twenty-two minute nautical delight. At the conclusion, the music and the voices fade as if wandering off over the horizon – never to return. This item ought to find its way on to anyone's desert island disc collection, because its duration would be the equivalent of six or seven lesser songs.

The UK Top 10 singles for the week ending December the 4th

1	Slade	Coz I Luv You
2	Benny Hill	Ernie (The Fastest Milkman In The West)
3	T. Rex	Jeepster
4	Cher	Gypsys, Tramps & Thieves
5	The Piglets	Johnny Reggae
6	John Kongos	Tokoloshe Man
7	Olivia Newton-John	Banks Of The Ohio
8	Tom Jones	Till
9	Springwater	I Will Return
10	The Newbeats	Run Baby Run

The US Number One single: Sly & The Family Stone – Family Affair
The US Number One album: Santana – Santana III
The UK Number One album: Led Zeppelin – Four Symbols
Also this week: Pakistan launches a full-scale war against India. (3rd)

The UK Top 10 singles for the week ending December the 11th

1	Benny Hill	Ernie (The Fastest Milkman In The West)
2	T. Rex	Jeepster
3	Slade	Coz I Luv You
4	John Kongos	Tokoloshe Man
5	Cher	Gypsys, Tramps & Thieves
6	Olivia Newton-John	Banks Of The Ohio
7	Isaac Hayes	Theme From Shaft
8	Tom Jones	Till
9	Gilbert O'Sullivan	No Matter How I Try
10	The Piglets	Johnny Reggae

The US Number One single: Sly & The Family Stone – Family Affair
The US Number One album: Santana – Santana III
The UK Number One album: Led Zeppelin – Four Symbols
Also this week: Indian planes bomb an orphanage, killing three hundred children. (9th)

The UK Top 10 singles for the week ending December the 18th

1	Benny Hill	Ernie (The Fastest Milkman In The West)
2	T. Rex	Jeepster
3	Slade	Coz I Luv You
4	Isaac Hayes	Theme From Shaft
5	Gilbert O'Sullivan	No Matter How I Try
6	John Kongos	Tokoloshe Man
7	Cilla Black	Something Tells Me
8	Cher	Gypsys, Tramps & Thieves
9	Olivia Newton-John	Banks Of The Ohio
10	Tom Jones	Till

The US Number One single: Sly & The Family Stone – Family Affair
The US Number One album: Sly & The Family Stone – There's A Riot Goin' On
The UK Number One album: T.Rex – Electric Warrior
Also this week: Pakistan capitulates and accepts India's cease-fire ultimatum. (17th)

The UK Top 10 singles for the week ending December the 25th

1	Benny Hill	Ernie (The Fastest Milkman In The West)
2	T. Rex	Jeepster
3	Cilla Black	Something Tells Me
4	New Seekers	I'd Like To Teach The World To Sing
5	Isaac Hayes	Theme From Shaft
6	The Congregation	Softly Whispering I Love You
7	John Kongos	Tokoloshe Man
8	Gilbert O'Sullivan	No Matter How I Try
9	Middle Of The Road	Soley Soley
10	Cher	Gypsys, Tramps & Thieves

The US Number One single: Melanie – Brand New Key
The US Number One album: Sly & The Family Stone – There's A Riot Goin' On
The UK Number One album: T.Rex – Electric Warrior
Also this week: Austria's Dr Kurt Waldheim is appointed UN Secretary-General.
(21st)

Song of the month for December 1971

Theme From 'Shaft' by Isaac Hayes (peak chart position: No.4)

Performer of 'hot buttered soul', Isaac Hayes served up a treat with the outstanding theme to 'Shaft'. The song oozes sex appeal and is one of the coolest anthems to be delivered to the airwaves. Unfortunately, Hayes was never able to repeat this American chart-topper, but who can ever forget those strings and his spoken words? Nothing that the performer would subsequently record would ever stand any chance of a favourable comparison.

Listed Below are the Top 10 Best Selling UK Singles of 1971

1	My Sweet Lord	George Harrison
2	Maggie May	Rod Stewart
3	Chirpy Chirpy Cheep Cheep	Middle of the Road
4	Knock Three Times	Dawn
5	Hot Love	T.Rex
6	The Pushbike Song	The Mixtures
7	Never Ending Song Of Love	The New Seekers
8	I'm Still Waiting	Diana Ross
9	Get It On	T.Rex
10	Hey Girl Don't Bother Me	The Tams

1971's CONCERTS OF THE YEAR

Led Zeppelin braved the deteriorating situation in Ulster to perform at the Ulster Hall in Belfast in March. The band took the opportunity to treat the audience to the first public performances of 'Black Dog' and 'Stairway To Heaven'. However, the most noteworthy concert of 1971 is undoubtedly the event organised by George Harrison to raise money for the famine-stricken citizens of the new state of Bangladesh. Held at Madison Square Garden in New York City, the ex-Beatle guitarist recruited such acts as Eric Clapton, Bob Dylan, Billy Preston, Ravi Shankar, and Ringo Starr who all made contributions to the gig, which was subsequently translated onto vinyl. To quote from 'The Song For Today' (by Jimmie Oliver) "this historic event [on August the 1st] was a prototype Live Aid, and it was the first notable occasion when performers from the rock and pop aristocracy assembled to raise funds for others less fortunate."

1971's ALBUM OF THE YEAR

Sticky Fingers by The Rolling Stones
(released in April; reached No.1 in the UK)

SIDE ONE:

1. Brown Sugar; 3:50
2. Sway; 3:52
3. Wild Horses; 5:44
4. Can't You Hear Me Knocking; 7:15
5. You Gotta Move; 2:34

SIDE TWO:

1. Bitch; 3:37
2. I Got the Blues; 3:54
3. Sister Morphine; 5:34
4. Dead Flowers; 4:05
5. Moonlight Mile; 5:56

The landscape on Planet Stones had changed considerably since the issue of 'Let It Bleed' at the end of the 'sixties. For a start, the talented young Mick Taylor was now firmly ensconced in the role of guitarist, filling the void of the departed Brian Jones. Secondly, the Rolling Stones were now liberated from their contractual obligations to Decca Records and thus able to form their very own record label. Thirdly, these new rock aristocrats were now effectively tax exiles. However, one thing that did not change was the quality of their music. In fact, 'Sticky Fingers' is frequently hailed as the band's finest three-quarters of an hour, and it is hard not to agree. The album boasted the presence of the group's signature rocker, 'Brown Sugar', which dominated the charts on both sides of the Atlantic. The highlights however don't end there. The long player also contains such gems as 'Wild Horses', though much of the content dwells on drugs, pain, and vulnerability, as typified on 'Sister Morphine', 'I Got The Blues', and the magnificent 'Moonlight Mile', so the project is hardly overflowing with joie de vivre. Whatever the negativity of such items as 'Bitch', the album with the Andy Warhol-inspired cover met with the royal seal of approval from fans and critics alike.

SPORT IN 1971

English Division One football champions: Arsenal; runners-up: Leeds United

English FA Cup final: Arsenal 2 Liverpool 1 (after extra time)

English League Cup Final: Tottenham Hotspur 2 Aston Villa 0

Scotiish Division One football champions: Glasgow Celtic; runners-up: Aberdeen

Scottish FA Cup final: Glasgow Celtic 2 Glasgow Rangers 1 (in a replay)

Scottish League Cup final: Glasgow Rangers 1 Glasgow Celtic 0

Irish League football champions: Linfield; Irish Cup final: Distillery 3 Derry City 0

League Of Ireland football champions: Cork Hibernians; cup winners: Limerick

European Cup final: Ajax Amsterdam 2 Panathinaikos 0

European Cup-Winners' Cup final: Chelsea 2 Real Madrid 1 (in a replay)

European Fairs Cup final: Leeds United beat Juventus on away goals rule (3–3 on aggregate)

English county cricket champions: Surrey

Five Nations' rugby union champions: Wales (the Grand Slam); runners-up: France

Formula One world drivers' champion: Jackie Stewart (United Kingdom) in a Tyrrell car

Gaelic football All-Ireland champions: Offaly; runners-up: Galway

British Open golf champion: Lee Trevino (at Royal Birkdale)

US Masters golf champion: Charles Coody

US Open golf champion: Lee Trevino

USPGA golf champion: Jack Nicklaus

Rugby league Challenge Cup final: Leigh 24 Leeds 7

Wimbledon men's singles tennis final: J Newcombe beat S Smith 6–3, 5–7, 2–6, 6–4, 6–4

Wimbledon ladies' singles tennis final:E Goolagong beat M Court 6–4, 6–1

World snooker final: John Spencer (England) beat Warren Simpson (Australia) 37–29

The Aintree Grand National steeplechase winner: Specify; price 28–1

The Epsom Derby winner: Mill Reef; jockey – Geoff Lewis; price 100–30F

The Ryder Cup golf contest: United States 18.5 Great Britain And Ireland 13.5

1971's DEATHS

January 5th: Sonny Liston (US boxer), aged 38

January 10th: Gabrielle 'Coco' Chanel (French designer), aged 87

March 8th: Harold Lloyd (US actor), aged 77

March 16th: Thomas Dewey (US politician), aged 68

April 6th: Igor Stravinsky (Russian composer), aged 88

April 21st: 'Papa Doc' Duvalier (Haitian dictator), aged 64

May 19th: Ogden Nash (US poet), aged 68

June 4th: Gyorgy Lukacs (Hungarian politician), aged 86

June 16th: Baron Reith (BBC pioneer), aged 81

July 3rd: Jim Morrison (US singer), aged 27

July 6th: Louis Armstrong (US entertainer), aged 71

August 14th: Georg Von Opel (German car manufacturer), aged 59

September 11th: Nikita Khrushchev (Soviet statesman), aged 77

October 12th: Gene Vincent (US singer), aged 36

October 29th: Duane Allman (US musician), aged 24

December 18th: Bobby Jones (US golfer), aged 69

The UK Top 10 singles for the week ending January the 1st

1	Benny Hill	Ernie (The Fastest Milkman In The West)
2	T. Rex	Jeepster
3	Cilla Black	Something Tells Me
4	New Seekers	I'd Like To Teach The World To Sing
5	Isaac Hayes	Theme From Shaft
6	The Congregation	Softly Whispering I Love You
7	John Kongos	Tokoloshe Man
8	Gilbert O'Sullivan	No Matter How I Try
9	Middle Of The Road	Soley Soley
10	Cher	Gypsys Tramps And Thieves

The US Number One single: Melanie – Brand New Key
The US Number One album: Carole King – Music
The UK Number One album: T.Rex – Electric Warrior
Also this week: The Iraqi government expels thousands of Iranians. (31st)

The UK Top 10 singles for the week ending January the 8th

1	New Seekers	I'd Like To Teach The World To Sing
2	Benny Hill	Ernie (The Fastest Milkman In The West)
3	T. Rex	Jeepster
4	The Congregation	Softly Whispering I Love You
5	Middle Of The Road	Soley Soley
6	Isaac Hayes	Theme From Shaft
7	Cilla Black	Something Tells Me
8	Johnny Pearson Orchestra	Sleepy Shores
9	Gilbert O'Sullivan	No Matter How I Try
10	Elvis Presley	I Just Can't Help Believing

The US Number One single: Melanie – Brand New Key
The US Number One album: Carole King – Music
The UK Number One album: T.Rex – Electric Warrior
Also this week: Richard Nixon grants his approval to space shuttle research. (5th)

The UK Top 10 singles for the week ending January the 15th

1	New Seekers	I'd Like To Teach The World To Sing
2	Neil Reid	Mother Of Mine
3	Benny Hill	Ernie (The Fastest Milkman In The West)
4	The Congregation	Softly Whispering I Love You
5	Middle Of The Road	Soley Soley
6	Cilla Black	Something Tells Me
7	Elvis Presley	I Just Can't Help Believing
8	Melanie	Brand New Key
9	Johnny Pearson Orchestra	Sleepy Shores
10	T. Rex	Jeepster

The US Number One single: Don McLean – American Pie
The US Number One album: Carole King – Music
The UK Number One album: T.Rex – Electric Warrior
Also this week: A coal–miners' strike begins in Britain. (9th)

The UK Top 10 singles for the week ending January the 22nd

1	New Seekers	I'd Like To Teach The World To Sing
2	Neil Reid	Mother Of Mine
3	America	A Horse With No Name
4	Melanie	Brand New Key
5	The Congregation	Softly Whispering I Love You
6	Elvis Presley	I Just Can't Help Believing
7	Middle Of The Road	Soley Soley
8	Faces	Stay With Me
9	Johnny Pearson Orchestra	Sleepy Shores
10	Cat Stevens	Morning Has Broken

The US Number One single: Don McLean – American Pie
The US Number One album: Don McLean – American Pie
The UK Number One album: T.Rex – Electric Warrior
Also this week: Britain's entry into the Common Market is ratified in Brussels. (22nd)

The UK Top 10 singles for the week ending January the 29th

1	New Seekers	I'd Like To Teach The World To Sing
2	Neil Reid	Mother Of Mine
3	T. Rex	Telegram Sam
4	America	A Horse With No Name
5	Melanie	Brand New Key
6	Elvis Presley	I Just Can't Help Believing
7	Faces	Stay With Me
8	Donnie Elbert	Where Did Our Love Go
9	Cat Stevens	Morning Has Broken
10	Al Green	Let's Stay Together

The US Number One single: Don McLean – American Pie
The US Number One album: Don McLean – American Pie
The UK Number One album: George Harrison & Friends – Concert For Bangladesh
Also this week: The Soviet Union accepts Bangladesh as a nation–state. (24th)

The song of the month for January 1972
Let's Stay Together by Al Green (peak chart position: No.7)

Perhaps immortalised from its inclusion on the 'Pulp Fiction' movie, Al Green's magnificent love song, decorated by an excellent horns section, deservedly climbed to the top of the tree in the Billboard singles list. British record–buyers were slightly less appreciative, but few observers and listeners three decades later can argue that this is perhaps the greatest soul recording to emerge from North America in the 1970s.

The UK Top 10 singles for the week ending February the 5th

1	T. Rex	Telegram Sam
2	New Seekers	I'd Like To Teach The World To Sing
3	Neil Reid	Mother Of Mine
4	America	A Horse With No Name
5	Melanie	Brand New Key
6	Faces	Stay With Me
7	Chi-Lites	Have You Seen Her
8	Donnie Elbert	Where Did Our Love Go
9	Al Green	Let's Stay Together
10	Elvis Presley	I Just Can't Help Believing

The US Number One single: Don McLean – American Pie
The US Number One album: Don McLean – American Pie
The UK Number One album: T.Rex – Electric Warrior
Also this week: British paratroopers kill thirteen people at a civil rights march. (30th)

The UK Top 10 singles for the week ending February the 12th

1	T. Rex	Telegram Sam
2	Chicory Tip	Son Of My Father
3	Neil Reid	Mother Of Mine
4	New Seekers	I'd Like To Teach The World To Sing
5	Chi-Lites	Have You Seen Her
6	America	A Horse With No Name
7	Al Green	Let's Stay Together
8	Melanie	Brand New Key
9	Slade	Look Wot You Dun
10	Sonny And Cher	All I Ever Need Is You

The US Number One single: Al Green – Let's Stay Together
The US Number One album: Don McLean – American Pie
The UK Number One album: T.Rex – Electric Warrior
Also this week: Another civil rights march takes place in Newry. (6th)

The UK Top 10 singles for the week ending February the 19th

1	Chicory Tip	Son Of My Father
2	T. Rex	Telegram Sam
3	Chi-Lites	Have You Seen Her
4	Slade	Look Wot You Dun
5	Neil Reid	Mother Of Mine
6	Don McLean	American Pie
7	New Seekers	I'd Like To Teach The World To Sing
8	Sonny And Cher	All I Ever Need Is You
9	Fortunes	Storm In A Teacup
10	Al Green	Let's Stay Together

The US Number One single: Nilsson – Without You
The US Number One album: Don McLean – American Pie
The UK Number One album: Neil Reid – Neil Reid
Also this week: The Wilberforce inquiry recommends a pay rise for Britain's miners. (18th)

The UK Top 10 singles for the week ending February the 26th

1	Chicory Tip	Son Of My Father
2	T. Rex	Telegram Sam
3	Don McLean	American Pie
4	Slade	Look Wot You Dun
5	Nilsson	Without You
6	Chi-Lites	Have You Seen Her
7	Fortunes	Storm In A Teacup
8	Michael Jackson	Got To Be There
9	Neil Reid	Mother Of Mine
10	Badfinger	Day After Day

The US Number One single: Nilsson – Without You
The US Number One album: Don McLean – American Pie
The UK Number One album: Neil Reid – Neil Reid
Also this week: President Nixon arrives in China on a state visit. (21st)

The song of the month for February 1972

Without You by Nilsson (peak chart position: No.1)

This tearjerker is steeped in tragedy.the composer, Pete Ham (from the group Badfinger) took his own life a few years later, whilst the singer Harry Nilsson also died rather prematurely in the mid–1990s after his hard living caught up with him. Nevertheless, this 'bad luck charm' proved to be one of the most successful sad songs of all time, as it proceeded to sit on the top perch of the charts on both sides of the Atlantic Ocean.

The UK Top 10 singles for the week ending March the 4th

1   Chicory Tip   Son Of My Father
2   Don McLean   American Pie
3   Nilsson   Without You
4   Slade   Look Wot You Dun
5   Michael Jackson   Got To Be There
6   Chi-Lites   Have You Seen Her
7   Paul Simon   Mother And Child Reunion
8   Fortunes   Storm In A Teacup
9   Chelsea Football Team Blue Is The Colour
10 Badfinger   Day After Day

The US Number One single: Nilsson – Without You
The US Number One album: Don McLean – American Pie
The UK Number One album: Neil Reid – Neil Reid
Also this week: Michael Manley's Labour Party wins Jamaica's general election. (3rd)

The UK Top 10 singles for the week ending March the 11th

1 Nilsson   Without You
2 Don McLean   American Pie
3 Chicory Tip   Son Of My Father
4 New Seekers   Beg Steal Or Borrow
5 Chelsea Football Team   Blue Is The Colour
6 Michael Jackson   Got To Be There
7 Paul Simon   Mother And Child Reunion
8 Slade   Look Wot You Dun
9 Gilbert O'Sullivan   Alone Again (Naturally)
10 Lindisfarne   Meet Me On The Corner

The US Number One single: Nilsson – Without You
The US Number One album: Neil Young – Harvest
The UK Number One album: Neil Young – Harvest
Also this week: Walter Dejaco, the designer of Auschwitz's gas chambers, is freed. (10th)

The UK Top 10 singles for the week ending March the 18th

1 Nilsson   Without You
2 Don McLean   American Pie
3 New Seekers   Beg Steal Or Borrow
4 Chicory Tip   Son Of My Father
5 Paul Simon   Mother And Child Reunion
6 Gilbert O'Sullivan   Alone Again (Naturally)
7 Michael Jackson   Got To Be There
8 Chelsea Football Team   Blue Is The Colour
9 Lindisfarne   Meet Me On The Corner
10 Neil Reid   Mother Of Mine

The US Number One single: Neil Young – Heart Of Gold
The US Number One album: Neil Young – Harvest
The UK Number One album: Paul Simon – Paul Simon
Also this week: Millionaire recluse Howard Hughes meets Nicaragua's President Somoza. (14th)

The UK Top 10 singles for the week ending March the 25th

1	Nilsson	Without You
2	New Seekers	Beg Steal Or Borrow
3	Don McLean	American Pie
4	Gilbert O'Sullivan	Alone Again (Naturally)
5	Lindisfarne	Meet Me On The Corner
6	Paul Simon	Mother And Child Reunion
7	Argent	Hold Your Head Up
8	Michael Jackson	Got To Be There
9	Les Crane	Desiderata
10	The Supremes	Floy Joy

The US Number One single: America – A Horse With No Name
The US Number One album: America – America
The UK Number One album: Lindisfarne – Fog On The Tyne
Also this week: Edward Heath announces direct British rule for Northern Ireland. (24th)

The song of the month for March 1972

Smoke On The Water by Deep Purple (peak chart position: No.21 in 1977)

This album track from the newly–released 'Machine Head' never featured prominently in the hit parade, but it unquestionably rates as one of the great rock songs of the twentieth century. Recounting the story of their appearance at Montreux where the casino was wrecked by a fire, Deep Purple treat the listener to one of the greatest instrumental breaks in popular music as well as a memorable intro. Some songs are just too good for the charts, and this rock milestone was clearly one of them.

The UK Top 10 singles for the week ending April the 1st

1 Nilsson   Without You
2 New Seekers   Beg Steal Or Borrow
3 Gilbert O'Sullivan   Alone Again (Naturally)
4 Don McLean   American Pie
5 Argent   Hold Your Head Up
6 Lindisfarne   Meet Me On The Corner
7 Les Crane   Desiderata
8 Paul Simon   Mother And Child Reunion
9 The Supremes   Floy Joy
10 Michael Jackson   Got To Be There

The US Number One single: America – A Horse With No Name
The US Number One album: America – America
The UK Number One album: Lindisfarne – Fog On The Tyne
Also this week: Thousands of Ulster loyalists protest against direct British rule. (28th)

The UK Top 10 singles for the week ending April the 8th

1 Nilsson   Without You
2 New Seekers   Beg Steal Or Borrow
3 The Royal Scots Dragoon Guards   Amazing Grace
4 Gilbert O'Sullivan   Alone Again (Naturally)
5 Argent   Hold Your Head Up
6 Lindisfarne   Meet Me On The Corner
7 Don McLean   American Pie
8 The Chiffons   Sweet Talking Guy
9 Les Crane   Desiderata
10 The Supremes   Floy Joy

The US Number One single: America – A Horse With No Name
The US Number One album: America – America
The UK Number One album: Lindisfarne – Fog On The Tyne
Also this week: Egypt cuts diplomatic ties with Jordan. (6th)

The UK Top 10 singles for the week ending April the 15th

1 The Royal Scots Dragoon Guards   Amazing Grace
2 Nilsson   Without You
3 New Seekers   Beg Steal Or Borrow
4 Ringo Starr   Back Off Boogaloo
5 The Chiffons   Sweet Talking Guy
6 Argent   Hold Your Head Up
7 Tom Jones   The Young New Mexican Puppeteer
8 Gilbert O'Sullivan   Alone Again (Naturally)
9 Les Crane   Desiderata
10 Neil Young   Heart Of Gold

The US Number One single: Roberta Flack – The First Time Ever I Saw Your Face
The US Number One album: America – America
The UK Number One album: Lindisfarne – Fog On The Tyne
Also this week: Roy Jenkins resigns as the Labour Party's deputy leader. (6th)

The UK Top 10 singles for the week ending April the 22nd

1 The Royal Scots Dragoon Guards   Amazing Grace
2 Nilsson   Without You
3 Ringo Starr   Back Off Boogaloo
4 The Chiffons   Sweet Talking Guy
5 Elvis Presley   Until It's Time For You To Go
6 New Seekers   Beg Steal Or Borrow
7 Tom Jones   The Young New Mexican Puppeteer
8 Argent   Hold Your Head Up
9 Jo Jo Gunne   Run Run Run
10 Gilbert O'Sullivan   Alone Again (Naturally)

The US Number One single: Roberta Flack – The First Time Ever I Saw Your Face
The US Number One album: America – America
The UK Number One album: Deep Purple – Machine Head
Also this week: Long–distance rowers, Fairfax and Cook, complete their Pacific voyage. (22nd)

The UK Top 10 singles for the week ending April the 29th

1 The Royal Scots Dragoon Guards   Amazing Grace
2 Ringo Starr   Back Off Boogaloo
3 Nilsson   Without You
4 The Chiffons   Sweet Talking Guy
5 Vicky Leandros   Come What May
6 Tom Jones   The Young New Mexican Puppeteer
7 Tyrannosaurus Rex   Debora
8 Jo Jo Gunne   Run Run Run
9 Marmalade   Radancer
10 Elvis Presley   Until It's Time For You To Go

The US Number One single: Roberta Flack – The First Time Ever I Saw Your Face
The US Number One album: Roberta Flack – First Take
The UK Number One album: Deep Purple – Machine Head
Also this week: A French referendum accepts the Treaty of Brussels. (23rd)

The song of the month for April 1972

Amazing Grace by The Royal Scots Dragoon Guards
(peak chart position: No.1)

It was certainly one of the most unexpected of chart–toppers, but an instrumental version of the Christian hymn, 'Amazing Grace', dominated the British hit parade throughout the spring of 1972. Five weeks at Number One and a mere 27 weeks on the singles chart tells its own story. Long before the likes of the Bay City Rollers and Rod Stewart popularized tartan fashion, the Pipes And Drums Of The Military Band Of The Royal Scots Dragoon Guards got there first!

The UK Top 10 singles for the week ending May the 6th

1	The Royal Scots Dragoon Guards	Amazing Grace
2	Ringo Starr	Back Off Boogaloo
3	Vicky Leandros	Come What May
4	David Cassidy	Could It Be Forever
5	The Chiffons	Sweet Talking Guy
6	Jo Jo Gunne	Run Run Run
7	Johnny Cash	A Thing Called Love
8	Tyrannosaurus Rex	Debora
9	Marmalade	Radancer
10	Nilsson	Without You

The US Number One single: Roberta Flack – The First Time Ever I Saw Your Face
The US Number One album: Roberta Flack – First Take
The UK Number One album: Tyrannosaurus Rex – Prophets, Seers And Sages The Angels Of The Ages
Also this week: Hue in Vietnam is evacuated as Communist forces draw near. (3rd)

The UK Top 10 singles for the week ending May the 13th

1	The Royal Scots Dragoon Guards	Amazing Grace
2	Vicky Leandros	Come What May
3	David Cassidy	Could It Be Forever
4	Johnny Cash	A Thing Called Love
5	Rolling Stones	Tumbling Dice
6	Marmalade	Radancer
7	Elton John	Rocket Man
8	Jo Jo Gunne	Run Run Run
9	T. Rex	Metal Guru
10	The Chiffons	Sweet Talking Guy

The US Number One single: Roberta Flack – The First Time Ever I Saw Your Face
The US Number One album: Roberta Flack – First Take
The UK Number One album: Deep Purple – Machine Head
Also this week: An Irish referendum approves the Treaty of Brussels. (11th)

The UK Top 10 singles for the week ending May the 20th

1	T. Rex	Metal Guru
2	The Royal Scots Dragoon Guards	Amazing Grace
3	David Cassidy	Could It Be Forever
4	Vicky Leandros	Come What May
5	Elton John	Rocket Man
6	Johnny Cash	A Thing Called Love
7	Rolling Stones	Tumbling Dice
8	Drifters	At The Club/Saturday Night At The Movies
9	Marmalade	Radancer
10	Jo Jo Gunne	Run Run Run

The US Number One single: Roberta Flack – The First Time Ever I Saw Your Face
The US Number One album: Roberta Flack – First Take
The UK Number One album: T. Rex – Bolan Boogie
Also this week: Governor George Wallace is wounded by a gunman. (16th)

The UK Top 10 singles for the week ending May the 27th

1	T. Rex	Metal Guru
2	David Cassidy	Could It Be Forever
3	The Royal Scots Dragoon Guards	Amazing Grace
4	Vicky Leandros	Come What May
5	Elton John	Rocket Man
6	Hurricane Smith	Oh Babe What Would You Say
7	Johnny Cash	A Thing Called Love
8	Drifters	At The Club/Saturday Night At The Movies
9	Rolling Stones	Tumbling Dice
10	Leeds United	Leeds United FC

The US Number One single: Chi–Lites – Oh Girl
The US Number One album: Roberta Flack – First Take
The UK Number One album: T. Rex – Bolan Boogie
Also this week: Richard Nixon arrives in the Soviet Union for talks. (22nd)

The song of the month for May 1972

Happy by The Rolling Stones (album track)

After the critical success of 'Sticky Fingers', the Fab Five delivered an hour of music in a similarly murky vein that would comprise the 'Exile On Main St.' album. Whilst many of the songs were a bit seedy, there were a few rays of light. One such item was 'Happy' in which Keef has another bash at lead vocals, having previously sang 'You Got The Silver' on the 'Let It Bleed' project. Richards was singing "I need your love to keep me happy", but if this was directed at his partner, Anita Pallenberg, it would be closer to the truth to suggest that they had a mutual suicide pact, given their dangerous flirtation with hard drugs.

The UK Top 10 singles for the week ending June the 3rd

1	T. Rex	Metal Guru
2	Elton John	Rocket Man
3	Drifters	At The Club/Saturday Night At The Movies
4	Hurricane Smith	Oh Babe What Would You Say
5	Don McLean	Vincent
6	Lindisfarne	Lady Eleanor
7	David Cassidy	Could It Be Forever
8	The Royal Scots Dragoon Guards	Amazing Grace
9	Johnny Cash	A Thing Called Love
10	Vicky Leandros	Come What May

The US Number One single: The Staple Singers – I'll Take You There
The US Number One album: Jethro Tull – Thick As A Brick
The UK Number One album: T. Rex – Bolan Boogie
Also this week: Three Japanese terrorists massacre 25 at Tel Aviv airport. (30th)

The UK Top 10 singles for the week ending June the 10th

1	T. Rex	Metal Guru
2	Don McLean	Vincent
3	Lindisfarne	Lady Eleanor
4	Hurricane Smith	Oh Babe What Would You Say
5	Elton John	Rocket Man
6	Drifters	At The Club/Saturday Night At The Movies
7	David Cassidy	Could It Be Forever
8	The Move	California Man
9	New World	Sister Jane
10	Michael Jackson	Rockin' Robin

The US Number One single: Sammy Davis, Jr. – The Candy Man
The US Number One album: Jethro Tull – Thick As A Brick
The UK Number One album: Rolling Stones – Exile On Main St.
Also this week: A pit explosion in Rhodesia kills four hundred miners. (8th)

The UK Top 10 singles for the week ending June the 17th

1	Don McLean	Vincent
2	T. Rex	Metal Guru
3	Slade	Take Me Bak 'Ome
4	Drifters	At The Club/Saturday Night At The Movies
5	Michael Jackson	Rockin' Robin
6	Lindisfarne	Lady Eleanor
7	The Move	California Man
8	Hurricane Smith	Oh Babe What Would You Say
9	New World	Sister Jane
10	Wings	Mary Had A Little Lamb

The US Number One single: Sammy Davis, Jr. – The Candy Man
The US Number One album: Rolling Stones – Exile On Main St.
The UK Number One album: Various Artist Compilation – 20 Dynamic Hits
Also this week: Five 'burglars' are arrested at Washington's Watergate offices. (17th)

The UK Top 10 singles for the week ending June the 24th

1	Don McLean	Vincent
2	Slade	Take Me Bak 'Ome
3	Michael Jackson	Rockin' Robin
4	T. Rex	Metal Guru
5	Drifters	At The Club/Saturday Night At The Movies
6	Gary Glitter	Rock And Roll-Parts 1 & 2
7	The Move	California Man
8	Sweet	Little Willy
9	Wings	Mary Had A Little Lamb
10	Lindisfarne	Lady Eleanor

The US Number One single: Sammy Davis, Jr. – The Candy Man

The US Number One album: Rolling Stones – Exile On Main St.

The UK Number One album: Various Artist Compilation – 20 Dynamic Hits

Also this week: Anthony Barber, the Conservative Chancellor, decides to float the pound. (23rd)

The song of the month for June 1972

American Trilogy by Elvis Presley (peak chart position: No.8)

As the 1970s unfolded, the behaviour and performances of Elvis Presley became increasingly erratic. However, what was good was exceptionally good. The King's rendition of an 'American Trilogy' simply takes the breath away and helps to explain why this 'has–been' remained one of the greatest live attractions. Sourcing 'Dixieland', 'All My Trials', and 'The Battle Hymn Of The Republic', Elvis sings straight from the depths of his soul. Only the coldest heart could fail to be moved or impressed by four and a half minutes of this emotional piece.

The UK Top 10 singles for the week ending July the 1st

1	Slade	Take Me Bak 'Ome
2	Don McLean	Vincent
3	Donny Osmond	Puppy Love
4	Sweet	Little Willy
5	Gary Glitter	Rock And Roll-Parts 1 & 2
6	Michael Jackson	Rockin' Robin
7	The Move	California Man
8	Elvis Presley	American Trilogy
9	Wings	Mary Had A Little Lamb
10	Drifters	At The Club/Saturday Night At The Movies

The US Number One single: Neil Diamond – Song Sung Blue
The US Number One album: Rolling Stones – Exile On Main St.
The UK Number One album: Various Artist Compilation – 20 Dynamic Hits
Also this week: John Mitchell resigns as President Nixon's election campaign manager. (1st)

The UK Top 10 singles for the week ending July the 8th

1	Donny Osmond	Puppy Love
2	Gary Glitter	Rock And Roll–Parts 1 & 2
3	Slade	Take Me Bak 'Ome
4	Sweet	Little Willy
5	Don McLean	Vincent
6	New Seekers	Circles
7	Michael Jackson	Rockin' Robin
8	Gilbert O'Sullivan	Ooh–Wakka–Doo–Wakka–Day
9	Elvis Presley	American Trilogy
10	The Move	California Man

The US Number One single: Bill Withers – Lean On Me
The US Number One album: Rolling Stones – Exile On Main St.
The UK Number One album: Various Artist Compilation – 20 Dynamic Hits
Also this week: Jacques Chaban-Delmas resigns as France's Prime Minister. (5th)

The UK Top 10 singles for the week ending July the 15th

1	Donny Osmond	Puppy Love
2	Gary Glitter	Rock And Roll-Parts 1 & 2
3	Slade	Take Me Bak 'Ome
4	Dr Hook And The Medicine Show	Sylvia's Mother
5	New Seekers	Circles
6	Sweet	Little Willy
7	Johnny Nash	I Can See Clearly Now
8	Don McLean	Vincent
9	Elvis Presley	American Trilogy
10	Michael Jackson	Rockin' Robin

The US Number One single: Bill Withers – Lean On Me
The US Number One album: Elton John – Honky Chateau
The UK Number One album: Various Artist Compilation – 20 Dynamic Hits
Also this week: George McGovern wins the Democrat's nomination for the
November election. (13th)

The UK Top 10 singles for the week ending July the 22nd

1	Donny Osmond	Puppy Love
2	Gary Glitter	Rock And Roll-Parts 1 & 2
3	Dr Hook And The Medicine Show	Sylvia's Mother
4	New Seekers	Circles
5	Johnny Nash	I Can See Clearly Now
6	Sweet	Little Willy
7	Partridge Family	Breaking Up Is Hard To Do
8	Slade	Take Me Bak 'Ome
9	The Who	Join Together
10	Elvis Presley	American Trilogy

The US Number One single: Bill Withers – Lean On Me
The US Number One album: Elton John – Honky Chateau
The UK Number One album: Various Artist Compilation – 20 Dynamic Hits
Also this week: Eleven are killed during Belfast's 'Bloody Friday'. (21st)

The UK Top 10 singles for the week ending July the 29th

1	Donny Osmond	Puppy Love
2	Dr Hook And The Medicine Show	Sylvia's Mother
3	Gary Glitter	Rock And Roll-Parts 1 & 2
4	Partridge Family	Breaking Up Is Hard To Do
5	Terry Dactyl And The Dinosaurs	Seaside Shuffle
6	Alice Cooper	School's Out
7	Johnny Nash	I Can See Clearly Now
8	New Seekers	Circles
9	Bruce Ruffin	Mad About You
10	David Bowie	Starman

The US Number One single: Gilbert O'Sullivan – Alone Again (Naturally)
The US Number One album: Elton John – Honky Chateau
The UK Number One album: Various Artist Compilation – 20 Dynamic Hits
Also this week: A nationwide dock strike begins in Britain. (28th)

The song of the month for July 1972

All The Young Dudes by Mott The Hoople (peak chart position: No.3)

Flavour of the month David Bowie stepped in to rescue the flagging career of Mott The Hoople by offering a composition of his own which he then produced for the combo. Not content with this, he weighed in with backing vocals. The group for their part rose to the challenge with a landmark rock song which opens wonderfully and goes from strength to strength, culminating in a formidable arms-swaying outro, during which Ian Hunter ad-libs "Hey you with the glasses/I want you/I want you up at the front." They just don't make them like this anymore.

The UK Top 10 singles for the week ending August the 5th

1   Donny Osmond   Puppy Love
2   Alice Cooper   School's Out
3   Dr Hook And The Medicine Show Sylvia's Mother
4   Terry Dactyl And The Dinosaurs Seaside Shuffle
5   Partridge Family   Breaking Up Is Hard To Do
6   Gary Glitter   Rock And Roll-Parts 1 & 2
7   Hawkwind   Silver Machine
8   Johnny Nash   I Can See Clearly Now
9   New Seekers   Circles
10 The Supremes   Automatically Sunshine

The US Number One single: Gilbert O'Sullivan – Alone Again (Naturally)
The US Number One album: Elton John – Honky Chateau
The UK Number One album: Various Artist Compilation – 20 Dynamic Hits
Also this week: British troops launch 'Operation Motorman' in Northern Ireland. (31st)

The UK Top 10 singles for the week ending August the 12th

1   Alice Cooper   School's Out
2   Terry Dactyl And The Dinosaurs Seaside Shuffle
3   Partridge Family   Breaking Up Is Hard To Do
4   Donny Osmond   Puppy Love
5   Dr Hook And The Medicine Show Sylvia's Mother
6   Hot Butter   Popcorn
7   Hawkwind   Silver Machine
8   Johnny Nash   I Can See Clearly Now
9   Gary Glitter   Rock And Roll-Parts 1 & 2
10 New Seekers   Circles

The US Number One single: Gilbert O'Sullivan – Alone Again (Naturally)
The US Number One album: Elton John – Honky Chateau
The UK Number One album: Various Artist Compilation – 20 Fantastic Hits
Also this week: General Idi Amin announces plans to expel many Ugandan Asians. (6th)

The UK Top 10 singles for the week ending August the 19th

1 Alice Cooper — School's Out
2 Terry Dactyl And The Dinosaurs — Seaside Shuffle
3 Hawkwind — Silver Machine
4 Donny Osmond — Puppy Love
5 Hot Butter — Popcorn
6 Partridge Family — Breaking Up Is Hard To Do
7 Rod Stewart — You Wear It Well
8 Dr Hook And The Medicine Show — Sylvia's Mother
9 Bee Gees — Run To Me
10 Faron Young — It's Four In The Morning

The US Number One single: Gilbert O'Sullivan – Alone Again (Naturally)
The US Number One album: Chicago – Chicago V
The UK Number One album: Various Artist Compilation – 20 Fantastic Hits
Also this week: King Hassan of Morocco survives another coup attempt. (16th)

The UK Top 10 singles for the week ending August the 26th

1 Alice Cooper — School's Out
2 Rod Stewart — You Wear It Well
3 Hawkwind — Silver Machine
4 Mott The Hoople — All The Young Dudes
5 Terry Dactyl And The Dinosaurs — Seaside Shuffle
6 Hot Butter — Popcorn
7 Derek And The Dominoes — Layla
8 Partridge Family — Breaking Up Is Hard To Do
9 E.L.O. — 10538 Overture
10 Donny Osmond — Puppy Love

The US Number One single: Looking Glass – Brandy (You're A Fine Girl)
The US Number One album: Chicago – Chicago V
The UK Number One album: Various Artist Compilation – 20 Fantastic Hits
Also this week: The twentieth Olympic Games opens in Munich. (26th)

The song of the month for August 1972

Virginia Plain by Roxy Music (peak chart position: No.4)

Former teacher Bryan Ferry joined forces all too briefly with Brian Eno as their new combo Roxy Music were at the forefront of art rock. The new act hit the ground running with the marvel that was 'Virginia Plain' which ought to be short–listed for the best debut single of all time. The song possesses a plethora of amusing lyrics featuring "you're so chic/teenage rebel of the week" with references to flamingoes, a studebaker, and a rollercoaster ride. What a pity that Eno subsequently jumped ship, but the rest of the crew coped more than adequately in his subsequent absence.

The UK Top 10 singles for the week ending September the 2nd

1	Rod Stewart	You Wear It Well
2	Slade	Mama Weer All Crazee Now
3	Alice Cooper	School's Out
4	Hawkwind	Silver Machine
5	Mott The Hoople	All The Young Dudes
6	Faron Young	It's Four In The Morning
7	Derek And The Dominoes	Layla
8	Hot Butter	Popcorn
9	Blackfoot Sue	Standing In The Road
10	Terry Dactyl And The Dinosaurs	Seaside Shuffle

The US Number One single: Gilbert O'Sullivan – Alone Again (Naturally)
The US Number One album: Chicago – Chicago V
The UK Number One album: Various Artist Compilation – 20 Fantastic Hits
Also this week: Twenty–two die in a Montreal night club bomb attack. (2nd)

The UK Top 10 singles for the week ending September the 9th

1	Slade	Mama Weer All Crazee Now
2	Rod Stewart	You Wear It Well
3	Mott The Hoople	All The Young Dudes
4	Blackfoot Sue	Standing In The Road
5	Faron Young	It's Four In The Morning
6	Lynsey De Paul	Sugar Me
7	Hawkwind	Silver Machine
8	Roxy Music	Virginia Plain
9	Derek And The Dominoes	Layla
10	Jackie Wilson	I Get The Sweetest Feeling

The US Number One single: Gilbert O'Sullivan – Alone Again (Naturally)
The US Number One album: Chicago – Chicago V
The UK Number One album: Various Artist Compilation – 20 Fantastic Hits
Also this week: 'Black September' Arab terrorists seize Israeli hostages at Munich. (5th)

The UK Top 10 singles for the week ending September the 16th

1	Slade	Mama Weer All Crazee Now
2	Rod Stewart	You Wear It Well
3	Faron Young	It's Four In The Morning
4	Roxy Music	Virginia Plain
5	Lynsey De Paul	Sugar Me
6	Blackfoot Sue	Standing In The Road
7	Mott The Hoople	All The Young Dudes
8	Michael Jackson	Ain't No Sunshine
9	Jackie Wilson	I Get The Sweetest Feeling
10	David Cassidy	How Can I Be Sure

The US Number One single: Three Dog Night – Black And White
The US Number One album: Chicago – Chicago V
The UK Number One album: Rod Stewart – Never A Dull Moment
Also this week: An Icelandic gunboat sinks two British trawlers. (12th)

The UK Top 10 singles for the week ending September the 23rd

1	Slade	Mama Weer All Crazee Now
2	T. Rex	Children Of The Revolution
3	David Cassidy	How Can I Be Sure
4	Rod Stewart	You Wear It Well
5	Lynsey De Paul	Sugar Me
6	Faron Young	It's Four In The Morning
7	Roxy Music	Virginia Plain
8	Michael Jackson	Ain't No Sunshine
9	Donny Osmond	Too Young
10	Drifters	Come On Over To My Place

The US Number One single: Mac Davis – Baby, Don't Get Hooked On Me
The US Number One album: Chicago – Chicago V
The UK Number One album: Rod Stewart – Never A Dull Moment
Also this week: Martial law is declared in the Philippines. (23rd)

The UK Top 10 singles for the week ending September the 30th

1	David Cassidy	How Can I Be Sure
2	T. Rex	Children Of The Revolution
3	Slade	Mama Weer All Crazee Now
4	Lieutenant Pigeon	Mouldy Old Dough
5	Donny Osmond	Too Young
6	Sweet	Wig-Wam Bam
7	Faron Young	It's Four In The Morning
8	Michael Jackson	Ain't No Sunshine
9	Drifters	Come On Over To My Place
10	Roxy Music	Virginia Plain

The US Number One single: Mac Davis – Baby, Don't Get Hooked On Me
The US Number One album: Chicago – Chicago V
The UK Number One album: Various Artist Compilation – 20 Fantastic Hits
Also this week: Norway votes against joining the Common Market. (25th)

The song of the month for September 1972

Mouldy Old Dough by Lieutenant Pigeon (peak chart position: No.1)

British record–purchasers have always been logic–defying suckers for novelty records, and good old Lieutenant Pigeon stepped forth with the mother of all novelty singles. Featuring a marching drum, a flute, and a fabulous piano contribution, this home–made recording stomped to the top of the UK charts. It was the kind of record that would have driven music critics to distraction, but I do confess to a liking for this bizarre smash hit.

The UK Top 10 singles for the week ending October the 7th

1	David Cassidy	How Can I Be Sure
2	T. Rex	Children Of The Revolution
3	Lieutenant Pigeon	Mouldy Old Dough
4	Sweet	Wig-Wam Bam
5	Donny Osmond	Too Young
6	Peter Skellern	You're A Lady
7	Slade	Mama Weer All Crazee Now
8	Gary Glitter	I Didn't Know I Loved You (Till I Saw You Rock 'N' Roll)
9	Faron Young	It's Four In The Morning
10	Drifters	Come On Over To My Place

The US Number One single: Mac Davis – Baby, Don't Get Hooked On Me
The US Number One album: Chicago – Chicago V
The UK Number One album: Various Artist Compilation – 20 All Time Hits Of The 50s
Also this week: Denmark votes in favour of the Treaty of Brussels. (2nd)

The UK Top 10 singles for the week ending October the 14th

1	Lieutenant Pigeon	Mouldy Old Dough
2	David Cassidy	How Can I Be Sure
3	Peter Skellern	You're A Lady
4	Gary Glitter	I Didn't Know I Loved You (Till I Saw You Rock 'N' Roll)
5	T. Rex	Children Of The Revolution
6	Sweet	Wig–Wam Bam
7	Donny Osmond	Too Young
8	Elvis Presley	Burning Love
9	Python Lee Jackson	In A Broken Dream
10	10cc	Donna

The US Number One single: Michael Jackson – Ben
The US Number One album: Chicago – Chicago V
The UK Number One album: Various Artist Compilation – 20 All Time Hits Of The 50s
Also this week: John Betjeman is appointed as Britain's poet laureate. (10th)

The UK Top 10 singles for the week ending October the 21st

1	Lieutenant Pigeon	Mouldy Old Dough
2	10cc	Donna
3	Peter Skellern	You're A Lady
4	David Cassidy	How Can I Be Sure
5	Gary Glitter	I Didn't Know I Loved You (Till I Saw You Rock 'N' Roll)
6	Python Lee Jackson	In A Broken Dream
7	Elvis Presley	Burning Love
8	Sweet	Wig–Wam Bam
9	Alice Cooper	Elected
10	T. Rex	Children Of The Revolution

The US Number One single: Chuck Berry – My Ding-A-Ling
The US Number One album: Curtis Mayfield/Soundtrack – Super Fly
The UK Number One album: Various Artist Compilation – 20 All Time Hits Of The 50s
Also this week: The Queen pays a state visit to communist Yugoslavia. (17th)

The UK Top 10 singles for the week ending October the 28th

1	Lieutenant Pigeon	Mouldy Old Dough
2	10cc	Donna
3	Python Lee Jackson	In A Broken Dream
4	Alice Cooper	Elected
5	Gilbert O'Sullivan	Clair
6	Gary Glitter	I Didn't Know I Loved You (Till I Saw You Rock 'N' Roll)
7	Peter Skellern	You're A Lady
8	Elvis Presley	Burning Love
9	Johnny Nash	There Are More Questions Than Answers
10	Sweet	Wig–Wam Bam

The US Number One single: Chuck Berry – My Ding–A–Ling
The US Number One album: Curtis Mayfield/Soundtrack – Super Fly
The UK Number One album: Various Artist Compilation – 20 All Time Hits Of The 50s
Also this week: The 'Cod War' intensifies as Iceland boycotts British goods. (25th)

The song of the month for October 1972

Clair by Gilbert O'Sullivan (peak chart position: No.1)

Gilbert O'Sullivan was a prolific hit–maker in the early 'seventies. His finest four minutes are almost certainly 'Clair'. I have an ambiguous attitude to this chart-topper. On a purely naive level, this is a sweet piece with beautiful strings music, but in the changed times of the twenty-first century it is doubtful whether O'Sullivan would get away with a song in which his intense affection for his niece Clair is perhaps questionable: "Nothing means more to me than hearing you say I'm going to marry you/Will you marry me, Uncle Ray?"

The UK Top 10 singles for the week ending November the 4th

1	Lieutenant Pigeon	Mouldy Old Dough
2	Gilbert O'Sullivan	Clair
3	10cc	Donna
4	Python Lee Jackson	In A Broken Dream
5	Alice Cooper	Elected
6	The Shangri-Las	Leader Of The Pack
7	Shag	Loop Di Love
8	Peter Skellern	You're A Lady
9	Elvis Presley	Burning Love
10	Johnny Nash	There Are More Questions Than Answers

The US Number One single: Johnny Nash – I Can See Clearly Now
The US Number One album: Curtis Mayfield/Soundtrack – Super Fly
The UK Number One album: Various Artist Compilation – 20 All Time Hits Of The 50s
Also this week: An Israeli bombing raid in Syria leaves fifty dead. (30th)

The UK Top 10 singles for the week ending November the 11th

1	Gilbert O'Sullivan	Clair
2	Lieutenant Pigeon	Mouldy Old Dough
3	10cc	Donna
4	Alice Cooper	Elected
5	Shag	Loop Di Love
6	Chuck Berry	My Ding-A-Ling
7	Python Lee Jackson	In A Broken Dream
8	The Shangri-Las	Leader Of The Pack
9	Carpenters	Goodbye To Love
10	Junior Campbell	Hallelujah Freedom

The US Number One single: Johnny Nash – I Can See Clearly Now
The US Number One album: Curtis Mayfield/Soundtrack – Super Fly
The UK Number One album: Various Artist Compilation – 20 All Time Hits Of The 50s
Also this week: Richard Nixon trounces George McGovern in the Presidential election. (7th)

The UK Top 10 singles for the week ending November the 18th

1	Gilbert O'Sullivan	Clair
2	Chuck Berry	My Ding-A-Ling
3	The Shangri-Las	Leader Of The Pack
4	Shag	Loop Di Love
5	Lieutenant Pigeon	Mouldy Old Dough
6	Donny Osmond	Why
7	Osmonds	Crazy Horses
8	Elton John	Crocodile Rock
9	Chris Montez	Let's Dance
10	Stylistics	I'm Stone In Love With You

The US Number One single: Johnny Nash – I Can See Clearly Now
The US Number One album: Cat Stevens – Catch Bull At Four
The UK Number One album: Various Artist Compilation – 20 All Time Hits Of The 50s
Also this week: Juan Peron returns to Argentina after seventeen years in exile. (17th)

The UK Top 10 singles for the week ending November the 25th

1	Chuck Berry	My Ding–A–Ling
2	Osmonds	Crazy Horses
3	Gilbert O'Sullivan	Clair
4	Donny Osmond	Why
5	Elton John	Crocodile Rock
6	The Shangri-Las	Leader Of The Pack
7	Shag	Loop Di Love
8	Slade	Gudbuy T'Jane
9	Stylistics	I'm Stone In Love With You
10	Rod Stewart	Angel/What Made Milwaukee Famous (Has Made A Loser Out Of Me)

The US Number One single: Johnny Nash – I Can See Clearly Now
The US Number One album: Cat Stevens – Catch Bull At Four
The UK Number One album: Various Artist Compilation – 20 All Time Hits Of The 50s
Also this week: The IRA leader Sean MacStiofain is arrested. (19th)

The song of the month for November 1972
Long Haired Lover From Liverpool by Little Jimmy Osmond
(peak chart position: No.1)

Having allowed the likes of Rolf Harris, Clive Dunn, and Benny Hill to reach Number One, it was hardly surprising that Britain's record–buyers were bowled over by Little Jimmy Osmond's delightful little ditty. It was perhaps fitting that the year of Osmond mania should finish with the youngest of their clan sitting on the top chart perch. In one crazy December week, the Osmonds and their rivals in the Jackson family were responsible for no fewer than five of the UK Top Ten singles. Little Jimmy himself was only nine years of age and thus made history as the youngest act to perform a British chart–topper!

The UK Top 10 singles for the week ending December the 2nd

1	Chuck Berry	My Ding-A-Ling
2	Osmonds	Crazy Horses
3	Donny Osmond	Why
4	Slade	Gudbuy T'Jane
5	Elton John	Crocodile Rock
6	Rod Stewart	Angel/What Made Milwaukee Famous (Has Made A Loser Out Of Me)
7	Gilbert O'Sullivan	Clair
8	The Shangri-Las	Leader Of The Pack
9	Jackson 5	Lookin' Through The Windows
10	Stylistics	I'm Stone In Love With You

The US Number One single: Temptations – Papa Was A Rollin' Stone
The US Number One album: Cat Stevens – Catch Bull At Four
The UK Number One album: Various Artist Compilation – 25 Rockin' And Rollin' Greats
Also this week: The Labour Party wins Australia's general election. (2nd)

The UK Top 10 singles for the week ending December the 9th

1 Chuck Berry — My Ding-A-Ling
2 Osmonds — Crazy Horses
3 Slade — Gudbuy T'Jane
4 Rod Stewart — Angel/What Made Milwaukee Famous (Has Made A Loser Out Of Me)
5 Elton John — Crocodile Rock
6 Donny Osmond — Why
7 Michael Jackson — Ben
8 T. Rex — Solid Gold Easy Action
9 Little Jimmy Osmond — Long Haired Lover From Liverpool
10 Jackson 5 — Lookin' Through The Windows

The US Number One single: Helen Reddy – I Am Woman
The US Number One album: Moody Blues – Seventh Sojourn
The UK Number One album: Various Artist Compilation – 25 Rockin' And Rollin' Greats
Also this week: Four members of the Angry Brigade are sentenced to prison. (6th)

The UK Top 10 singles for the week ending December the 16th

1 Chuck Berry — My Ding-A-Ling
2 Slade — Gudbuy T'Jane
3 Osmonds — Crazy Horses
4 T. Rex — Solid Gold Easy Action
5 Little Jimmy Osmond — Long Haired Lover From Liverpool
6 Donny Osmond — Why
7 Elton John — Crocodile Rock
8 Michael Jackson — Ben
9 Rod Stewart — Angel/What Made Milwaukee Famous (Has Made A Loser Out Of Me)
10 Roy C — Shotgun Wedding

The US Number One single: Billy Paul – Me And Mrs. Jones
The US Number One album: Moody Blues – Seventh Sojourn
The UK Number One album: Various Artist Compilation – 25 Rockin' And Rollin' Greats
Also this week: The Nobel Prize ceremony does not include a peace prize. (10th)

The UK Top 10 singles for the week ending December the 23rd

1 Little Jimmy Osmond   Long Haired Lover From Liverpool
2 Chuck Berry   My Ding-A-Ling
3 T. Rex   Solid Gold Easy Action
4 John & Yoko And The Plastic Ono Band   Happy Xmas (War Is Over)
5 Osmonds   Crazy Horses
6 Slade   Gudbuy T'Jane
7 Elton John   Crocodile Rock
8 Michael Jackson   Ben
9 Donny Osmond   Why
10 Moody Blues   Nights In White Satin

The US Number One single: Billy Paul – Me And Mrs. Jones
The US Number One album: Moody Blues – Seventh Sojourn
The UK Number One album: Various Artist Compilation – 20 All Time Hits Of The 50s
Also this week: B-52s inflict heavy damage whilst bombing Hanoi. (18th)

The UK Top 10 singles for the week ending December the 30th

1 Little Jimmy Osmond   Long Haired Lover From Liverpool
2 Chuck Berry   My Ding-A-Ling
3 T. Rex   Solid Gold Easy Action
4 John & Yoko And The Plastic Ono Band   Happy Xmas (War Is Over)
5 Osmonds   Crazy Horses
6 Slade   Gudbuy T'Jane
7 Elton John   Crocodile Rock
8 Michael Jackson   Ben
9 Donny Osmond   Why
10 Moody Blues   Nights In White Satin

The US Number One single: Billy Paul – Me And Mrs. Jones
The US Number One album: Moody Blues – Seventh Sojourn
The UK Number One album: Various Artist Compilation – 20 All Time Hits Of The 50s
Also this week: President Nixon halts the air offensive against Hanoi. (30th)

The song of the month for December 1972

The Jean Genie by David Bowie (peak chart position: No.2)

David Bowie followed his friend Marc Bolan down the path of re–inventing himself from previous mod and then hippie into a fictional glam rock star, Ziggy Stardust. Bowie's very own version of glam rock was critically better received than the less arty offerings from the likes of Slade and the Sweet. Ironically, Bowie's great rocker, 'The Jean Genie' contained a fabulous riff from the great Mick Ronson which appeared to re–surface shortly afterwards on the Sweet's 'Block Buster'. Although 'The Jean Genie' didn't quite match the heights of the Sweet's effort, it remains one of the very best recordings from arguably the decade's most important act.

Listed Below are the Top 10 Best Selling UK Singles of 1972

1	Amazing Grace	Royal Scots Dragoon Guards
2	Mouldy Old Dough	Lieutenant Pigeon
3	Puppy Love	Donny Osmond
4	Without You	Nilsson
5	I'd Like To Teach The World To Sing	The New Seekers
6	Son Of My Father	Chicory Tip
7	Rock & Roll	Gary Glitter
8	Metal Guru	T.Rex
9	Mother Of Mine	Neil Reid
10	American Pie	Don McLean

1972's CONCERTS OF THE YEAR

Whilst Ziggy Stardust and his Spiders From Mars were thrilling British concert-goers, Led Zeppelin and the Rolling Stones resumed their sonic onslaught of North America. Back in the United Kingdom, teenage audiences were in near hysteria at Marc Bolan and T. Rex, while Mr.Paul McCartney took his new band Wings out on the road as they traversed the university circuit, a far cry from Shea Stadium and Candlestick Park. McCartney's estranged musical partner, John Lennon, also took to the stage in his adopted home of New York, performing live for the first time in six years (an Apple rooftop appearance aside). Meanwhile in London an altogether different rock group, Pink Floyd, were introducing the assembled mass at Earl's Court to some new sounds which would later form the bedrock of 'The Dark Side Of The Moon', released a year later. The rest is history.

1972's ALBUM OF THE YEAR

Harvest by Neil Young
(released in February; reached No.1 in the UK)

Side One:

1. Out on the Weekend; 4:34
2. Harvest; 3:11
3. A Man Needs a Maid; 4:05
4. Heart of Gold; 3:07
5. Are You Ready for the Country?; 3:23

Side Two:

1. Old Man; 3:24
2. There's a World; 2:59
3. Alabama; 4:02
4. The Needle and the Damage Done; 2:03
5. Words (Between the Lines of Age); 6:40

Canada's Neil Young had emerged in recent years as one of the most respected singer–songwriters, both as a solo artist and in collaboration with Crosby, Stills, and Nash. His reputation was cemented by his appearance at Woodstock and further enhanced by the success of the 'After The Goldrush' album. Young's 'Harvest' project drew upon the assistance of his Stray Gators backing band as the singer veered off in the direction of country music as he attempted to follow the path of Gram Parsons in bringing country music to a rock audience. This big–selling long player is characterised by mellow music, though the theme is frequently one of loneliness, as illustrated on 'A Man Needs A Maid', 'Out On The Weekend', and 'Old Man'. Young actually recorded this cycle of songs from a wheelchair, as a result of a car accident. Whatever physical pain he was in perhaps doesn't compare with the emotional anguish he lays bare on 'The Needle And The Damage Done' as he sings of his departed guitarist Danny Whitten who was fighting a losing battle against heroin addiction. Harvest's massive commercial success was due in no small part to the fact that it contained 'Heart Of Gold' which provided Young with a rare presence amongst the higher echelons of the singles charts on both sides of the 'big pond'.

SPORT IN 1972

English Division One football champions: Derby County; runners–up: Leeds United

English FA Cup final: Leeds United 1 Arsenal 0

English League Cup Final: Stoke City 2 Chelsea 1

Scottish Division One football champions: Glasgow Celtic; runners–up: Aberdeen

Scottish FA Cup final: Glasgow Celtic 6 Hibernian 1

Scottish League Cup final: Partick Thistle 4 Glasgow Celtic 1

Irish League football champions: Glentoran; Irish Cup final: Coleraine 2 Portadown 1

League Of Ireland football champions: Waterford; cup winners: Cork Hibernians

European Cup final: Ajax Amsterdam 2 Inter Milan 0

European Cup-Winners' Cup final: Glasgow Rangers 3 Dynamo Moscow 2

UEFA Cup final: Tottenham Hotspur beat Wolverhampton Wanderers 3–2 on aggregate

English county cricket champions: Warwickshire

Five Nations' rugby union champions: none, due to the troubles in Ireland

Formula One world drivers' champion: Emerson Fittipaldi (Brazil) in a Lotus car

Gaelic football All–Ireland champions: Offaly; runners-up: Kerry

British Open golf champion: Lee Trevino (at Muirfield)

US Masters golf champion: Jack Nicklaus

US Open golf champion: Jack Nicklaus

USPGA golf champion: Gary Player

Rugby league Challenge Cup final: St Helens 16 Leeds 13

Wimbledon men's singles tennis final: S Smith beat I Nastase 4–6, 6–3, 6–3, 4–6, 7–5

Wimbledon ladies' singles tennis final: B-J King beat E Goolagong 6–3, 6–3

World snooker final: Alex Higgins (Northern Ireland) beat John Spencer (England) 37–32

The Aintree Grand National steeplechase winner: Well To Do; price 14–1

The Epsom Derby winner: Roberto; jockey – Lester Piggott; price 3–1F

European Championship final: West Germany 3 USSR 0

1972's DEATHS

January 1st: Maurice Chevalier (French singer), aged 83

January 14th: King Frederik IX of Denmark, aged 72

February 5th: Marianne Moore (US poet), aged 84

February 15th: Edgar Snow (US writer), aged 66

April 9th: James Byrne (US judge), aged 92

April 27th: Kwame Nkrumah (Ghana's ex-President), aged 62

May 2nd: John Edgar Hoover (US FBI chief), aged 77

May 22nd: Cecil Day Lewis (British poet laureate), aged 68

May 22nd: Dame Margaret Rutherford (British actress), aged 80

May 28th: Duke of Windsor, aged 77

June 8th: Jimmy Rushing (US singer), aged 69

June 13th: Clyde McPhatter (US singer), aged 39

August 26th: Sir Francis Chichester (British yachtsman), aged 70

August 28th: Prince William of Gloucester, aged 30

August 29th: Lale Andersen (German singer), aged 67

September 14th: Geoffrey Fisher (Archbishop of Canterbury), aged 85

October 1st: Dr Louis Leakey (British anthropologist), aged 69

October 26th: Igor Sikorsky (Russian aviation pioneer), aged 83

November 1st: Ezra Pound (US poet), aged 86

November 11th: Berry Oakley (US musician), aged 24

November 18th: Danny Whitten (US musician), aged 29

November 30th: Sir Compton Mackenzie (British author), aged 89

December 23rd: Andrei Tupolev (Soviet aviation pioneer), aged 84

December 26th: Harry S. Truman (ex-US President), aged 88

The UK Top 10 singles for the week ending January the 6th

1 Little Jimmy Osmond   Long Haired Lover From Liverpool
2 T.Rex   Solid Gold Easy Action
3 Osmonds   Crazy Horses
4 David Bowie   The Jean Genie
5 Slade   Gudbye T'Jane
6 John & Yoko And The Plastic Ono Band Happy Xmas (War Is Over)
7 Chuck Berry   My Ding-A-Ling
8 Roy C   Shotgun Wedding
9 Moody Blues   Nights In White Satin
10 Wings   Hi Hi Hi/C.Moon

The US Number One single: Carly Simon – You're So Vain
The US Number One album: The Moody Blues – Seventh Sojourn
The UK Number One album: Various Artist Compilation – 20 All Time Hits Of The 50s
Also this week: Britain, Denmark, and the Irish Republic join the EEC. (1st)

The UK Top 10 singles for the week ending January the 13th

1 Little Jimmy Osmond   Long Haired Lover From Liverpool
2 David Bowie   The Jean Genie
3 T.Rex   Solid Gold Easy Action
4 Osmonds   Crazy Horses
5 Wings   Hi Hi Hi/C. Moon
6 Wizzard   Ball Park Incident
7 Carly Simon   You're So Vain
8 Judge Dread   Big Seven
9 Slade   Gudbye T' Jane
10 Elvis Presley   Always On My Mind

The US Number One single: Carly Simon – You're So Vain
The US Number One album: Carly Simon – No Secrets
The UK Number One album: Slade – Slayed?
Also this week: The Open University awards its first degrees. (11th)

The UK Top 10 singles for the week ending January the 20th

1	Little Jimmy Osmond	Long Haired Lover From Liverpool
2	Sweet	Blockbuster
3	David Bowie	The Jean Genie
4	Carly Simon	You're So Vain
5	Wings	Hi Hi Hi/C. Moon
6	Wizzard	Ball Park Incident
7	T.Rex	Solid Gold Easy Action
8	Osmonds	Crazy Horses
9	Elvis Presley	Always On My Mind
10	Judge Dread	Big Seven

The US Number One single: Carly Simon – You're So Vain
The US Number One album: Carly Simon – No Secrets
The UK Number One album: Gilbert O'Sullivan – Back To Front
Also this week: Richard Nixon is sworn in for his second Presidential term. (20th)

The UK Top 10 singles for the week ending January the 27th

1	Sweet	Blockbuster
2	Little Jimmy Osmond	Long Haired Lover From Liverpool
3	David Bowie	The Jean Genie
4	Carly Simon	You're So Vain
5	Gary Glitter	Do You Wanna Touch Me (Oh Yeah)
6	Wizzard	Ball Park Incident
7	Wings	Hi Hi Hi/C. Moon
8	Free	Wishing Well
9	Harold Melvin And The Bluenotes	If You Don't Know Me By Now
10	Elton John	Daniel

The US Number One single: Stevie Wonder – Superstition
The US Number One album: Carly Simon – No Secrets
The UK Number One album: Slade – Slayed?
Also this week: The USA and North Vietnam agree to a ceasefire. (23rd)

The song of the month for January 1973

Blockbuster by The Sweet (peak chart position: No.1)

Glitter and platform shoes were very much to the fore when the Sweet stepped forth with the ultimate glam rock composition. Borrowing a remarkably similar guitar riff to David Bowie's 'The Jean Genie', Brian Connolly and the gang thrilled the teenage market with this energetic piece. A siren was thrown in for good measure as this single went on to occupy Number One in the British charts for five weeks, until fellow rockers Slade dislodged them with the rabble-rousing 'Cum On Feel The Noize'.

The UK Top 10 singles for the week ending February the 3rd

1	Sweet	Blockbuster
2	Gary Glitter	Do You Wanna Touch Me (Oh Yeah)
3	Carly Simon	You're So Vain
4	Little Jimmy Osmond	Long Haired Lover From Liverpool
5	David Bowie	The Jean Genie
6	Elton John	Daniel
7	Strawbs	Part Of The Union
8	Free	Wishing Well
9	Harold Melvin And The Bluenotes	If You Don't Know Me By Now
10	Wizzard	Ball Park Incident

The US Number One single: Elton John – Crocodile Rock

The US Number One album: Carly Simon – No Secrets

The UK Number One album: Slade – Slayed?

Also this week: A 'Bloody Sunday' anniversary rally takes place in Derry. (28th)

The UK Top 10 singles for the week ending February the 10th

1	Sweet	Blockbuster
2	Gary Glitter	Do You Wanna Touch Me (Oh Yeah)
3	Strawbs	Part Of The Union
4	Carly Simon	You're So Vain
5	Elton John	Daniel
6	Little Jimmy Osmond	Long Haired Lover From Liverpool
7	Free	Wishing Well
8	Status Quo	Paper Plane
9	Focus	Sylvia
10	E.L.O.	Roll Over Beethoven

The US Number One single: Elton John – Crocodile Rock
The US Number One album: Carly Simon – No Secrets
The UK Number One album: Elton John – Don't Shoot Me I'm Only The Piano Player
Also this week: A loyalist general strike takes place in Northern Ireland. (7th)

The UK Top 10 singles for the week ending February the 17th

1	Sweet	Blockbuster
2	Strawbs	Part Of The Union
3	Gary Glitter	Do You Wanna Touch Me (Oh Yeah)
4	Elton John	Daniel
5	Focus	Sylvia
6	E.L.O.	Roll Over Beethoven
7	Thin Lizzy	Whiskey In The Jar
8	Carly Simon	You're So Vain
9	Little Jimmy Osmond	Long Haired Lover From Liverpool
10	Status Quo	Paper Plane

The US Number One single: Elton John – Crocodile Rock
The US Number One album: War – The World Is A Ghetto
The UK Number One album: Elton John – Don't Shoot Me I'm Only The Piano Player
Also this week: The USA and North Vietnam begin exchanging prisoners. (14th)

The UK Top 10 singles for the week ending February the 24th

1	Sweet	Blockbuster
2	Strawbs	Part Of The Union
3	Gary Glitter	Do You Wanna Touch Me (Oh Yeah)
4	Focus	Sylvia
5	Faces	Cindy Incidentally
6	Thin Lizzy	Whiskey In The Jar
7	Elton John	Daniel
8	E.L.O.	Roll Over Beethoven
9	Partridge Family	Looking Thru' The Eyes Of Love
10	Dave Edmunds	Baby I Love You

The US Number One single: Roberta Flack – Killing Me Softly With His Song
The US Number One album: War – The World Is A Ghetto
The UK Number One album: Elton John – Don't Shoot Me I'm Only The Piano Player
Also this week: Israelis shoot down a Libyan Boeing 727 airliner. (22nd)

The song of the month for February 1973

Killing Me Softly With His Song by Roberta Flack
(peak chart position: No.6)

This love song only had a brief flirtation with the UK Top Ten, but in the United States, 'Killing Me Softly With His Song' softly killed off all competitors as it sat on the summit of the Billboard listings for a commendable five weeks. While the Osmond family, the Jackson family, and glam rock dominated the British pop scene, the intrusion of Roberta Flack's beautiful ballad upon the airwaves was a welcome distraction.

The UK Top 10 singles for the week ending March the 3rd

1	Slade	Cum On Feel The Noize
2	Strawbs	Part Of The Union
3	Sweet	Blockbuster
4	Focus	Sylvia
5	Faces	Cindy Incidentally
6	Gary Glitter	Do You Wanna Touch Me (Oh Yeah)
7	Thin Lizzy	Whiskey In The Jar
8	Dave Edmunds	Baby I Love You
9	Partridge Family	Looking Thru' The Eyes Of Love
10	Detroit Emeralds	Feel The Need In Me

The US Number One single: Roberta Flack – Killing Me Softly With His Song
The US Number One album: Elton John – Don't Shoot Me I'm Only The Piano Player
The UK Number One album: Elton John – Don't Shoot Me I'm Only The Piano Player
Also this week: A Fine Gael-Labour coalition wins the Irish general election. (1st)

The UK Top 10 singles for the week ending March the 10th

1	Slade	Cum On Feel The Noize
2	Faces	Cindy Incidentally
3	T.Rex	20th Century Boy
4	Strawbs	Part Of The Union
5	Sweet	Blockbuster
6	Detroit Emeralds	Feel The Need In Me
7	Alice Cooper	Hello Hurray
8	Roberta Flack	Killing Me Softly With His Song
9	Jackson Five	Doctor My Eyes
10	Thin Lizzy	Whiskey In The Jar

The US Number One single: Roberta Flack – Killing Me Softly With His Song
The US Number One album: Elton John – Don't Shoot Me I'm Only The Piano Player
The UK Number One album: Elton John – Don't Shoot Me I'm Only The Piano Player
Also this week: Bangladesh holds its first general election. (7th)

The UK Top 10 singles for the week ending March the 17th

1	Slade	Cum On Feel The Noize
2	Donny Osmond	The Twelfth Of Never
3	T.Rex	20th Century Boy
4	Detroit Emeralds	Feel The Need In Me
5	Faces	Cindy Incidentally
6	Alice Cooper	Hello Hurray
7	Roberta Flack	Killing Me Softly With His Song
8	Jimmy Helms	Gonna Make You An Offer You Can't Refuse
9	Focus	Sylvia
10	Dave Edmunds	Baby I Love You

The US Number One single: Roberta Flack – Killing Me Softly With His Song
The US Number One album: Eric Weissberg and Steve Mandell – Dueling Banjos
The UK Number One album: Elton John – Don't Shoot Me I'm Only The Piano Player
Also this week: The Queen opens the new London Bridge. (16th)

The UK Top 10 singles for the week ending March the 24th

1	Slade	Cum On Feel The Noize
2	Donny Osmond	The Twelfth Of Never
3	T.Rex	20th Century Boy
4	Cliff Richard	Power To All Our Friends
5	Detroit Emeralds	Feel The Need In Me
6	Roberta Flack	Killing Me Softly With His Song
7	Gilbert O'Sullivan	Get Down
8	Alice Cooper	Hello Hurray
9	Faces	Cindy Incidentally
10	Jimmy Helms	Gonna Make You An Offer You Can't Refuse

The US Number One single: The O'Jays – Love Train
The US Number One album: Eric Weissberg and Steve Mandell – Dueling Banjos
The UK Number One album: Alice Cooper – Billion Dollar Babies
Also this week: An Icelandic gunboat fires live ammunition at a British boat. (18th)

The UK Top 10 singles for the week ending March the 31st

1 Donny Osmond   The Twelfth Of Never
2 Slade   Cum On Feel The Noize
3 Gilbert O'Sullivan   Get Down
4 Cliff Richard   Power To All Our Friends
5 T.Rex   20th Century Boy
6 Detroit Emeralds   Feel The Need In Me
7 Dawn   Tie A Yellow Ribbon Round The Ole Oak Tree
8 David Cassidy   I'm A Clown/Some Kind Of Summer
9 Roberta Flack   Killing Me Softly With His Song
10 Shirley Bassey   Never Never Never

The US Number One single: Roberta Flack – Killing Me Softly With His Song
The US Number One album: Eric Weissberg and Steve Mandell – Dueling Banjos
The UK Number One album: Various Artist Compilation – 20 Flashback Greats Of The Sixties
Also this week: Marlon Brando refuses to accept his Oscar. (28th)

The song of the month for March 1973
The Great Gig In The Sky by Pink Floyd (album track)

If there was an accolade for the best album track of all time, then Rick Wright's 'The Great Gig In The Sky' would be a front-runner. It is bizarrely ironic that whilst this piece concerns the taboo subject of death, many folk chose this item as a soundtrack for making love to, such is its orgasmic sound. This is due largely to the session singer Clare Torry who was asked to stand at the microphone and make some sort of vocal response to the music. She then wails and returns to the studio booth sheepishly and apologises for her efforts. The band however were hugely impressed, although less amused by her eventual claim for co-composing royalties.

The UK Top 10 singles for the week ending April the 7th

1	Gilbert O'Sullivan	Get Down
2	Donny Osmond	The Twelfth Of Never
3	Dawn	Tie A Yellow Ribbon Round The Ole Oak Tree
4	Cliff Richard	Power To All Our Friends
5	David Cassidy	I'm A Clown/Some Kind Of Summer
6	Little Jimmy Osmond	Tweedle Dee
7	Slade	Cum On Feel The Noize
8	Shirley Bassey	Never Never Never
9	O'Jays	Love Train
10	Roberta Flack	Killing Me Softly With His Song

The US Number One single: Vicki Lawrence – The Night The Lights Went Out In Georgia
The US Number One album: Diana Ross/Soundtrack – Lady Sings The Blues
The UK Number One album: Various Artist Compilation – 20 Flashback Greats Of The Sixties
Also this week: Value Added Tax is introduced in the United Kingdom. (5th)

The UK Top 10 singles for the week ending April the 14th

1	Gilbert O'Sullivan	Get Down
2	Dawn	Tie A Yellow Ribbon Round The Ole Oak Tree
3	David Cassidy	I'm A Clown/Some Kind Of Summer
4	Donny Osmond	The Twelfth Of Never
5	Gary Glitter	Hello Hello I'm Back Again
6	Little Jimmy Osmond	Tweedle Dee
7	Cliff Richard	Power To All Our Friends
8	Shirley Bassey	Never Never Never
9	O'Jays	Love Train
10	Roxy Music	Pyjamarama

The US Number One single: Vicki Lawrence – The Night The Lights Went Out In Georgia
The US Number One album: Diana Ross/Soundtrack – Lady Sings The Blues
The UK Number One album: Led Zeppelin – Houses Of The Holy
Also this week: 105 people die in an aeroplane disaster in Switzerland. (10th)

The UK Top 10 singles for the week ending April the 21st

1	Dawn	Tie A Yellow Ribbon Round The Ole Oak Tree
2	Gary Glitter	Hello Hello I'm Back Again
3	Gilbert O'Sullivan	Get Down
4	Little Jimmy Osmond	Tweedle Dee
5	David Cassidy	I'm A Clown/Some Kind Of Summer
6	Donny Osmond	The Twelfth Of Never
7	Cliff Richard	Power To All Our Friends
8	David Bowie	Drive In Saturday
9	Shirley Bassey	Never Never Never
10	Roxy Music	Pyjamarama

The US Number One single: Dawn featuring Tony Orlando – Tie A Yellow Ribbon Round The Ole Oak Tree
The US Number One album: Alice Cooper – Billion Dollar Babies
The UK Number One album: Led Zeppelin – Houses Of The Holy
Also this week: The United States resumes its bombing campaign in Laos. (16th)

The UK Top 10 singles for the week ending April the 28th

1	Dawn	Tie A Yellow Ribbon Round The Ole Oak Tree
2	Gary Glitter	Hello Hello I'm Back Again
3	Gilbert O'Sullivan	Get Down
4	David Cassidy	I'm A Clown/Some Kind Of Summer
5	Little Jimmy Osmond	Tweedle Dee
6	Geordie	All Because Of You
7	David Bowie	Drive In Saturday
8	Donny Osmond	The Twelfth Of Never
9	Wings	My Love
10	Roxy Music	Pyjamarama

The US Number One single: Dawn featuring Tony Orlando – Tie A Yellow Ribbon Round The Ole Oak Tree
The US Number One album: Pink Floyd – The Dark Side Of The Moon
The UK Number One album: The Faces – Ooh-La-La
Also this week: An Icelandic gunboat opens fire on two British trawlers. (24th)

The song of the month for April 1973

My Love by Wings (peak chart position: No.9)

Paul McCartney's solo path fluctuated initially from the radical politics of 'Give Ireland Back To The Irish' to the 'markedly different' 'Mary Had A Little Lamb'. Eventually Wings soared high when Macca recorded perhaps his best love song since 'Revolver'. John Lennon may have scoffed at McCartney's muzak, but 'My Love' is a song of outstanding beauty and compares favourably with anything the Beatles ever released. Uncle Sam clearly agreed as Wings were rewarded with a Stateside chart-topper.

The UK Top 10 singles for the week ending May the 5th

1	Dawn	Tie A Yellow Ribbon Round The Ole Oak Tree
2	Gary Glitter	Hello Hello I'm Back Again
3	David Bowie	Drive In Saturday
4	Sweet	Hell Raiser
5	Little Jimmy Osmond	Tweedle Dee
6	Wizzard	See My Baby Jive
7	Geordie	All Because Of You
8	Gilbert O'Sullivan	Get Down
9	Hot Chocolate	Brother Louie
10	David Cassidy	I'm A Clown/Some Kind Of Summer

The US Number One single: Dawn featuring Tony Orlando – Tie A Yellow Ribbon Round The Ole Oak Tree

The US Number One album: Elvis Presley – Aloha From Hawaii: Via Satellite

The UK Number One album: David Bowie – Aladdin Sane

Also this week: Four members of the Nixon administration are obliged to resign. (30th)

The UK Top 10 singles for the week ending May the 12th

1 Dawn — Tie A Yellow Ribbon Round The Ole Oak Tree
2 Sweet — Hell Raiser
3 Gary Glitter — Hello Hello I'm Back Again
4 Wizzard — See My Baby Jive
5 Roger Daltrey — Giving It All Away
6 Perry Como — And I Love You So
7 Hot Chocolate — Brother Louie
8 David Bowie — Drive In Saturday
9 Wings — My Love
10 Alice Cooper — No More Mr. Nice Guy

The US Number One single: Dawn featuring Tony Orlando – Tie A Yellow Ribbon Round The Ole Oak Tree
The US Number One album: Led Zeppelin – Houses Of The Holy
The UK Number One album: David Bowie – Aladdin Sane
Also this week: Red Indians end their occupation of Wounded Knee. (8th)

The UK Top 10 singles for the week ending May the 19th

1 Wizzard — See My Baby Jive
2 Sweet — Hell Raiser
3 Dawn — Tie A Yellow Ribbon Round The Ole Oak Tree
4 Gary Glitter — Hello Hello I'm Back Again
5 Perry Como — And I Love You So
6 David Bowie — Drive In Saturday
7 Roger Daltrey — Giving It All Away
8 Hot Chocolate — Brother Louie
9 Deodato — Also Sprach Zarathustra (2001)
10 Alice Cooper — No More Mr. Nice Guy

The US Number One single: Stevie Wonder – You Are The Sunshine Of My Life
The US Number One album: Led Zeppelin – Houses Of The Holy
The UK Number One album: David Bowie – Aladdin Sane
Also this week: The Senate hearings into the Watergate affair begin. (17th)

The UK Top 10 singles for the week ending May the 26th

1	Wizzard	See My Baby Jive
2	Sweet	Hell Raiser
3	Perry Como	And I Love You So
4	Dawn	Tie A Yellow Ribbon Round The Ole Oak Tree
5	Suzi Quatro	Can The Can
6	Medicine Head	One And One Is One
7	Deodato	Also Sprach Zarathustra (2001)
8	Gary Glitter	Hello Hello I'm Back Again
9	Hot Chocolate	Brother Louie
10	Roger Daltrey	Giving It All Away

The US Number One single: The Edgar Winter Group – Frankenstein
The US Number One album: The Beatles – 1967–1970
The UK Number One album: David Bowie – Aladdin Sane
Also this week: President Nixon admits there was a Watergate cover-up. (22nd)

The song of the month for May 1973
Can The Can by Suzi Quatro (peak chart position: No.1)

American chick Suzi Quatro demonstrated that glam rock was not merely a boys' game as she elbowed another glam outfit, Wizzard off the British pop summit. Quatro was a beneficiary of the hugely successful Chinn and Chapman songwriting partnership. With the production expertise of Mickie Most, Quatro was well on the way to success. Above all, Quatro's high-pitched vocals and the drumbeat ensured a UK smash hit.

The UK Top 10 singles for the week ending June the 2nd

1 Wizzard   See My Baby Jive
2 Suzi Quatro   Can The Can
3 Perry Como   And I Love You So
4 Medicine Head   One And One Is One
5 Sweet   Hell Raiser
6 Dawn   Tie A Yellow Ribbon Round The Ole Oak Tree
7 Stevie Wonder   You Are The Sunshine Of My Life
8 Deodato   Also Sprach Zarathustra (2001)
9 Nazareth   Broken Down Angel
10 Lou Reed   Walk On The Wild Side

The US Number One single: Paul McCartney & Wings – My Love
The US Number One album: Paul McCartney & Wings – Red Rose Speedway
The UK Number One album: David Bowie – Aladdin Sane
Also this week: The Greek government abolishes the monarchy. (1st)

The UK Top 10 singles for the week ending June the 9th

1 Wizzard   See My Baby Jive
2 Suzi Quatro   Can The Can
3 Medicine Head   One And One Is One
4 Perry Como   And I Love You So
5 10cc   Rubber Bullets
6 Fleetwood Mac   Albatross
7 Stevie Wonder   You Are The Sunshine Of My Life
8 Sweet   Hell Raiser
9 Dawn   Tie A Yellow Ribbon Round The Ole Oak Tree
10 Partridge Family   Walking In The Rain

The US Number One single: Paul McCartney & Wings – My Love
The US Number One album: Paul McCartney & Wings – Red Rose Speedway
The UK Number One album: Various Artist Compilation – Pure Gold
Also this week: General Franco appoints Admiral Luis Blanco as Spain's President. (8th)

The UK Top 10 singles for the week ending June the 16th

1	Suzi Quatro	Can The Can
2	10cc	Rubber Bullets
3	Wizzard	See My Baby Jive
4	Medicine Head	One And One Is One
5	Fleetwood Mac	Albatross
6	T.Rex	The Groover
7	Perry Como	And I Love You So
8	Stealers Wheel	Stuck In The Middle
9	Stevie Wonder	You Are The Sunshine Of My Life
10	Partridge Family	Walking In The Rain

The US Number One single: Paul McCartney & Wings – My Love
The US Number One album: Paul McCartney & Wings – Red Rose Speedway
The UK Number One album: Various Artist Compilation – Pure Gold
Also this week: Russia's Leonid Brezhnev arrives in the United States. (16th)

The UK Top 10 singles for the week ending June the 23rd

1	10cc	Rubber Bullets
2	Fleetwood Mac	Albatross
3	Suzi Quatro	Can The Can
4	T.Rex	The Groover
5	Peters And Lee	Welcome Home
6	Wizzard	See My Baby Jive
7	Hotshots	Snoopy Versus The Red Baron
8	Stealers Wheel	Stuck In The Middle
9	Medicine Head	One And One Is One
10	George Harrison	Give Me Love (Give Me Peace On Earth)

The US Number One single: Paul McCartney & Wings – My Love
The US Number One album: George Harrison – Living In The Material World
The UK Number One album: Various Artist Compilation – Pure Gold
Also this week: Various tennis players reveal their plans to boycott Wimbledon. (22nd)

The UK Top 10 singles for the week ending June the 30th

1	Slade	Skweeze Me Pleeze Me
2	10cc	Rubber Bullets
3	Fleetwood Mac	Albatross
4	Peters And Lee	Welcome Home
5	T.Rex	The Groover
6	Hotshots	Snoopy Versus The Red Baron
7	Suzi Quatro	Can The Can
8	George Harrison	Give Me Love (Give Me Peace On Earth)
9	Wings	Live And Let Die
10	Stealers Wheel	Stuck In The Middle

The US Number One single: George Harrison – Give Me Love (Give Me Peace On Earth)
The US Number One album: George Harrison – Living In The Material World
The UK Number One album: Original Soundtrack – That'll Be The Day
Also this week: President de Valera of the Irish Republic resigns, aged ninety. (24th)

The song of the month for June 1973

Life On Mars by David Bowie (peak chart position: No.3)

This classic 'seventies single had originally been recorded almost two years earlier for the seminal 'Hunky Dory' long player, but eventually non-album buyers were allowed the opportunity to purchase this four minute wonder. What may have confused many observers was that this was not a Ziggy Stardust song, but a more mellow item, which featured Rick Wakeman on piano. One thing was for certain: this Top Three marvel with its sailors fighting in the dance halls was not a "God-awful small affair."

The UK Top 10 singles for the week ending July the 7th

1	Slade	Skweeze Me Pleeze Me
2	Peters And Lee	Welcome Home
3	10cc	Rubber Bullets
4	David Bowie	Life On Mars
5	Fleetwood Mac	Albatross
6	Hotshots	Snoopy Versus The Red Baron
7	Dave Edmunds	Born To Be With You
8	T.Rex	The Groover
9	Paul Simon	Take Me To The Mardi Gras
10	George Harrison	Give Me Love (Give Me Peace On Earth)

The US Number One single: Billy Preston – Will It Go Round In Circles
The US Number One album: George Harrison – Living In The Material World
The UK Number One album: Original Soundtrack – That'll Be The Day
Also this week: Elizabeth Taylor announces her separation from Richard Burton. (3rd)

The UK Top 10 singles for the week ending July the 14th

1	Slade	Skweeze Me Pleeze Me
2	Peters And Lee	Welcome Home
3	David Bowie	Life On Mars
4	Hotshots	Snoopy Versus The Red Baron
5	Dave Edmunds	Born To Be With You
6	10cc	Rubber Bullets
7	Paul Simon	Take Me To The Mardi Gras
8	Fleetwood Mac	Albatross
9	Elton John	Saturday Night's Alright For Fighting
10	George Harrison	Give Me Love (Give Me Peace On Earth)

The US Number One single: Billy Preston – Will It Go Round In Circles
The US Number One album: George Harrison – Living In The Material World
The UK Number One album: Original Soundtrack – That'll Be The Day
Also this week: The Bahamas become independent of Britain. (10th)

The UK Top 10 singles for the week ending July the 21st

1 Peters And Lee   Welcome Home
2 Gary Glitter   I'm The Leader Of The Gang (I Am)
3 David Bowie   Life On Mars
4 Slade   Skweeze Me Pleeze Me
5 Mungo Jerry   Alright Alright Alright
6 Osmonds   Going Home
7 Elton John   Saturday Night's Alright For Fighting
8 Dave Edmunds   Born To Be With You
9 Paul Simon   Take Me To The Mardi Gras
10 Hotshots   Snoopy Versus The Red Baron

The US Number One single: Jim Croce – Bad, Bad Leroy Brown
The US Number One album: George Harrison – Living In The Material World
The UK Number One album: Original Soundtrack – That'll Be The Day
Also this week: France tests the Hydrogen bomb near the Mururoa Atoll. (21st)

The UK Top 10 singles for the week ending July the 28th

1 Gary Glitter   I'm The Leader Of The Gang (I Am)
2 Peters And Lee   Welcome Home
3 David Bowie   Life On Mars
4 Mungo Jerry   Alright Alright Alright
5 Osmonds   Going Home
6 Slade   Skweeze Me Pleeze Me
7 Elton John   Saturday Night's Alright For Fighting
8 Clifford T. Ward   Gaye
9 Blue Mink   Randy
10 Dave Edmunds   Born To Be With You

The US Number One single: Jim Croce – Bad, Bad Leroy Brown
The US Number One album: Chicago – Chicago VI
The UK Number One album: Original Soundtrack – That'll Be The Day
Also this week: Colonel Gaddafi withdraws his resignation as Libya's leader. (23rd)

The song of the month for July 1973

Saturday Night's Alright For Fighting by Elton John
(peak chart position: No.7)

Recognising the fact that variety in your repertoire was the best means of sustaining a music career, Elton John drifted away from the tender 'Your Song' and the sensitive 'Daniel' in favour of a slice of alpha male musical machismo. Bernie Taupin supplied the rabble-rousing lyrics about the need to "get a belly full of beer" and Elton's pumping piano and Davey Jonstone's guitar did the raucous rest. This bar-room favourite was the first single from the 'Goodbye Yellow Brick Road' album. When it came to glam rock, Elton proved that he could cut it too.

The UK Top 10 singles for the week ending August the 4th

1	Gary Glitter	I'm The Leader Of The Gang (I Am)
2	Peters And Lee	Welcome Home
3	Mungo Jerry	Alright Alright Alright
4	Osmonds	Going Home
5	David Bowie	Life On Mars
6	Suzi Quatro	48 Crash
7	Carpenters	Yesterday Once More
8	Al Martino	Spanish Eyes
9	Diana Ross	Touch Me In The Morning
10	Blue Mink	Randy

The US Number One single: Maureen McGovern – The Morning After
The US Number One album: Chicago – Chicago VI
The UK Number One album: Original Soundtrack – That'll Be The Day
Also this week: The Isle of Man's Summerland complex catches fire, causing death. (2nd)

The UK Top 10 singles for the week ending August the 11th

1	Gary Glitter	I'm The Leader Of The Gang (I Am)
2	Peters And Lee	Welcome Home
3	Mungo Jerry	Alright Alright Alright
4	Suzi Quatro	48 Crash
5	Carpenters	Yesterday Once More
6	Osmonds	Going Home
7	David Bowie	Life On Mars
8	Al Martino	Spanish Eyes
9	Goons	Ying Tong Song
10	Nazareth	Bad Bad Boy

The US Number One single: Maureen McGovern – The Morning After
The US Number One album: Chicago – Chicago VI
The UK Number One album: Original Soundtrack – That'll Be The Day
Also this week: Arab terrorists open fire at Athens airport. (5th)

The UK Top 10 singles for the week ending August the 18th

1	Gary Glitter	I'm The Leader Of The Gang (I Am)
2	Carpenters	Yesterday Once More
3	Suzi Quatro	48 Crash
4	Peters And Lee	Welcome Home
5	Al Martino	Spanish Eyes
6	Mungo Jerry	Alright Alright Alright
7	Limmie And The Family Cookin'	You Can Do Magic
8	Barry Blue	Dancing On A Saturday Night
9	Goons	Ying Tong Song
10	Osmonds	Going Home

The US Number One single: Diana Ross – Touch Me In The Morning
The US Number One album: Jethro Tull – A Passion Play
The UK Number One album: Peters & Lee – We Can Make It
Also this week: The American bombing of Cambodia officially ends. (14th)

The UK Top 10 singles for the week ending August the 25th

1	Donny Osmond	Young Love
2	Carpenters	Yesterday Once More
3	Gary Glitter	I'm The Leader Of The Gang (I Am)
4	Barry Blue	Dancing On A Saturday Night
5	Limmie And The Family Cookin'	You Can Do Magic
6	Al Martino	Spanish Eyes
7	Suzi Quatro	48 Crash
8	Peters And Lee	Welcome Home
9	First Choice	Smarty Pants
10	Mungo Jerry	Alright Alright Alright

The US Number One single: The Stories – Brother Louie

The US Number One album: Chicago – Chicago VI

The UK Number One album: Peters & Lee – We Can Make It

Also this week: An open verdict is pronounced on the Bloody Sunday tragedy. (21st)

The song of the month for August 1973
Angie by The Rolling Stones (peak chart position: No.5)

Although their musical career was beginning to take something of a nosedive, Mick and his associates could still offer the occasional gem. The ballad 'Angie' (possibly Angie Bowie) was proof of this. It may have dismayed some Stones followers who cared only for a constant diet of riffs, but this acoustic piece found favour in the United States where it peaked at Number One. This was the highlight of the new 'Goat's Head Soup' project. Regrettably, the Stones started rolling downhill hereafter until the arrival of Ron Wood injected new life.

The UK Top 10 singles for the week ending September the 1st

1 Donny Osmond — Young Love
2 Barry Blue — Dancing On A Saturday Night
3 Limmie And The Family Cookin' — You Can Do Magic
4 Carpenters — Yesterday Once More
5 Al Martino — Spanish Eyes
6 Gary Glitter — I'm The Leader Of The Gang (I Am)
7 Drifters — Like Sister And Brother
8 Peters And Lee — Welcome Home
9 Bobby Goldsboro — Summer (The First Time)
10 First Choice — Smarty Pants

The US Number One single: The Stories – Brother Louie
The US Number One album: Chicago – Chicago VI
The UK Number One album: Rod Stewart – Sing It Again Rod
Also this week: Bride-to-be Princess Anne pays a visit to Russia. (28th)

The UK Top 10 singles for the week ending September the 8th

1 Donny Osmond — Young Love
2 Barry Blue — Dancing On A Saturday Night
3 Wizzard — Angel Fingers
4 Carpenters — Yesterday Once More
5 Al Martino — Spanish Eyes
6 David Essex — Rock On
7 Limmie And The Family Cookin' — You Can Do Magic
8 Drifters — Like Sister And Brother
9 Rolling Stones — Angie
10 Hudson Ford — Pick Up The Pieces

The US Number One single: Marvin Gaye – Let's Get It On
The US Number One album: The Allman Brothers Band – Brothers And Sisters
The UK Number One album: Rod Stewart – Sing It Again Rod
Also this week: Jackie Stewart announces his retirement from Formula One racing. (7th)

The UK Top 10 singles for the week ending September the 15th

1	Donny Osmond	Young Love
2	Wizzard	Angel Fingers
3	David Essex	Rock On
4	Barry Blue	Dancing On A Saturday Night
5	Rolling Stones	Angie
6	Al Martino	Spanish Eyes
7	Rod Stewart	Oh No Not My Baby
8	Hudson Ford	Pick Up The Pieces
9	Limmie And The Family Cookin'	You Can Do Magic
10	10cc	The Dean And I

The US Number One single: Helen Reddy – Delta Dawn
The US Number One album: The Allman Brothers Band – Brothers And Sisters
The UK Number One album: Rod Stewart – Sing It Again Rod
Also this week: The Chilean democratically-elected Marxist government is
overthrown. (11th)

The UK Top 10 singles for the week ending September the 22nd

1	Wizzard	Angel Fingers
2	Sweet	Ballroom Blitz
3	David Essex	Rock On
4	Bobby (Boris) Pickett & The Crypt Kickers	Monster Mash
5	Rolling Stones	Angie
6	Rod Stewart	Oh No Not My Baby
7	Donny Osmond	Young Love
8	Barry Blue	Dancing On A Saturday Night
9	Al Martino	Spanish Eyes
10	Perry Como	For The Good Times

The US Number One single: Marvin Gaye – Let's Get It On
The US Number One album: The Allman Brothers Band – Brothers And Sisters
The UK Number One album: The Rolling Stones – Goat's Head Soup
Also this week: Jordan declares a general amnesty and releases Palestinian
prisoners. (19th)

The UK Top 10 singles for the week ending September the 29th

1	Simon Park Orchestra	Eye Level
2	Sweet	Ballroom Blitz
3	Wizzard	Angel Fingers
4	Bobby (Boris) Pickett & The Crypt Kickers	Monster Mash
5	David Essex	Rock On
6	Rod Stewart	Oh No Not My Baby
7	Rolling Stones	Angie
8	Ike And Tina Turner	Nutbush City Limits
9	Perry Como	For The Good Times
10	Mott The Hoople	All The Way From Memphis

The US Number One single: Grand Funk – We're An American Band
The US Number One album: The Allman Brothers Band – Brothers And Sisters
The UK Number One album: The Rolling Stones – Goat's Head Soup
Also this week: Juan Peron regains power, becoming Argentina's President. (23rd)

The song of the month for September 1973
Eye Level by Simon Park Orchestra (peak chart position: No.1)

From time to time British record-buyers are seduced by something 'different'. The theme tune to the detective series 'Van der Valk' was one such piece of music that prompted droves of young and old to proceed to their local records retail outlet and invest in a wondrous little black plastic item called a 'single'. This particular single had made an unsuccessful incursion into the UK hit parade a year earlier, but eventually the Simon Park Orchestra re-appeared with a vengeance as their magical composition remained in the chart for 22 weeks.

The UK Top 10 singles for the week ending October the 6th

1	Simon Park Orchestra	Eye Level
2	Sweet	Ballroom Blitz
3	Bobby (Boris) Pickett & The Crypt Kickers	Monster Mash
4	Slade	My Friend Stan
5	Ike And Tina Turner	Nutbush City Limits
6	Wizzard	Angel Fingers
7	Perry Como	For The Good Times
8	David Bowie	Laughing Gnome
9	Manfred Mann's Earthband	Joybringer
10	David Essex	Rock On

The US Number One single: Cher – Half-Breed
The US Number One album: The Allman Brothers Band – Brothers And Sisters
The UK Number One album: Slade – Sladest
Also this week: Egypt and Syria launch surprise attacks upon Israel. (6th)

The UK Top 10 singles for the week ending October the 13th

1	Simon Park Orchestra	Eye Level
2	Slade	My Friend Stan
3	Sweet	Ballroom Blitz
4	Ike And Tina Turner	Nutbush City Limits
5	Bobby (Boris) Pickett & The Crypt Kickers	Monster Mash
6	David Bowie	Laughing Gnome
7	Perry Como	For The Good Times
8	David Cassidy	Daydreamer/Puppy Song
9	Status Quo	Caroline
10	Manfred Mann's Earthband	Joybringer

The US Number One single: Cher – Half-Breed
The US Number One album: The Rolling Stones – Goat's Head Soup
The UK Number One album: Slade – Sladest
Also this week: London's Capital Radio goes on air for the first time. (8th)

The UK Top 10 singles for the week ending October the 20th

1	Simon Park Orchestra	Eye Level
2	David Cassidy	Daydreamer/Puppy Song
3	Slade	My Friend Stan
4	Ike And Tina Turner	Nutbush City Limits
5	Bobby (Boris) Pickett & The Crypt Kickers	Monster Mash
6	David Bowie	Laughing Gnome
7	Sweet	Ballroom Blitz
8	Status Quo	Caroline
9	Perry Como	For The Good Times
10	Elton John	Goodbye Yellow Brick Road

The US Number One single: The Rolling Stones – Angie
The US Number One album: The Rolling Stones – Goat's Head Soup
The UK Number One album: Slade – Sladest
Also this week: Oil prices are drastically increased during the Yom Kippur War. (17th)

The UK Top 10 singles for the week ending October the 27th

1	David Cassidy	Daydreamer/Puppy Song
2	Simon Park Orchestra	Eye Level
3	Slade	My Friend Stan
4	David Bowie	Sorrow
5	Status Quo	Caroline
6	Elton John	Goodbye Yellow Brick Road
7	Perry Como	For The Good Times
8	David Bowie	Laughing Gnome
9	Ike And Tina Turner	Nutbush City Limits
10	Bryan Ferry	A Hard Rain's Gonna Fall

The US Number One single: Gladys Knight & The Pips – Midnight Train To Georgia
The US Number One album: The Rolling Stones – Goat's Head Soup
The UK Number One album: Status Quo – Hello
Also this week: The Yom Kippur War ends in victory for Israel. (25th)

The song of the month for October 1973

Hallelujah Time by The Wailers (album track)

This Bunny Livingstone (or Wailer) track was merely confined to Side One of the new 'Burnin' album. What a pity that many music aficionados have perhaps not yet familiarised themselves with it. Bunny Wailer had a supremely beautiful voice and this soulful, spiritual offering is a joy to listen to. 'Burnin' was the Wailers' second assignment for Island Records but it would also bring the curtain down on the ace trio of Bob, Bunny, and Peter Tosh, as the latter two went solo, leaving Bob Marley to recruit new Wailers for his backing band.

The UK Top 10 singles for the week ending November the 3rd

1	David Cassidy	Daydreamer/Puppy Song
2	Simon Park Orchestra	Eye Level
3	David Bowie	Sorrow
4	Osmonds	Let Me In
5	Status Quo	Caroline
6	Elton John	Goodbye Yellow Brick Road
7	Detroit Spinners	Ghetto Child
8	Slade	My Friend Stan
9	Carpenters	Top Of The World
10	Perry Como	For The Good Times

The US Number One single: Gladys Knight & The Pips – Midnight Train To Georgia
The US Number One album: The Rolling Stones – Goat's Head Soup
The UK Number One album: David Bowie – Pin-Ups
Also this week: The underground magazine, Oz, is issued for the last time. (1st)

The UK Top 10 singles for the week ending November the 10th

1 David Cassidy   Daydreamer/Puppy Song
2 Osmonds   Let Me In
3 David Bowie   Sorrow
4 Mud   Dyna-Mite
5 Carpenters   Top Of The World
6 Simon Park Orchestra   Eye Level
7 Status Quo   Caroline
8 Detroit Spinners   Ghetto Child
9 Perry Como   For The Good Times
10 Elton John   Goodbye Yellow Brick Road

The US Number One single: Eddie Kendricks – Keep On Truckin' (Part One)
The US Number One album: Elton John – Goodbye Yellow Brick Road
The UK Number One album: David Bowie – Pin-Ups
Also this week: The six Watergate 'burglars' are sentenced to prison. (9th)

The UK Top 10 singles for the week ending November the 17th

1 Gary Glitter   I Love You Love Me Love
2 Osmonds   Let Me In
3 David Cassidy   Daydreamer/Puppy Song
4 David Bowie   Sorrow
5 Mud   Dyna-Mite
6 Donny Osmond   When I Fall In Love
7 Carpenters   Top Of The World
8 Ringo Starr   Photograph
9 Barry Blue   Do You Wanna Dance
10 Detroit Spinners   Ghetto Child

The US Number One single: Eddie Kendricks – Keep On Truckin' (Part One)
The US Number One album: Elton John – Goodbye Yellow Brick Road
The UK Number One album: David Bowie – Pin-Ups
Also this week: Princess Anne marries Captain Mark Phillips at Westminster Abbey. (14th)

The UK Top 10 singles for the week ending November the 24th

1	Gary Glitter	I Love You Love Me Love
2	Osmonds	Let Me In
3	Marie Osmond	Paper Roses
4	Mud	Dyna-Mite
5	David Bowie	Sorrow
6	Donny Osmond	When I Fall In Love
7	Barry Blue	Do You Wanna Dance
8	Alvin Stardust	My Coo Ca Choo
9	Carpenters	Top Of The World
10	Ringo Starr	Photograph

The US Number One single: Ringo Starr – Photograph
The US Number One album: Elton John – Goodbye Yellow Brick Road
The UK Number One album: David Bowie – Pin-Ups
Also this week: Ulster unionists and nationalists agree to share power. (21st)

The song of the month for November 1973

You Won't Find Another Fool Like Me by The New Seekers
(peak chart position: No.1)

Not to be confused with a successful Australian outfit of the mid-sixties, the New Seekers were also seeking out success in the singles lists. Lightning would indeed strike twice as 'You Won't Find Another Fool Like Me' would be their second UK Number One, emulating two chart-toppers accumulated by the ('old') Seekers. This composition stalled just short of the top spot for several weeks, before peaking in January 1974. In my semi-humble opinion it rates as one of the greatest pop songs of the twentieth century, nothing more, nothing less.

The UK Top 10 singles for the week ending December the 1st

1 Gary Glitter   I Love You Love Me Love
2 Alvin Stardust   My Coo Ca Choo
3 Marie Osmond   Paper Roses
4 Donny Osmond   When I Fall In Love
5 Mud   Dyna-Mite
6 Gilbert O'Sullivan   Why Oh Why Oh Why
7 New Seekers   You Won't Find Another Fool Like Me
8 David Essex   Lamplight
9 Barry Blue   Do You Wanna Dance
10 Osmonds   Let Me In

The US Number One single: The Carpenters – Top Of The World
The US Number One album: Elton John – Goodbye Yellow Brick Road
The UK Number One album: David Bowie – Pin-Ups
Also this week: Armed forces seize power again in Greece. (25th)

The UK Top 10 singles for the week ending December the 8th

1 Gary Glitter   I Love You Love Me Love
2 Marie Osmond   Paper Roses
3 New Seekers   You Won't Find Another Fool Like Me
4 Alvin Stardust   My Coo Ca Choo
5 Osmonds   Let Me In
6 Mud   Dyna-Mite
7 David Essex   Lamplight
8 Mott The Hoople   Roll Away The Stone
9 Gilbert O'Sullivan   Why Oh Why Oh Why
10 Barry Blue   Do You Wanna Dance

The US Number One single: The Carpenters – Top Of The World
The US Number One album: Elton John – Goodbye Yellow Brick Road
The UK Number One album: Roxy Music – Stranded
Also this week: Gerald Ford replaces Spiro Agnew as Nixon's Vice-President. (6th)

The UK Top 10 singles for the week ending December the 15th

1	Slade	Merry Xmas Everybody
2	Gary Glitter	I Love You Love Me Love
3	Alvin Stardust	My Coo Ca Choo
4	New Seekers	You Won't Find Another Fool Like Me
5	Marie Osmond	Paper Roses
6	Wizzard	I Wish It Could Be Christmas Everyday
7	David Essex	Lamplight
8	Mott The Hoople	Roll Away The Stone
9	Roxy Music	Street Life
10	Gilbert O'Sullivan	Why Oh Why Oh Why

The US Number One single: Charlie Rich – The Most Beautiful Girl
The US Number One album: Elton John – Goodbye Yellow Brick Road
The UK Number One album: David Cassidy – Dreams Are Nuthin' More Than Wishes
Also this week: Idi Amin starts his 'Save Britain' fundraising campaign. (14th)

The UK Top 10 singles for the week ending December the 22nd

1	Slade	Merry Xmas Everybody
2	Gary Glitter	I Love You Love Me Love
3	New Seekers	You Won't Find Another Fool Like Me
4	Wizzard	I Wish It Could Be Christmas Everyday
5	Alvin Stardust	My Coo Ca Choo
6	Marie Osmond	Paper Roses
7	Leo Sayer	The Show Must Go On
8	David Essex	Lamplight
9	Mott The Hoople	Roll Away The Stone
10	Roxy Music	Street Life

The US Number One single: Charlie Rich – The Most Beautiful Girl
The US Number One album: Elton John – Goodbye Yellow Brick Road
The UK Number One album: Elton John – Goodbye Yellow Brick Road
Also this week: Spain's Prime Minister is killed by a terrorist bomb. (20th)

The UK Top 10 singles for the week ending December the 29th

1	Slade	Merry Xmas Everybody
2	Gary Glitter	I Love You Love Me Love
3	New Seekers	You Won't Find Another Fool Like Me
4	Wizzard	I Wish It Could Be Christmas Everyday
5	Alvin Stardust	My Coo Ca Choo
6	Marie Osmond	Paper Roses
7	Leo Sayer	The Show Must Go On
8	David Essex	Lamplight
9	Mott The Hoople	Roll Away The Stone
10	Roxy Music	Street Life

The US Number One single: Jim Croce – Time In A Bottle
The US Number One album: Elton John – Goodbye Yellow Brick Road
The UK Number One album: Elton John – Goodbye Yellow Brick Road
Also this week: Arab oil producers in Iran double their oil prices. (23rd)

The song of the month for December 1973

I Wish It Could Be Christmas Everyday by Wizzard
(peak chart position: No.4)

1973 was a hugely successful year for the eye-catching Roy Wood as his Wizzard combo helped themselves to two British Number Ones, thus vindicating Wood's 'move' from The Move and E.L.O. This Christmas Top Five failed to reach the summit in the face of stiff opposition from the likes of Slade's dreadful 'Merry Xmas Everybody' but it remains a constant feature of shopping arcades throughout the land every November and December. The song is a fusion of glam with a Spectoresque 'wall of sound'. It does possess a certain charm.

Listed Below are the Top 10 Best Selling UK Singles of 1973

1	Tie A Yellow Ribbon	Dawn
2	Eye Level	The Simon Park Orchestra
3	Welcome Home	Peters and Lee
4	Blockbuster	The Sweet
5	Cum On Feel The Noize	Slade
6	I Love You Love Me Love	Gary Glitter
7	See My Baby Jive	Wizzard
8	I'm The Leader Of The Gang	Gary Glitter
9	The Twelfth of Never	Donny Osmond
10	Daydreamer / Puppy Song	David Cassidy

1973's CONCERTS OF THE YEAR

A new musical phenomenon that hailed from Jamaica called Bob Marley was beginning to deliver his message to 'Babylon'. Speaking of Babylon, the United States was treated to another Led Zeppelin tour, whereupon the awesome foursome showcased their damp squib 'Houses Of The Holy' album. The Zep's performances at Madison Square Garden would later surface on the disappointing 'The Song Remains The Same' live soundtrack. Gig of the year however was almost certainly Elvis Presley's 'Aloha From Hawaii' in January. It is one of the great injustices in the history of popular music that 'the King' was never able to delight his international followers in the flesh. A concert in Hawaii was the nearest that the burger king came to a foreign gig. The mid-Pacific venue had been shrewdly chosen by the wily Colonel Tom Parker to cash in on the far east audience, as well as enchanting the globe via satellite. It was regarded as Elvis's last great outing before self-destruction took its toll.

1973's ALBUM OF THE YEAR

Goodbye Yellow Brick Road by Elton John
(released in October; reached No.1 in the UK)

Side One:

1. Funeral for a Friend/
   Love Lies Bleeding; 11:09
2. This Song Has No Title; 2:23
3. Bennie and the Jets; 5:23

Side Two:

1. Goodbye Yellow Brick Road; 3:13
2. Candle in the Wind; 3:49
3. Grey Seal; 4:00
4. Jamaica Jerk-Off; 3:38
5. I've Seen That Movie Too; 5:58

Side Three:

1. Sweet Painted Lady; 3:54

2. The Ballad of Danny Bailey (1909-34); 4:23

3. Dirty Little Girl; 5:01
4. All The Girls Love Alice; 5:09

Side Four:

1. Your Sister Can't Twist
   (But She Can Rock 'n Roll); 2:42
2. Saturday Night's Alright
   for Fighting; 4:53
3. Roy Rogers; 4:08
4. Social Disease; 3:43
5. Harmony; 2:46

If anyone should ever doubt the merits of music in the seventies, just respond with four words:'Goodbye Yellow Brick Road'. Elton's masterpiece incorporated a variety of musical styles such as love songs ('Harmony'), glam rock ('All The Girls Love Alice'), pseudo-reggae ('Jamaica Jerk-Off'), and country ('Roy Rogers'). However, the proceedings were dominated by the massive hits that were drawn from this project, namely 'Candle In The Wind' (the timeless tribute to Marilyn), the seminal title track, the US chart-topper 'Bennie And The Jets', not forgetting the energetic 'Saturday Night's Alright For Fighting'. The album, which was recorded in France, also benefited from marvellous artwork on the cover. Assisted by the orchestral arrangements of Del Newman and the allegedly suspiciously misogynistic lyrics of Bernie Taupin, this offering from Mr. Dwight is a joy to behold. Also worth checking out are such majestic items as 'The Ballad Of Danny Bailey (1909–1934)' and 'Sweet Painted Lady'. Until the emergence of 'London Calling' at the end of the decade, this piece of work was undoubtedly the finest double album of the 1970s.

SPORT IN 1973

English Division One football champions: Liverpool; runners-up: Arsenal

English FA Cup final: Sunderland 1 Leeds United 0

English League Cup Final: Tottenham Hotspur 1 Norwich City 0

Scottish Division One football champions: Glasgow Celtic; runners-up: Glasgow Rangers

Scottish FA Cup final: Glasgow Rangers 3 Glasgow Celtic 2

Scottish League Cup final: Hibernian 2 Glasgow Celtic 1

Irish League football champions: Crusaders; Irish Cup final: Glentoran 3 Linfield 2

League Of Ireland football champions: Waterford; cup winners: Cork Hibernians

European Cup final: Ajax Amsterdam 1 Juventus 0

European Cup-Winners' Cup final: AC Milan 1 Leeds United 0

UEFA Cup final: Liverpool beat Borussia Moenchengladbach 3–2 on aggregate

English county cricket champions: Hampshire

Five Nations' rugby union champions: all five countries finished with four points

Formula One world drivers' champion: Jackie Stewart (United Kingdom) in a Tyrrell car

Gaelic football All-Ireland champions: Cork; runners-up: Galway

British Open golf champion: Tom Weiskopf (at Royal Troon)

US Masters golf champion: Tommy Aaron

US Open golf champion: Johnny Miller

USPGA golf champion: Jack Nicklaus

Rugby league Challenge Cup final: Featherstone Rovers 33 Bradford Northern 14

Wimbledon men's singles tennis final: J Kodes beat A Metreveli 6–1, 9–8, 6–3

Wimbledon ladies' singles tennis final: B-J King beat C Evert 6–0, 7–5

World snooker final: Ray Reardon (Wales) beat Eddie Charlton (Australia) 38–32

The Aintree Grand National steeplechase winner: Red Rum; price 9–1

The Epsom Derby winner: Morston; jockey – Eddie Hide; price 25–1

The Ryder Cup golf contest: Great Britain And Ireland 13 United States 19

1973's DEATHS

January 22nd: Lyndon Baines Johnson (ex-US President), aged 64

January 26th: Edward G. Robinson (US actor), aged 79

February 11th: Hans Jensen (German physicist), aged 65

February 22nd: Elizabeth Bowen (Irish writer), aged 73

March 6th: Pearl S. Buck (US writer), aged 80

March 8th: Ron 'Pigpen' McKernan (US musician), aged 27

March 26th: Sir Noel Coward (British playwright), aged 73

April 8th: Pablo Picasso (Spanish painter), aged 91

May 18th: Jeannette Rankin (US politician), aged 92

May 26th: Jacques Lipchitz (French painter), aged 81

June 10th: William Inge (US poet), aged 60

June 26th: John Cranko (British dancer), aged 45

July 1st: Nancy Mitford (British novelist), aged 68

July 2nd: Betty Grable (US actress), aged 56

July 8th: Wilfred Rhodes (English cricketer), aged 95

July 19th: Bruce Lee (US actor), aged 32

August 1st: Walter Ulbricht (East German head of state), aged 80

August 6th: Fulgencio Batista (ex-Cuban dictator), aged 72

August 17th: Paul Williams (US singer), aged 34

August 31st: John Ford (US film director), aged 78

September 2nd: John Ronald Reuel Tolkien (British author), aged 81

September 11th: Salvador Allende (Chilean President), aged 65

September 15th: KIng Gustav VI of Sweden, aged 90

September 19th: Gram Parsons (US musician), aged 26

September 28th: Wystan Hugh Auden (British poet), aged 66

October 2nd: Paavo Nurmi (Finnish athlete), aged 76

October 22nd: Pablo Casals (Spanish cellist), aged 96

October 26th: Sir Roger Henry Hollis (British MI5 chief), aged 67

November 13th: Bruno Maderna (Italian composer), aged 53

November 13th: Elsa Schiaparelli (French fashion expert), aged 77

December 1st: David Ben-Gurion (Israeli statesman), aged 87

December 20th: Luis Carrero Blanco (Spanish statesman), aged 70

December 20th: Bobby Darin (US singer), aged 37

The UK Top 10 singles for the week ending January the 5th

1	Slade	Merry Xmas Everybody
2	New Seekers	You Won't Find Another Fool Like Me
3	Gary Glitter	I Love You Love Me Love
4	Wizzard	I Wish It Could Be Christmas Everyday
5	Alvin Stardust	My Coo Ca Choo
6	Marie Osmond	Paper Roses
7	Leo Sayer	The Show Must Go On
8	David Essex	Lamplight
9	Mott The Hoople	Roll Away The Stone
10	Roxy Music	Street Life

The US Number One single: Jim Croce – Time In A Bottle
The US Number One album: Carpenters – The Singles: 1969–1973
The UK Number One album: Yes – Tales From Topographic Oceans
Also this week: Golda Meir's Labour government is re-elected in Israel. (1st)

The UK Top 10 singles for the week ending January the 12th

1	Slade	Merry Xmas Everybody
2	New Seekers	You Won't Find Another Fool Like Me
3	Leo Sayer	The Show Must Go On
4	Wizzard	I Wish It Could Be Christmas Everyday
5	Alvin Stardust	My Coo Ca Choo
6	Cozy Powell	Dance With The Devil
7	Gary Glitter	I Love You Love Me Love
8	Faces	Pool Hall Richard / I Wish It Would Rain
9	Golden Earring	Radar Love
10	David Essex	Lamplight

The US Number One single: Steve Miller Band – The Joker
The US Number One album: Jim Croce – You Don't Mess Around With Jim
The UK Number One album: Yes – Tales From Topographic Oceans
Also this week: A train drivers' strike cripples Britain's rail services. (10th)

The UK Top 10 singles for the week ending January the 19th

1	New Seekers	You Won't Find Another Fool Like Me
2	Leo Sayer	The Show Must Go On
3	Slade	Merry Xmas Everybody
4	Cozy Powell	Dance With The Devil
5	Alvin Stardust	My Coo Ca Choo
6	Sweet	Teenage Rampage
7	Golden Earring	Radar Love
8	Marie Osmond	Paper Roses
9	Roy Wood	Forever
10	Mud	Tiger Feet

The US Number One single: Al Wilson – Show And Tell
The US Number One album: Jim Croce – You Don't Mess Around With Jim
The UK Number One album: Slade – Sladest
Also this week: Israel signs an agreement with Egypt. (18th)

The UK Top 10 singles for the week ending January the 26th

1	Mud	Tiger Feet
2	Sweet	Teenage Rampage
3	Leo Sayer	The Show Must Go On
4	Cozy Powell	Dance With The Devil
5	New Seekers	You Won't Find Another Fool Like Me
6	Alvin Stardust	My Coo Ca Choo
7	Golden Earring	Radar Love
8	Roy Wood	Forever
9	Andy Williams	Solitaire
10	Robert Knight	Love On A Mountain Top

The US Number One single: Ringo Starr – You're Sixteen
The US Number One album: Jim Croce – You Don't Mess Around With Jim
The UK Number One album: Perry Como – And I Love You So
Also this week: Israel begins troop withdrawls from Egypt. (23rd)

The song of the month for January 1974

All Of My Life by Diana Ross (peak chart position: No.9)

Diana Ross was proving to be as consistently successful as a solo artist as she had been in tandem with the Supremes. 'All Of My Life' may have only scraped into the British Top Ten, but it still ranks as one of her very finest love songs. Miss Ross then proceeded on to a couple of heavyweight collaborations with another American icon, Marvin Gaye, which yielded the excellent 'You Are Everything'. Regardless of the trends and fads which surfaced and then vanished, the recordings of Diana Ross remained constantly popular.

The UK Top 10 singles for the week ending February the 2nd

1	Mud	Tiger Feet
2	Sweet	Teenage Rampage
3	New Seekers	You Won't Find Another Fool Like Me
4	Leo Sayer	The Show Must Go On
5	Cozy Powell	Dance With The Devil
6	Andy Williams	Solitaire
7	Golden Earring	Radar Love
8	Alvin Stardust	My Coo Ca Choo
9	Roy Wood	Forever
10	Robert Knight	Love On A Mountain Top

The US Number One single: Barbra Streisand – The Way We Were
The US Number One album: Jim Croce – You Don't Mess Around With Jim
The UK Number One album: Carpenters – The Singles: 1969–1973
Also this week: The Great Train robber, Ronnie Biggs, is arrested in Brazil. (1st)

The UK Top 10 singles for the week ending February the 9th

1	Mud	Tiger Feet
2	Sweet	Teenage Rampage
3	Cozy Powell	Dance With The Devil
4	Andy Williams	Solitaire
5	Lulu	The Man Who Sold The World
6	Stylistics	Rockin' Roll Baby
7	Leo Sayer	The Show Must Go On
8	New Seekers	You Won't Find Another Fool Like Me
9	Diana Ross	All Of My Life
10	Roy Wood	Forever

The US Number One single: Love Unlimited Orchestra – Love's Theme
The US Number One album: Jim Croce – You Don't Mess Around With Jim
The UK Number One album: Carpenters – The Singles: 1969–1973
Also this week: The heiress, Patty Hearst, is kidnapped in San Francisco. (4th)

The UK Top 10 singles for the week ending February the 16th

1	Mud	Tiger Feet
2	Suzi Quatro	Devil Gate Drive
3	Lulu	The Man Who Sold The World
4	Sweet	Teenage Rampage
5	Andy Williams	Solitaire
6	Cozy Powell	Dance With The Devil
7	Wombles	The Wombling Song
8	Stylistics	Rockin' Roll Baby
9	Diana Ross	All Of My Life
10	Leo Sayer	The Show Must Go On

The US Number One single: Barbra Streisand – The Way We Were
The US Number One album: Bob Dylan – Planet Waves
The UK Number One album: Carpenters – The Singles: 1969–1973
Also this week: The author, Alexander Solzhenitsyn, is expelled from the Soviet Union. (14th)

The UK Top 10 singles for the week ending February the 23rd

1 Suzi Quatro — Devil Gate Drive
2 Mud — Tiger Feet
3 Alvin Stardust — Jealous Mind
4 Wombles — The Wombling Song
5 Lulu — The Man Who Sold The World
6 David Bowie — Rebel Rebel
7 Andy Williams — Solitaire
8 Hollies — The Air That I Breathe
9 Diana Ross — All Of My Life
10 Love Unlimited Orchestra — Love's Theme

The US Number One single: Barbra Streisand – The Way We Were
The US Number One album: Bob Dylan – Planet Waves
The UK Number One album: Carpenters – The Singles: 1969–1973
Also this week: Bangladesh is recognised by its former ruler, Pakistan. (22nd)

The song of the month for February 1974

Billy, Don't Be A Hero by Paper Lace (peak chart position: No.1)

This sad tale about a young soldier who ignored his fiancee's plea to keep his "pretty head low" also reached the American pop summit, but it was covered by Bo Donaldson and the Heywoods, who gave it an American Civil War setting. Even more strange was the fact that Paper Lace actually topped the Billboard singles chart later in the year with 'The Night Chicago Died'. This track will always be remembered for its military sound of a marching drum and an accompanying flute.

The UK Top 10 singles for the week ending March the 2nd

1	Suzi Quatro	Devil Gate Drive
2	Alvin Stardust	Jealous Mind
3	Hollies	The Air That I Breathe
4	Wombles	The Wombling Song
5	David Bowie	Rebel Rebel
6	Mud	Tiger Feet
7	Ringo Starr	You're Sixteen
8	Bay City Rollers	Remember (Sha-La-La-La)
9	Lulu	The Man Who Sold The World
10	Lena Zavaroni	Ma He's Making Eyes At Me

The US Number One single: Terry Jacks – Seasons In The Sun
The US Number One album: Bob Dylan – Planet Waves
The UK Number One album: Slade – Old New Borrowed And Blue
Also this week: The British general election results in a hung parliament. (1st)

The UK Top 10 singles for the week ending March the 9th

1	Alvin Stardust	Jealous Mind
2	Suzi Quatro	Devil Gate Drive
3	Hollies	The Air That I Breathe
4	Ringo Starr	You're Sixteen
5	David Bowie	Rebel Rebel
6	Bay City Rollers	Remember (Sha-La-La-La)
7	Wombles	The Wombling Song
8	Paper Lace	Billy Don't Be A Hero
9	Charlie Rich	The Most Beautiful Girl
10	Wings	Jet

The US Number One single: Terry Jacks – Seasons In The Sun
The US Number One album: Bob Dylan – Planet Waves
The UK Number One album: Carpenters – The Singles: 1969–1973
Also this week: Britain's miners' strike ends with a pay increase. (6th)

The UK Top 10 singles for the week ending March the 16th

1	Paper Lace	Billy Don't Be A Hero
2	Alvin Stardust	Jealous Mind
3	Hollies	The Air That I Breathe
4	Charlie Rich	The Most Beautiful Girl
5	Ringo Starr	You're Sixteen
6	Suzi Quatro	Devil Gate Drive
7	Bay City Rollers	Remember (Sha-La-La-La)
8	Wings	Jet
9	Freddie Starr	It's You
10	Wombles	The Wombling Song

The US Number One single: Terry Jacks – Seasons In The Sun
The US Number One album: Barbra Streisand – The Way We Were
The UK Number One album: Carpenters – The Singles: 1969–1973
Also this week: The architect, John Poulson, is jailed for corruption. (15th)

The UK Top 10 singles for the week ending March the 23rd

1	Paper Lace	Billy Don't Be A Hero
2	Hollies	The Air That I Breathe
3	Charlie Rich	The Most Beautiful Girl
4	Ringo Starr	You're Sixteen
5	Alvin Stardust	Jealous Mind
6	New Seekers	I Get A Little Sentimental Over You
7	Wings	Jet
8	Bay City Rollers	Remember (Sha-La-La-La)
9	Freddie Starr	It's You
10	Hot Chocolate	Emma

The US Number One single: Cher – Dark Lady
The US Number One album: Barbra Streisand – The Way We Were
The UK Number One album: Carpenters – The Singles: 1969–1973
Also this week: Princess Anne narrowly escapes a kidnap attempt. (20th)

The UK Top 10 singles for the week ending March the 30th

1	Paper Lace	Billy Don't Be A Hero
2	Charlie Rich	The Most Beautiful Girl
3	Terry Jacks	Seasons In The Sun
4	Hollies	The Air That I Breathe
5	New Seekers	I Get A Little Sentimental Over You
6	Hot Chocolate	Emma
7	Ringo Starr	You're Sixteen
8	Gary Glitter	Remember Me This Way
9	Glitter Band	Angel Face
10	Wings	Jet

The US Number One single: John Denver – Sunshine On My Shoulders
The US Number One album: John Denver – John Denver's Greatest Hits
The UK Number One album: Carpenters – The Singles: 1969–1973
Also this week: Fifty army officers are executed in Uganda. (25th)

The song of the month for March 1974

Seasons In The Sun by Terry Jacks (peak chart position: No.1)

Following shortly after the tearjerker that was 'Billy Don't Be A Hero' was perhaps the saddest song of them all. Yes, in spite of the title, 'Seasons In The Sun' was far from sunny. Instead it is sung from the point of view of a person contemplating an imminent death who recalls past times when he had joy and fun and seasons in the sun. Tissue paper manufacturers must surely have been doing a good trade in the spring of this year. 'Seasons In The Sun' was so popular that it became the second biggest-selling single of the year.

The UK Top 10 singles for the week ending April the 6th

1	Terry Jacks	Seasons In The Sun
2	Paper Lace	Billy Don't Be A Hero
3	Hot Chocolate	Emma
4	Gary Glitter	Remember Me This Way
5	Glitter Band	Angel Face
6	Slade	Everyday
7	New Seekers	I Get A Little Sentimental Over You
8	Charlie Rich	The Most Beautiful Girl
9	Diana Ross & Marvin Gaye	You Are Everything
10	Hollies	The Air That I Breathe

The US Number One single: Blue Swede – Hooked On A Feeling
The US Number One album: John Denver – John Denver's Greatest Hits
The UK Number One album: Carpenters – The Singles: 1969–1973
Also this week: Rutland 'disappears' as England's counties are re-structured. (1st)

The UK Top 10 singles for the week ending April the 13th

1	Terry Jacks	Seasons In The Sun
2	Paper Lace	Billy Don't Be A Hero
3	Gary Glitter	Remember Me This Way
4	Slade	Everyday
5	Glitter Band	Angel Face
6	Hot Chocolate	Emma
7	Diana Ross & Marvin Gaye	You Are Everything
8	Mud	The Cat Crept In
9	Charlie Rich	The Most Beautiful Girl
10	Queen	Seven Seas Of Rhye

The US Number One single: Elton John – Bennie And The Jets
The US Number One album: Paul McCartney & Wings – Band On The Run
The UK Number One album: Carpenters – The Singles: 1969–1973
Also this week: Golda Meir resigns as Israel's Prime Minister. (10th)

The UK Top 10 singles for the week ending April the 20th

1 Terry Jacks   Seasons In The Sun
2 Mud   The Cat Crept In
3 Slade   Everyday
4 Glitter Band   Angel Face
5 Diana Ross & Marvin Gaye   You Are Everything
6 Hot Chocolate   Emma
7 Gary Glitter   Remember Me This Way
8 Wombles   Remember You're A Womble
9 Sunny   Doctor's Orders
10 Paper Lace   Billy Don't Be A Hero

The US Number One single: MFSB Featuring The Three Degrees – TSOP (The Sound Of Philadelphia)
The US Number One album: John Denver – John Denver's Greatest Hits
The UK Number One album: Carpenters – The Singles: 1969–1973
Also this week: Andrei Sakharov urges the Soviet leadership to renounce Marxism. (14th)

The UK Top 10 singles for the week ending April the 27th

1 Terry Jacks   Seasons In The Sun
2 Abba   Waterloo
3 Mud   The Cat Crept In
4 Wombles   Remember You're A Womble
5 Glitter Band   Angel Face
6 Diana Ross & Marvin Gaye   You Are Everything
7 Slade   Everyday
8 Sunny   Doctor's Orders
9 Chi-Lites   Homely Girl
10 Limmie & The Family Cookin'   A Walkin' Miracle

The US Number One single: MFSB Featuring The Three Degrees – TSOP (The Sound Of Philadelphia)
The US Number One album: Chicago – Chicago VII
The UK Number One album: Carpenters – The Singles: 1969–1973
Also this week: General Spinola ousts Doctor Caetano in a coup in Portugal. (25th)

The song of the month for April 1974

Waterloo by Abba (peak chart position: No.1)

Continental Europe had never provided artists who could enjoy a durable chart career in Britain or the United States, but all that was to change with the Abba invasion from Sweden, which began with the glorious 'Waterloo'. The two men and two women singing act had been a well-worn formula, but this time the two guys were highly capable composers, so the group simply stuck to their own admirable material. What was remarkable was that after the success of 'Waterloo', Abba struggled to find a decent follow-up for eighteen months until their flagging fortunes were rescued by an 'S.O.S.'

The UK Top 10 singles for the week ending May the 4th

1	Abba	Waterloo
2	Mud	The Cat Crept In
3	Terry Jacks	Seasons In The Sun
4	Wombles	Remember You're A Womble
5	Chi-Lites	Homely Girl
6	Limmie & The Family Cookin'	A Walkin' Miracle
7	Sunny	Doctor's Orders
8	Diana Ross & Marvin Gaye	You Are Everything
9	Wizzard	Rock And Roll Winter
10	Glitter Band	Angel Face

The US Number One single: Grand Funk – The Loco-Motion
The US Number One album: Soundtrack – The Sting
The UK Number One album: Carpenters – The Singles: 1969–1973
Also this week: Sir Alf Ramsey is sacked as England's soccer manager. (1st)

The UK Top 10 singles for the week ending May the 11th

1 Abba — Waterloo
2 Rubettes — Sugar Baby Love
3 Wombles — Remember You're A Womble
4 Peters And Lee — Don't Stay Away Too Long
5 Bay City Rollers — Shang-A-Lang
6 Wizzard — Rock And Roll Winter
7 Chi-Lites — Homely Girl
8 Limmie & The Family Cookin' — A Walkin' Miracle
9 Terry Jacks — Seasons In The Sun
10 Stevie Wonder — He's Misstra Know It All

The US Number One single: Grand Funk – The Loco-Motion
The US Number One album: Soundtrack – The Sting
The UK Number One album: Carpenters – The Singles: 1969–1973
Also this week: Willy Brandt resigns as West Germany's Chancellor. (6th)

The UK Top 10 singles for the week ending May the 18th

1 Rubettes — Sugar Baby Love
2 Abba — Waterloo
3 Peters And Lee — Don't Stay Away Too Long
4 Bay City Rollers — Shang-A-Lang
5 Wombles — Remember You're A Womble
6 Wizzard — Rock And Roll Winter
7 Paper Lace — The Night Chicago Died
8 Chi-Lites — Homely Girl
9 Sparks — This Town Ain't Big Enough For Both Of Us
10 Alvin Stardust — Red Dress

The US Number One single: Ray Stevens – The Streak
The US Number One album: Soundtrack – The Sting
The UK Number One album: Carpenters – The Singles: 1969–1973
Also this week: Helmut Schmidt becomes West Germany's new Chancellor. (16th)

The UK Top 10 singles for the week ending May the 25th

1 Rubettes   Sugar Baby Love
2 Bay City Rollers   Shang-A-Lang
3 Sparks   This Town Ain't Big Enough For Both Of Us
4 Peters And Lee   Don't Stay Away Too Long
5 Paper Lace   The Night Chicago Died
6 Abba   Waterloo
7 Alvin Stardust   Red Dress
8 Status Quo   Break The Rules
9 R. Dean Taylor   There's A Ghost In My House
10 David Cassidy   If I Didn't Care

The US Number One single: Ray Stevens – The Streak
The US Number One album: Soundtrack – The Sting
The UK Number One album: Rick Wakeman – Journey To The Centre Of The Earth
Also this week: Valery Giscard d'Estaing is elected President of France. (19th)

The song of the month for May 1974

This Town Ain't Big Enough For Both Of Us by Sparks
(peak chart position: No.2)

One of the great injustices in human history was the fact that the Rubettes kept this charming rocker off the Number One position in the British singles listing. Nevertheless, the Sparks had delivered one of the biggest music thrills of the year with this eccentric piece, underpinned by the sound of gunfire, a falsetto singing voice, not to mention the 'Hitler moustache' of the keyboardist Ron Mael. Any 'seventies compilation that overlooks this magnificent museum piece deserves itself to be overlooked.

The UK Top 10 singles for the week ending June the 1st

1 Rubettes   Sugar Baby Love
2 Sparks   This Town Ain't Big Enough For Both Of Us
3 Paper Lace   The Night Chicago Died
4 R. Dean Taylor   There's A Ghost In My House
5 Peters And Lee   Don't Stay Away Too Long
6 Showaddywaddy   Hey Rock And Roll
7 Bay City Rollers   Shang-A-Lang
8 Gigliola Cinquetti   Go
9 David Cassidy   If I Didn't Care
10 Alvin Stardust   Red Dress

The US Number One single: Ray Stevens – The Streak
The US Number One album: Soundtrack – The Sting
The UK Number One album: Carpenters – The Singles: 1969–1973
Also this week: Northern Ireland's power-sharing executive resigns. (28th)

The UK Top 10 singles for the week ending June the 8th

1 Rubettes   Sugar Baby Love
2 Sparks   This Town Ain't Big Enough For Both Of Us
3 Showaddywaddy   Hey Rock And Roll
4 Ray Stevens   The Streak
5 R. Dean Taylor   There's A Ghost In My House
6 Paper Lace   The Night Chicago Died
7 Cockney Rebel   Judy Teen
8 Mouth And McNeal   I See A Star
9 David Cassidy   If I Didn't Care
10 Status Quo   Break The Rules

The US Number One single: Paul McCartney & Wings – Band On The Run
The US Number One album: Paul McCartney & Wings – Band On The Run
The UK Number One album: David Bowie – Diamond Dogs
Also this week: Yitzhak Rabin becomes Israel's new Prime Minister. (3rd)

The UK Top 10 singles for the week ending June the 15th

1	Ray Stevens	The Streak
2	Showaddywaddy	Hey Rock And Roll
3	R. Dean Taylor	There's A Ghost In My House
4	Sparks	This Town Aint Big Enough For Both Of Us
5	Gary Glitter	Always Yours
6	Rubettes	Sugar Baby Love
7	Cockney Rebel	Judy Teen
8	Alan Price	Jarrow Song
9	The Arrows	A Touch Too Much
10	Mouth And McNeal	I See A Star

The US Number One single: Bo Donaldson And The Heywoods – Billy Don't Be A Hero
The US Number One album: Paul McCartney & Wings – Band On The Run
The UK Number One album: David Bowie – Diamond Dogs
Also this week: Henry Kissinger threatens resignation over wire-tapping allegations. (11th)

The UK Top 10 singles for the week ending June the 22nd

1	Gary Glitter	Always Yours
2	Ray Stevens	The Streak
3	Showaddywaddy	Hey Rock And Roll
4	R. Dean Taylor	There's A Ghost In My House
5	Cockney Rebel	Judy Teen
6	Alan Price	Jarrow Song
7	The Scaffold	Liverpool Lou
8	The Arrows	A Touch Too Much
9	Sparks	This Town Aint Big Enough For Both Of Us
10	Lobo	I'd Love You To Want Me

The US Number One single: Bo Donaldson And The Heywoods – Billy Don't Be A Hero
The US Number One album: Gordon Lightfoot – Sundown
The UK Number One album: David Bowie – Diamond Dogs
Also this week: Inflation in Britain reaches a record sixteen per cent. (21st)

The UK Top 10 singles for the week ending June the 29th

1	Charles Aznavour	She
2	Gary Glitter	Always Yours
3	Ray Stevens	The Streak
4	Showaddywaddy	Hey Rock And Roll
5	R. Dean Taylor	There's A Ghost In My House
6	Leo Sayer	One Man Band
7	Lobo	I'd Love You To Want Me
8	Drifters	Kissin' In The Back Row Of The Movies
9	The Arrows	A Touch Too Much
10	Alan Price	Jarrow Song

The US Number One single: Gordon Lightfoot – Sundown

The US Number One album: Gordon Lightfoot – Sundown

The UK Number One album: David Bowie – Diamond Dogs

Also this week: Richard Nixon arrives in Moscow, whilst Watergate remains unresolved. (27th)

The song of the month for June 1974

Rock Your Baby by George McCrae (peak chart position: No.1)

The British record-buyers were mercifully beginning to tire of glam rock and turned instead in increasing numbers to the genre of disco. The only drawback was that for a few years anything with the word 'disco' in the song title found its way onto the charts, regardless of its dubious quality. Nevertheless, there were clearly a number of giant dancefloor classics, of which 'Rock Your Baby' is most certainly one. George McCrae reaches the high notes here and is deservedly rewarded with a Number One on both sides of the Atlantic.

The UK Top 10 singles for the week ending July the 6th

1	Charles Aznavour	She
2	Drifters	Kissin' In The Back Row Of The Movies
3	Gary Glitter	Always Yours
4	Slade	Banging Man
5	Showaddywaddy	Hey Rock And Roll
6	Lobo	I'd Love You To Want Me
7	Ray Stevens	The Streak
8	Leo Sayer	One Man Band
9	Gary Puckett And The Union Gap	Young Girl
10	The Pearls	Guilty

The US Number One single: Hues Corporation – Rock The Boat
The US Number One album: Paul McCartney & Wings – Band On The Run
The UK Number One album: Carpenters – The Singles: 1969–1973
Also this week: Don Revie becomes England's new soccer manager. (5th)

The UK Top 10 singles for the week ending July the 13th

1	Charles Aznavour	She
2	Drifters	Kissin' In The Back Row Of The Movies
3	Slade	Banging Man
4	George McCrae	Rock Your Baby
5	Lobo	I'd Love You To Want Me
6	Leo Sayer	One Man Band
7	Wings	Band On the Run
8	Gary Puckett And The Union Gap	Young Girl
9	Gary Glitter	Always Yours
10	10cc	Wall Street Shuffle

The US Number One single: George McCrae – Rock Your Baby
The US Number One album: Elton John – Caribou
The UK Number One album: Elton John – Caribou
Also this week: Pierre Trudeau's Liberal government is re-elected in Canada. (8th)

The UK Top 10 singles for the week ending July the 20th

1 Charles Aznavour — She
2 Drifters — Kissin' In The Back Row Of The Movies
3 George McCrae — Rock Your Baby
4 Wings — Band On The Run
5 Slade — Banging Man
6 Gary Puckett And The Union Gap — Young Girl
7 Lobo — I'd Love You To Want Me
8 Terry Jacks — If You Go Away
9 Wombles — Banana Rock
10 Gary Glitter — Always Yours

The US Number One single: George McCrae – Rock Your Baby
The US Number One album: Elton John – Caribou
The UK Number One album: Elton John – Caribou
Also this week: A coup breaks out to overthrow military rule in Greece. (15th)

The UK Top 10 singles for the week ending July the 27th

1 George McCrae — Rock Your Baby
2 Charles Aznavour — She
3 Stephanie De Sykes — Born With A Smile On My Face
4 Drifters — Kissin' In The Back Row Of The Movies
5 Wings — Band On the Run
6 Gary Puckett And The Union Gap — Young Girl
7 Three Degrees — When Will I See You Again
8 Slade — Banging Man
9 Sweet — The Six Teens
10 Lobo — I'd Love You To Want Me

The US Number One single: John Denver – Annie's Song
The US Number One album: Elton John – Caribou
The UK Number One album: Paul McCartney & Wings – Band On The Run
Also this week: Impeachment proceedings are initiated against President Nixon. (27th)

The song of the month for July 1974

Band On The Run by Wings (peak chart position: No.3)

The fertile imagination of Paul McCartney hit upon the crazy idea of fleeing to Africa to record an album there. The ensuing result of Macca's 'band on the run' was a long player that even the once scornful John Lennon approved of. Wings may have gone on to dwell at Number One for a staggering nine weeks with 'Mull Of Kintyre', but McCartney's jailbreak song represents his post-Beatles creative peak. The item switches cleverly between a wonderful acoustic guitar and electric guitar. Such is popular taste that McCartney has reached singles summits with songs that don't compare with the quality of this tune.

The UK Top 10 singles for the week ending August the 3rd

1	George McCrae	Rock Your Baby
2	Stephanie De Sykes	Born With A Smile On My Face
3	Wings	Band On The Run
4	Three Degrees	When Will I See You Again
5	Charles Aznavour	She
6	Drifters	Kissin' In The Back Row Of The Movies
7	Gary Puckett And The Union Gap	Young Girl
8	Stylistics	You Make Me Feel Brand New
9	Sparks	Amateur Hour
10	Terry Jacks	If You Go Away

The US Number One single: John Denver – Annie's Song

The US Number One album: Elton John – Caribou

The UK Number One album: Paul McCartney & Wings – Band On The Run

Also this week: The Supreme Court orders Nixon to hand over tape recordings. (30th)

The UK Top 10 singles for the week ending August the 10th

1	George McCrae	Rock Your Baby
2	Three Degrees	When Will I See You Again
3	Stephanie De Sykes	Born With A Smile On My Face
4	Stylistics	You Make Me Feel Brand New
5	Bay City Rollers	Summerlove Sensation
6	Mud	Rocket
7	Sparks	Amateur Hour
8	Wings	Band On The Run
9	Drifters	Kissin' In The Back Row Of The Movies
10	The Hues Corporation	Rock The Boat

The US Number One single: Roberta Flack – Feel Like Makin' Love
The US Number One album: John Denver – Back Home Again
The UK Number One album: Paul McCartney & Wings – Band On The Run
Also this week: Gerald Ford becomes American President after Nixon's resignation. (9th)

The UK Top 10 singles for the week ending August the 17th

1	Three Degrees	When Will I See You Again
2	George McCrae	Rock Your Baby
3	Stylistics	You Make Me Feel Brand New
4	Bay City Rollers	Summerlove Sensation
5	Stephanie De Sykes	Born With A Smile On My Face
6	The Hues Corporation	Rock The Boat
7	Mud	Rocket
8	Jimmy Ruffin	What Becomes Of The Broken Hearted?
9	Eric Clapton	I Shot The Sheriff
10	Rolling Stones	It's Only Rock 'N' Roll

The US Number One single: Paper Lace – The Night Chicago Died
The US Number One album: Eric Clapton – 461 Ocean Boulevard
The UK Number One album: Paul McCartney & Wings – Band On The Run
Also this week: Colonel Gaddafi orders the arrests of five hundred Egyptian troops. (14th)

The UK Top 10 singles for the week ending August the 24th

1	Three Degrees	When Will I See You Again
2	Stylistics	You Make Me Feel Brand New
3	Bay City Rollers	Summerlove Sensation
4	Jimmy Ruffin	What Becomes Of The Broken Hearted?
5	Donny And Marie Osmond	I'm Leaving It All Up To You
6	George McCrae	Rock Your Baby
7	The Hues Corporation	Rock The Boat
8	Mud	Rocket
9	Eric Clapton	I Shot The Sheriff
10	Glitter Band	Just For You

The US Number One single: Paul Anka And Odia Coates – (You're) Having My Baby
The US Number One album: Eric Clapton – 461 Ocean Boulevard
The UK Number One album: Paul McCartney & Wings – Band On The Run
Also this week: Nelson Rockefeller is appointed as Gerald Ford's Vice-President. (20th)

The UK Top 10 singles for the week ending August the 31st

1	Osmonds	Love Me For A Reason
2	Three Degrees	When Will I See You Again
3	Stylistics	You Make Me Feel Brand New
4	Donny And Marie Osmond	I'm Leaving It All Up To You
5	Bay City Rollers	Summerlove Sensation
6	Jimmy Ruffin	What Becomes Of The Broken Hearted?
7	Sylvia	Y Viva Espana
8	Cockney Rebel	Mr Soft
9	Carl Douglas	Kung Fu Fighting
10	Sweet Dreams	Honey Honey

The US Number One single: Paul Anka And Odia Coates – (You're) Having My Baby
The US Number One album: Eric Clapton – 461 Ocean Boulevard
The UK Number One album: Paul McCartney & Wings – Band On The Run
Also this week: The Soviet Union launches Soyuz Fifteen into orbit. (26th)

The song of the month for August 1974

Annie's Song by John Denver (peak chart position: No.1)

John Denver was no stranger to lofty chart positions in the United States, courtesy of the likes of 'Thank God I'm A Country Boy' but his only major British success story was the hugely listenable 'Annie's Song'. Here was one of those occasions when the adults closed ranks and purchased something which all the teenage record-buyers would not have warmed to. This delightful piece benefited from harmonies and a fine strings arrangement and re-appeared in the UK chart in 1978 when Irish flautist James Galway delivered his own version.

The UK Top 10 singles for the week ending September the 7th

1	Osmonds	Love Me For A Reason
2	Donny And Marie Osmond	I'm Leaving It All Up To You
3	Three Degrees	When Will I See You Again
4	Carl Douglas	Kung Fu Fighting
5	Sylvia	Y Viva Espana
6	Stylistics	You Make Me Feel Brand New
7	John Denver	Annie's Song
8	Jimmy Ruffin	What Becomes Of The Broken Hearted?
9	Cockney Rebel	Mr Soft
10	Sweet Dreams	Honey Honey

The US Number One single: Paul Anka And Odia Coates – (You're) Having My Baby
The US Number One album: Eric Clapton – 461 Ocean Boulevard
The UK Number One album: Paul McCartney & Wings – Band On The Run
Also this week: General Somoza is appointed as the President of Nicaragua. (1st)

The UK Top 10 singles for the week ending September the 14th

1	Osmonds	Love Me For A Reason
2	Carl Douglas	Kung Fu Fighting
3	Donny And Marie Osmond	I'm Leaving It All Up To You
4	Sylvia	Y Viva Espana
5	John Denver	Annie's Song
6	Johnny Bristol	Hang On In There Baby
7	Three Degrees	When Will I See You Again
8	Jimmy Ruffin	What Becomes Of The Broken Hearted?
9	Alvin Stardust	You You You
10	Cozy Powell	Na Na Na

The US Number One single: Eric Clapton – I Shot The Sheriff
The US Number One album: Stevie Wonder – Fulfillingness' First Finale
The UK Number One album: Mike Oldfield – Hergest Ridge
Also this week: Chou En-lai resigns as China's Prime Minister. (10th)

The UK Top 10 singles for the week ending September the 21st

1	Carl Douglas	Kung Fu Fighting
2	Osmonds	Love Me For A Reason
3	John Denver	Annie's Song
4	Johnny Bristol	Hang On In There Baby
5	Donny And Marie Osmond	I'm Leaving It All Up To You
6	Sylvia	Y Viva Espana
7	Alvin Stardust	You You You
8	Barry White	Can't Get Enough Of Your Love, Babe
9	KC And The Sunshine Band	Queen Of Clubs
10	Cozy Powell	Na Na Na

The US Number One single: Barry White – Can't Get Enough Of Your Love, Babe
The US Number One album: Stevie Wonder – Fulfillingness' First Finale
The UK Number One album: Mike Oldfield – Hergest Ridge
Also this week: President Ford grants a pardon to his predecessor, Richard Nixon. (16th)

The UK Top 10 singles for the week ending September the 28th

1	Carl Douglas	Kung Fu Fighting
2	John Denver	Annie's Song
3	Johnny Bristol	Hang On In There Baby
4	Osmonds	Love Me For A Reason
5	Sylvia	Y Viva Espana
6	Alvin Stardust	You You You
7	KC And The Sunshine Band	Queen Of Clubs
8	Barry White	Can't Get Enough Of Your Love, Babe
9	Andy Kim	Rock Me Gently
10	Leo Sayer	Long Tall Glasses

The US Number One single: Andy Kim – Rock Me Gently
The US Number One album: Bad Company – Bad Company
The UK Number One album: Mike Oldfield – Hergest Ridge
Also this week: The BBC Ceefax teletext service is first transmitted. (23rd)

The song of the month for September 1974

Sad Sweet Dreamer by Sweet Sensation (peak chart position: No.1)

ITV's hugely popular 'Opportunity Knocks' was the breeding ground for many new acts in the world of showbusiness. One such instance was the emergence of the Sweet Sensation who were regarded as Britain's very own answer to the Jacksons. This young group never fulfilled the high expectations, which is all the more surprising since they made a majestic splash with the beautiful 'Sad Sweet Dreamer'. Here is another candidate for one of the best-ever pop songs. Yet again record-buyers were seduced by a sad, sweet composition.

The UK Top 10 singles for the week ending October the 5th

1	Carl Douglas	Kung Fu Fighting
2	John Denver	Annie's Song
3	Johnny Bristol	Hang On In There Baby
4	Leo Sayer	Long Tall Glasses
5	Sweet Sensation	Sad Sweet Dreamer
6	Peter Shelley	Gee Baby
7	Alvin Stardust	You You You
8	Andy Kim	Rock Me Gently
9	Barry White	Can't Get Enough Of Your Love, Babe
10	KC And The Sunshine Band	Queen Of Clubs

The US Number One single: Olivia Newton-John – I Honestly Love You
The US Number One album: Beach Boys – Endless Summer
The UK Number One album: Mike Oldfield – Tubular Bells
Also this week: The IRA explodes bombs in two Guildford pubs. (5th)

The UK Top 10 singles for the week ending October the 12th

1	John Denver	Annie's Song
2	Andy Kim	Rock Me Gently
3	Sweet Sensation	Sad Sweet Dreamer
4	Carl Douglas	Kung Fu Fighting
5	Peter Shelley	Gee Baby
6	Leo Sayer	Long Tall Glasses
7	Johnny Bristol	Hang On In There Baby
8	Alvin Stardust	You You You
9	Barry White	Can't Get Enough Of Your Love, Babe
10	David Bowie	Knock On Wood

The US Number One single: Olivia Newton-John – I Honestly Love You
The US Number One album: Olivia Newton-John – If You Love Me, Let Me Know
The UK Number One album: Bay City Rollers – Rollin'
Also this week: The Labour Party narrowly wins the British general election. (11th)

The UK Top 10 singles for the week ending October the 19th

1	Sweet Sensation	Sad Sweet Dreamer
2	Ken Boothe	Everything I Own
3	Slade	Far Far Away
4	Peter Shelley	Gee Baby
5	John Denver	Annie's Song
6	Leo Sayer	Long Tall Glasses
7	Rod Stewart	Farewell/Bring It On Home To Me
8	Andy Kim	Rock Me Gently
9	Gary Shearston	I Get A Kick Out Of You
10	Andy Fairweather-Low	Reggae Tune

The US Number One single: Billy Preston – Nothing From Nothing
The US Number One album: Bachman-Turner Overdrive – Not Fragile
The UK Number One album: Rod Stewart – Smiler
Also this week: The Maze Prison is set on fire by Republican prisoners. (16th)

The UK Top 10 singles for the week ending October the 26th

1	Ken Boothe	Everything I Own
2	Slade	Far Far Away
3	Sweet Sensation	Sad Sweet Dreamer
4	Bay City Rollers	All Of Me Loves All Of You
5	Peter Shelley	Gee Baby
6	Paul Anka And Odia Coates	(You're) Having My Baby
7	Gary Shearston	I Get A Kick Out Of You
8	Andy Kim	Rock Me Gently
9	George McCrae	I Can't Leave You Alone
10	David Essex	Gonna Make You A Star

The US Number One single: Dionne Warwicke And Spinners – Then Came You
The US Number One album: Barry White – Can't Get Enough
The UK Number One album: Bay City Rollers – Rollin'
Also this week: Moscow is selected to host the 1980 Olympic Games. (26th)

The song of the month for October 1974

Killer Queen by Queen (peak chart position: No.2)

Queen carved out their very own niche on planet pop by shrewdly offering material that was more accessible than heavy metal and yet they were correctly labelled as a 'rock band'. They made an impressive start with the 'Seven Seas Of Rhye' and it was becoming apparent that they would be a prolific act when they then issued 'Killer Queen'. Failing narrowly to hit the Number One spot, this is an entertaining tale of a femme fatale, decorated with tongue-in-cheek lyrics while Brian May's guitar weighs in with its customary excellence.

The UK Top 10 singles for the week ending November the 2nd

1	Ken Boothe	Everything I Own
2	Slade	Far Far Away
3	David Essex	Gonna Make You A Star
4	Bay City Rollers	All Of Me Loves All Of You
5	Queen	Killer Queen
6	Sweet Sensation	Sad Sweet Dreamer
7	Paul Anka And Odia Coates	(You're) Having My Baby
8	Drifters	Down On The Beach Tonight
9	George McCrae	I Can't Leave You Alone
10	Glitter Band	Let's Get Together Again

The US Number One single: Stevie Wonder – You Haven't Done Nothin'
The US Number One album: Crosby, Stills, Nash & Young – So Far
The UK Number One album: Rod Stewart – Smiler
Also this week: Muhammad Ali defeats George Foreman in the 'jungle' in Zaire. (29th)

The UK Top 10 singles for the week ending November the 9th

1	Ken Boothe	Everything I Own
2	David Essex	Gonna Make You A Star
3	Queen	Killer Queen
4	Bay City Rollers	All Of Me Loves All Of You
5	Slade	Far Far Away
6	Eddie Holman	Hey There Lonely Girl
7	Drifters	Down On The Beach Tonight
8	Glitter Band	Let's Get Together Again
9	Paul Anka And Odia Coates	(You're) Having My Baby
10	Stylistics	Let's Put It All Together

The US Number One single: Bachman-Turner Overdrive – You Ain't Seen Nothing Yet
The US Number One album: Carole King – Wrap Around Joy
The UK Number One album: Bay City Rollers – Rollin'
Also this week: The convicted bomber, Judith Ward, is jailed for thirty years. (4th)

The UK Top 10 singles for the week ending November the 16th

1	David Essex	Gonna Make You A Star
2	Queen	Killer Queen
3	Ken Boothe	Everything I Own
4	Eddie Holman	Hey There Lonely Girl
5	Barry White	You're The First, The Last, My Everything
6	Slade	Far Far Away
7	Bay City Rollers	All Of Me Loves All Of You
8	Drifters	Down On The Beach Tonight
9	Stylistics	Let's Put It All Together
10	The Peppers	Pepper Box

The US Number One single: John Lennon – Whatever Gets You Thru The Night
The US Number One album: John Lennon – Walls And Bridges
The UK Number One album: Bay City Rollers – Rollin'
Also this week: Yassir Arafat makes a speech to the United Nations Assembly. (13th)

The UK Top 10 singles for the week ending November the 23rd

1	David Essex	Gonna Make You A Star
2	Queen	Killer Queen
3	Barry White	You're The First, The Last, My Everything
4	Eddie Holman	Hey There Lonely Girl
5	Ken Boothe	Everything I Own
6	The Peppers	Pepper Box
7	Lynsey De Paul	No Honestly
8	Rubettes	Juke Box Jive
9	Stylistics	Let's Put It All Together
10	Bay City Rollers	All Of Me Loves All Of You

The US Number One single: Billy Swan – I Can Help
The US Number One album: Rolling Stones – It's Only Rock 'n' Roll
The UK Number One album: Elton John – Elton John's Greatest Hits
Also this week: The IRA kills seventeen people in two Birmingham pub bombs. (21st)

The UK Top 10 singles for the week ending November the 30th

1	David Essex	Gonna Make You A Star
2	Barry White	You're The First, The Last, My Everything
3	Gary Glitter	Oh Yes You're Beautiful
4	Rubettes	Juke Box Jive
5	Queen	Killer Queen
6	Bachman-Turner Overdrive	You Ain't Seen Nothing Yet
7	Suzi Quatro	The Wild One
8	Eddie Holman	Hey There Lonely Girl
9	The Peppers	Pepper Box
10	Chi-Lites	Too Good To Be Forgotten

The US Number One single: Billy Swan – I Can Help
The US Number One album: Elton John – Elton John's Greatest Hits
The UK Number One album: Elton John – Elton John's Greatest Hits
Also this week: The Prevention of Terrorism Act becomes law in Britain. (29th)

The song of the month for November 1974

You Ain't Seen Nothing Yet by Bachman-Turner Overdrive
(peak chart position: No.2)

This monumental rock song was one of Canadian music's finest moments. Taking its cue from 'All Right Now', the recording has amusing seduction lyrics. It certainly struck a chord with music aficionados on both sides of the 'big pond'. The item was later popularized by spoof disc jockeys 'Smashy' and 'Nicey' who were rather fond of it. The trouble for Randy Bachman and his team were that they will forever be remembered for this one song, but then when you record one of the great rock anthems, you only have yourself to blame.

The UK Top 10 singles for the week ending December the 7th

1	Barry White	You're The First, The Last, My Everything
2	David Essex	Gonna Make You A Star
3	Rubettes	Juke Box Jive
4	Gary Glitter	Oh Yes You're Beautiful
5	Bachman-Turner Overdrive	You Ain't Seen Nothing Yet
6	Hello	Tell Him
7	Eddie Holman	Hey There Lonely Girl
8	Elvis Presley	My Boy
9	Queen	Killer Queen
10	Rupie Edwards	Ire Feelings

The US Number One single: Carl Douglas – Kung Fu Fighting
The US Number One album: Elton John – Elton John's Greatest Hits
The UK Number One album: Elton John – Elton John's Greatest Hits
Also this week: Australia win the first Ashes test in Brisbane. (4th)

The UK Top 10 singles for the week ending December the 14th

1	Barry White	You're The First, The Last, My Everything
2	Gary Glitter	Oh Yes You're Beautiful
3	Bachman-Turner Overdrive	You Ain't Seen Nothing Yet
4	Mud	Lonely This Christmas
5	David Essex	Gonna Make You A Star
6	Elvis Presley	My Boy
7	Hello	Tell Him
8	Rubettes	Juke Box Jive
9	Rupie Edwards	Ire Feelings
10	Elton John	Lucy In The Sky With Diamonds

The US Number One single: Carl Douglas – Kung Fu Fighting
The US Number One album: Elton John – Elton John's Greatest Hits
The UK Number One album: Elton John – Elton John's Greatest Hits
Also this week: Alexander Solzhenitsyn collects his Nobel Prize, awarded back in 1970. (10th)

The UK Top 10 singles for the week ending December the 21st

1	Mud	Lonely This Christmas
2	Bachman-Turner Overdrive	You Ain't Seen Nothing Yet
3	Rubettes	Juke Box Jive
4	Barry White	You're The First, The Last, My Everything
5	Wombles	Wombling Merry Christmas
6	Ralph McTell	Streets Of London
7	Elvis Presley	My Boy
8	Disco Tex And The Sex-O-Lettes	Get Dancing
9	Gary Glitter	Oh Yes You're Beautiful
10	Hello	Tell Him

The US Number One single: Harry Chapin – Cat's In The Cradle
The US Number One album: Elton John – Elton John's Greatest Hits
The UK Number One album: Elton John – Elton John's Greatest Hits
Also this week: Australia trounce England in the second Ashes test at Perth. (17th)

The UK Top 10 singles for the week ending December the 28th

1	Mud	Lonely This Christmas
2	Bachman-Turner Overdrive	You Ain't Seen Nothing Yet
3	Rubettes	Juke Box Jive
4	Barry White	You're The First, The Last, My Everything
5	Wombles	Wombling Merry Christmas
6	Ralph McTell	Streets Of London
7	Elvis Presley	My Boy
8	Disco Tex And The Sex-O-Lettes	Get Dancing
9	Gary Glitter	Oh Yes You're Beautiful
10	Hello	Tell Him

The US Number One single: Helen Reddy – Angie Baby
The US Number One album: Elton John – Elton John's Greatest Hits
The UK Number One album: Elton John – Elton John's Greatest Hits
Also this week: The vanishing MP, John Stonehouse, is seized in Australia. (24th)

The song of the month for December 1974
Help Me Make It Through The Night by John Holt
(peak chart position: No.6)

Bob Marley was slowly beginning to emerge as one of the world's most important performers, but in the mean time a plethora of acts still took turns to fly the flag for Jamaican music. Stepping up to the mark for his four minutes of fame this time was John Holt, a renowned exponent of love songs in Caribbean circles. Holt expertly covered Kris Kristofferson's delightful song of seduction and eventually helped himself to a British Top Ten position in early 1975. Both the vocals and the musical accompaniment were of the highest order.

Listed Below are the Top 10 Best Selling UK Singles of 1974

1	Tiger Feet	Mud
2	Seasons In The Sun	Terry Jacks
3	Billy, Don't Be A Hero	Paper Lace
4	When Will I See You Again	The Three Degrees
5	Rock Your Baby	George McCrae
6	Gonna Make You A Star	David Essex
7	Kung Fu Fighting	Carl Douglas
8	She	Charles Aznavour
9	Sugar Baby Love	The Rubettes
10	Everything I Own	Ken Boothe

1974's CONCERTS OF THE YEAR

The Beatles once insisted that they would not tour the United States until they had achieved a Stateside Number One. 'I Want To Hold Your Hand' resolved that potential impasse. Eleven years later, John Lennon made a similar pronouncement to his new buddy, Elton John. Lennon stated that he would not take to the stage unless his new disco release, 'Whatever Gets You Through The Night', should reach the top of the Billboard charts. To Lennon's astonishment, his new single did indeed climb to the American pop summit, whereupon he kept his word and joined Elton John on stage at Madison Square Garden in November where the two Johns (Elton and Lennon) performed versions of 'Lucy In The Sky With Diamonds' and 'I Saw Her Standing There', as well as Lennon's current US chart-topper. It would be the last time that one of the icons of popular music would sing live. Meanwhile, back in the spring, a different musical gathering at Brighton, on England's south coast, witnessed the birth of pop world's next 'big thing' when Sweden's Abba conquered the Eurovision Song Contest, en route to global domination in the ensuing seven years.

1974's ALBUM OF THE YEAR

Natty Dread by Bob Marley & The Wailers
(released in October; reached No.43 in the UK)

Side One:

1. Lively Up Yourself; 5:11
2. No Woman, No Cry; 3:46
3. Them Belly Full (But We Hungry); 3:13
4. Rebel Music (3 O'Clock Roadblock); 6:45

Side Two:

1. So Jah Seh; 4:27
2. Natty Dread; 3:35
3. Bend Down Low; 3:22
4. Talkin' Blues; 4:06
5. Revolution; 4:23

Robert Nesta Marley was entering new territory with his 'Natty Dread' recording, as his act was now billed as Bob Marley And The Wailers. The recent departure of his closest collaborators Bunny Livingstone and Peter Tosh to pursue their own solo paths had necessitated this new state of affairs. Bob recruited his wife Rita as well as singers Judy Mowatt and Marcia Griffiths to form the backing band, the I-Threes, whilst American blues guitarist Al Anderson was hired to assist the Barrett brothers who comprised the Wailers' rhythm section. The result was Marley's first breakthrough into the British album charts. The long player visited Marley's main concerns of inequality ('Them Belly Full') and oppression ('Rebel Music'). It also possessed the first outing of 'No Woman, No Cry', as well as a fans' favourite, 'Lively Up Yourself'. On the road to becoming reggae's first superstar and an ambassador for the Third World, Bob Marley was already setting out his stall with his musical anxieties about 'Babylon'. This isn't by any means his best album, but it was a signpost of what was to follow from Jamaica's most famous son who quickly became one of the most important recording stars of the 1970s.

SPORT IN 1974

English Division One football champions: Leeds United; runners-up: Liverpool

English FA Cup final: Liverpool 3 Newcastle United 0

English League Cup Final: Wolverhampton Wanderers 2 Manchester City 1

Scottish Division One football champions: Glasgow Celtic; runners-up: Hibernian

Scottish FA Cup final: Glasgow Celtic 3 Dundee United 0

Scottish League Cup final: Dundee 1 Glasgow Celtic 0

Irish League football champions: Coleraine; Irish Cup final: Ards 2 Ballymena United 1

League Of Ireland football champions: Cork Celtic; cup winners: Finn Harps

European Cup final: Bayern Munich 4 Atletico Madrid 0 (in a replay)

European Cup-Winners' Cup final: FC Magdeburg 2 AC Milan 0

UEFA Cup final: Feyenoord beat Tottenham Hotspur 4–2 on aggregate

English county cricket champions: Worcestershire

Five Nations' rugby union champions: Ireland (five points)

Formula One world drivers' champion: Emerson Fittipaldi (Brazil) in a McLaren car

Gaelic football All-Ireland champions: Dublin; runners-up: Galway

British Open golf champion: Gary Player (at Royal Lytham & St Annes)

US Masters golf champion: Gary Player

US Open golf champion: Hale Irwin

USPGA golf champion: Lee Trevino

Rugby league Challenge Cup final: Warrington 24 Featherstone Rovers 9

Wimbledon men's singles tennis final: J Connors beat K Rosewall 6–1, 6–1, 6–4

Wimbledon ladies' singles tennis final: C Evert beat O Morozova 6–0, 6–4

World snooker final: Ray Reardon (Wales) beat Graham Miles (England) 22–12

The Aintree Grand National steeplechase winner: Red Rum; price 11–1

The Epsom Derby winner: Snow Knight; jockey – Brian Taylor; price 50–1

World Cup final: West Germany 2 Holland 1

1974's DEATHS

January 6th: David Siqueiros (Mexican painter), aged 77

January 25th: James Pope-Hennessy (British author), aged 57

January 31st: Samuel Goldwyn (US film producer), aged 91

April 2nd: Georges Pompidou (France's President), aged 62

April 5th: Richard Crossman (British politician), aged 66

May 24th: Duke Ellington (US musician), aged 75

June 10th: Duke of Gloucester, aged 74

June 18th: Marshal Georgi Zhukov (Soviet soldier), aged 77

July 1st: Juan Domingo Peron (Argentina's President), aged 78

July 5th: Georgette Heyer (British novelist), aged 71

July 9th: Earl Warren (US judge), aged 83

July 29th: Mama Cass Elliot (US singer), aged 32

August 13th: Kate O'Brien (Irish novelist), aged 76

August 22nd: Dr. Jacob Bronowski (Polish biologist), aged 66

September 23rd: Robbie McIntosh (British musician), aged 24

October 24th: David Oistrakh (Soviet violinist), aged 66

November 7th: Eric Linklater (British novelist), aged 75

November 13th: Vittorio de Sica (Italian film director), aged 72

November 24th: Cornelius Ryan (Irish writer), aged 54

November 25th: Nick Drake (British singer), aged 26

November 25th: U Thant (Burmese UN Secretary-General), aged 65

December 14th: Walter Lippman (US journalist), aged 75

The UK Top 10 singles for the week ending January the 4th

1	Mud	Lonely This Christmas
2	Wombles	Wombling Merry Christmas
3	Rubettes	Jukebox Jive
4	Ralph McTell	Streets Of London
5	Elvis Presley	My Boy
6	Bachman-Turner Overdrive	You Ain't Seen Nothing Yet
7	Goodies	The Inbetweenies/ Father Christmas Do Not Touch Me
8	Barry White	You're The First, The Last, My Everything
9	Gary Glitter	Oh Yes You're Beautiful
10	Status Quo	Down Down

The US Number One single: Elton John – Lucy In The Sky With Diamonds
The US Number One album: Elton John – Elton John's Greatest Hits
The UK Number One album: Elton John – Elton John's Greatest Hits
Also this week: Charlie Chaplin is selected for a knighthood. (2nd)

The UK Top 10 singles for the week ending January the 11th

1	Mud	Lonely This Christmas
2	Ralph McTell	Streets Of London
3	Status Quo	Down Down
4	Kenny	The Bump
5	Wombles	Wombling Merry Christmas
6	Gloria Gaynor	Never Can Say Goodbye
7	Tymes	Ms. Grace
8	Disco Tex & The Sex-O-Lettes	Get Dancing
9	Billy Swan	I Can Help
10	Rubettes	Jukebox Jive

The US Number One single:Elton John – Lucy In The Sky With Diamonds
The US Number One album: Elton John – Elton John's Greatest Hits
The UK Number One album: Elton John – Elton John's Greatest Hits
Also this week: Australia retain the Ashes after defeating England in Sydney. (9th)

The UK Top 10 singles for the week ending January the 18th

1	Status Quo	Down Down
2	Ralph McTell	Streets Of London
3	Kenny	The Bump
4	Gloria Gaynor	Never Can Say Goodbye
5	Tymes	Ms. Grace
6	Billy Swan	I Can Help
7	David Essex	Stardust
8	Mud	Lonely This Christmas
9	Disco Tex & The Sex-O-Lettes	Get Dancing
10	Wizzard	Are You Ready To Rock

The US Number One single: Barry Manilow – Mandy
The US Number One album: Elton John – Elton John's Greatest Hits
The UK Number One album: Elton John – Elton John's Greatest Hits
Also this week: Portugal decides to give Angola its independence. (16th)

The UK Top 10 singles for the week ending January the 25th

1	Tymes	Ms. Grace
2	Gloria Gaynor	Never Can Say Goodbye
3	Kenny	The Bump
4	Ralph McTell	Streets Of London
5	Status Quo	Down Down
6	John Holt	Help Me Make It Through The Night
7	Donny & Marie Osmond	Morning Side Of The Mountain
8	Wizzard	Are You Ready To Rock
9	Pilot	January
10	David Essex	Stardust

The US Number One single: Carpenters – Please Mr.Postman
The US Number One album: Elton John – Elton John's Greatest Hits
The UK Number One album: Elton John – Elton John's Greatest Hits
Also this week: The Labour government abandons the Channel Tunnel project. (20th)

The song of the month for January 1975

January by Pilot (peak chart position: No.1)

It was wholly appropriate that this song should be released in January and find itself in the upper echelons of the UK singles list before the month's end. Before long it was at the pop summit, which is not surprising as this radio-friendly light rocker couldn't fail to arouse the interest of pop aficionados. Unfortunately for Pilot, they could not navigate their next 2 singles into the British Top Thirty and thus any hopes of a durable pop career crash landed when January 'disappeared' in March.

The UK Top 10 singles for the week ending February the 1st

1	Pilot	January
2	Tymes	Ms. Grace
3	Kenny	The Bump
4	Gloria Gaynor	Never Can Say Goodbye
5	Donny & Marie Osmond	Morning Side Of The Mountain
6	Status Quo	Down Down
7	John Holt	Help Me Make It Through The Night
8	Glitter Band	Goodbye My Love
9	Elvis Presley	Promised Land
10	Mac & Katie Kissoon	Sugar Candy Kisses

The US Number One single: Neil Sedaka – Laughter In The Rain

The US Number One album: Elton John – Elton John's Greatest Hits

The UK Number One album: Elton John – Elton John's Greatest Hits

Also this week: Five IRA bombs explode in London. (27th)

The UK Top 10 singles for the week ending February the 8th

1	Pilot	January
2	Glitter Band	Goodbye My Love
3	Mac & Katie Kissoon	Sugar Candy Kisses
4	Tymes	Ms. Grace
5	Gloria Gaynor	Never Can Say Goodbye
6	Donny & Marie Osmond	Morning Side Of The Mountain
7	Kenny	The Bump
8	Carpenters	Please Mr. Postman
9	John Holt	Help Me Make It Through The Night
10	Elvis Presley	Promised Land

The US Number One single: Ohio Players – Fire

The US Number One album: Ohio Players – Fire

The UK Number One album: Engelbert Humperdinck – His Greatest Hits

Also this week: Margaret Thatcher defeats Edward Heath in a Conservative leadership ballot. (4th)

The UK Top 10 singles for the week ending February the 15th

1	Pilot	January
2	Carpenters	Please Mr. Postman
3	Mac & Katie Kissoon	Sugar Candy Kisses
4	Glitter Band	Goodbye My Love
5	Helen Reddy	Angie Baby
6	Kenny	The Bump
7	Johnny Wakelin & The Kinshasa Band	Black Superman (Muhammad Ali)
8	Donny & Marie Osmond	Morning Side Of The Mountain
9	Steve Harley & Cockney Rebel	Make Me Smile (Come Up And See Me)
10	Wigan's Chosen Few	Footsee

The US Number One single: Linda Ronstadt – You're No Good

The US Number One album: Linda Ronstadt – Heart Like A Wheel

The UK Number One album: Engelbert Humperdinck – His Greatest Hits

Also this week: Margaret Thatcher is elected the new Conservative Party leader. (11th)

The UK Top 10 singles for the week ending February the 22nd

1 Steve Harley & Cockney Rebel   Make Me Smile (Come Up And See Me)
2 Pilot   January
3 Carpenters   Please Mr. Postman
4 Mac & Katie Kissoon   Sugar Candy Kisses
5 Mud   Secrets That You Keep
6 Glitter Band   Goodbye My Love
7 Shirley And Company   Shame Shame Shame
8 Helen Reddy   Angie Baby
9 Wigan's Chosen Few   Footsee
10 Johnny Wakelin & The Kinshasa Band   Black Superman (Muhammad Ali)

The US Number One single: Average White Band – Pick Up The Pieces
The US Number One album: Average White Band – AWB
The UK Number One album: Engelbert Humperdinck – His Greatest Hits
Also this week: Reginald Maudling is appointed as the Shadow Foreign Secretary. (18th)

The song of the month for February 1975

Number Nine Dream by John Lennon (peak chart position: No.23)

Released a few months previously on his 'Walls And Bridges' album, John Lennon's under-rated masterpiece made an all-too-brief appearance in the British singles chart in early 1975. With the help of Phil Spector, Lennon draws attention to the significance of the number 9 in his life. He was born on the ninth of October 1940 in the midst of a Luftwaffe air raid upon Liverpool. Fortunately the Luftwaffe missed Julia Lennon, or we would never have been treated to this piece which surely surpasses the hyped 'Imagine'.

The UK Top 10 singles for the week ending March the 1st

1 Steve Harley & Cockney Rebel   Make Me Smile (Come Up And See Me)
2 Telly Savalas   If
3 Carpenters   Please Mr. Postman
4 Mud   Secrets That You Keep
5 Fox   Only You Can
6 Shirley And Company   Shame Shame Shame
7 Frankie Valli   My Eyes Adored You
8 Mac & Katie Kissoon   Sugar Candy Kisses
9 Pilot   January
10 Wigan's Chosen Few   Footsee

The US Number One single: Eagles – Best Of My Love
The US Number One album: Bob Dylan – Blood On The Tracks
The UK Number One album: Status Quo – On The Level
Also this week:35 die in a crash at Moorgate underground station. (28th)

The UK Top 10 singles for the week ending March the 8th

1 Telly Savalas   If
2 Steve Harley & Cockney Rebel   Make Me Smile (Come Up And See Me)
3 Mud   Secrets That You Keep
4 Fox   Only You Can
5 Frankie Valli   My Eyes Adored You
6 Carpenters   Please Mr. Postman
7 Shirley And Company   Shame Shame Shame
8 Bay City Rollers   Bye Bye Baby
9 Average White Band   Pick Up The Pieces
10 Wigan's Chosen Few   Footsee

The US Number One single: Olivia Newton-John – Have You Never Been Mellow
The US Number One album: Bob Dylan – Blood On The Tracks
The UK Number One album: Status Quo – On The Level
Also this week: Zimbabwean black politician, Ndabaningi Sithole, is arrested. (4th)

The UK Top 10 singles for the week ending March the 15th

1	Telly Savalas	If
2	Bay City Rollers	Bye Bye Baby
3	Steve Harley & Cockney Rebel	Make Me Smile (Come Up And See Me)
4	Fox	Only You Can
5	Mud	Secrets That You Keep
6	Frankie Valli	My Eyes Adored You
7	Average White Band	Pick Up The Pieces
8	Dana	Please Tell Him That I Said Hello
9	Guys And Dolls	There's A Whole Lot Of Loving
10	Johnny Mathis	I'm Stone In Love With You

The US Number One single: Doobie Brothers – Black Water
The US Number One album: Olivia Newton-John – Have You Never Been Mellow
The UK Number One album: Led Zeppelin – Physical Graffiti
Also this week: A failed coup attempt occurs in Portugal. (12th)

The UK Top 10 singles for the week ending March the 22nd

1	Bay City Rollers	Bye Bye Baby
2	Telly Savalas	If
3	Fox	Only You Can
4	Guys And Dolls	There's A Whole Lot Of Loving
5	Barry White	What Am I Gonna Do With You
6	Average White Band	Pick Up The Pieces
7	Mud	Secrets That You Keep
8	Kenny	Fancy Pants
9	Moments And Whatnauts	Girls
10	Rubettes	I Can Do It

The US Number One single: Frankie Valli – My Eyes Adored You
The US Number One album: Led Zeppelin – Physical Graffiti
The UK Number One album: Tom Jones – 20 Greatest Hits
Also this week: The monarchy in Ethiopia is abolished. (21st)

The UK Top 10 singles for the week ending March the 29th

1	Bay City Rollers	Bye Bye Baby
2	Guys And Dolls	There's A Whole Lot Of Loving
3	Moments And Whatnauts	Girls
4	Telly Savalas	If
5	Barry White	What Am I Gonna Do With You
6	Kenny	Fancy Pants
7	Fox	Only You Can
8	Goodies	Funky Gibbon
9	Rubettes	I Can Do It
10	Sweet	Fox On The Run

The US Number One single: LaBelle – Lady Marmalade
The US Number One album: Led Zeppelin – Physical Graffiti
The UK Number One album: Tom Jones – 20 Greatest Hits
Also this week: King Faisal of Saudi Arabia is murdered by his nephew. (25th)

The song of the month for March 1975

Honey by Bobby Goldsboro (peak chart position: No.2)

'Honey' had previously made its sweet presence felt back in the spring of 1968 when it fell agonisingly short of the Number One position. History actually repeated itself when this beautiful item again came close to the coveted top spot. As a consequence of these two chart runs, this popular single spent a total of 27 weeks in the British singles lists. It was clearly Bobby Goldsboro's most successful release. Regrettably, the folks 'back then' had a stronger preference for 'Bye Bye Baby' by the Bay City Rollers. Dear oh dear.

The UK Top 10 singles for the week ending April the 5th

1 Bay City Rollers   Bye Bye Baby
2 Guys And Dolls   There's A Whole Lot Of Loving
3 Moments And Whatnauts   Girls
4 Kenny   Fancy Pants
5 Sweet   Fox On The Run
6 Barry White   What Am I Gonna Do With You
7 Rubettes   I Can Do It
8 Jim Gilstrap   Swing Your Daddy
9 Duane Eddy   Play Me Like You Play Your Guitar
10 Goodies   Funky Gibbon

The US Number One single: Minnie Riperton – Lovin' You
The US Number One album: Led Zeppelin – Physical Graffiti
The UK Number One album: Tom Jones – 20 Greatest Hits
Also this week: American embassy staff start to evacuate Phnom Penh. (3rd)

The UK Top 10 singles for the week ending April the 12th

1 Bay City Rollers   Bye Bye Baby
2 Sweet   Fox On The Run
3 Guys And Dolls   There's A Whole Lot Of Loving
4 Goodies   Funky Gibbon
5 Kenny   Fancy Pants
6 Moments And Whatnauts   Girls
7 Jim Gilstrap   Swing Your Daddy
8 Peter Shelley   Love Me Love My Dog
9 Rubettes   I Can Do It
10 Duane Eddy   Play Me Like You Play Your Guitar

The US Number One single: The Elton John Band – Philadelphia Freedom
The US Number One album: Led Zeppelin – Physical Graffiti
The UK Number One album: Tom Jones – 20 Greatest Hits
Also this week: Harold Wilson sacks his Industry Minister, Eric Heffer. (9th)

The UK Top 10 singles for the week ending April the 19th

1	Bay City Rollers	Bye Bye Baby
2	Sweet	Fox On The Run
3	Peter Shelley	Love Me Love My Dog
4	Jim Gilstrap	Swing Your Daddy
5	Goodies	Funky Gibbon
6	Guys And Dolls	There's A Whole Lot Of Loving
7	Moments And Whatnauts	Girls
8	Kenny	Fancy Pants
9	Bobby Goldsboro	Honey
10	Mike Reid	The Ugly Duckling

The US Number One single: The Elton John Band – Philadelphia Freedom
The US Number One album: Led Zeppelin – Physical Graffiti
The UK Number One album: Stylistics – The Best Of The Stylistics
Also this week: Phnom Penh surrenders to the besieging Khmer Rouge forces. (17th)

The UK Top 10 singles for the week ending April the 26th

1	Bay City Rollers	Bye Bye Baby
2	Bobby Goldsboro	Honey
3	Sweet	Fox On The Run
4	Peter Shelley	Love Me Love My Dog
5	Jim Gilstrap	Swing Your Daddy
6	Mud	Oh Boy
7	Minnie Riperton	Lovin' You
8	Goodies	Funky Gibbon
9	10cc	Life Is A Minestrone
10	Susan Cadogan	Hurt So Good

The US Number One single: B.J. Thomas – Another Somebody Done Somebody
Wrong Song
The US Number One album: Led Zeppelin – Physical Graffiti
The UK Number One album: Stylistics – The Best Of The Stylistics
Also this week: British embassy staff are advised to evacuate Saigon. (23rd)

The song of the month for April 1975

Lovin' You by Minnie Riperton (peak chart position: No.2)

Loving this is easy 'cos it's beautiful. Minnie Riperton excels here with a vocal performance that takes the breath away. Aside from the notable singing, the song is remembered for the bird constantly chirping in the background. For all the incurable romantics for whom flowers and chocolates are the order of the day, this American chart-topper would have been essential listening. Tragically, Minnie Riperton passed away in July of 1979 at the age of 31, a victim of breast cancer. What a waste.

The UK Top 10 singles for the week ending May the 3rd

1	Mud	Oh Boy
2	Minnie Riperton	Lovin' You
3	Bobby Goldsboro	Honey
4	Susan Cadogan	Hurt So Good
5	Bay City Rollers	Bye Bye Baby
6	Peter Shelley	Love Me Love My Dog
7	10cc	Life Is A Minestrone
8	Glitter Band	The Tears I Cried
9	Three Degrees	Take Good Care Of Yourself
10	Sweet	Fox On The Run

The US Number One single: Tony Orlando And Dawn – He Don't Love You (Like I Love You)

The US Number One album: Chicago – Chicago VIII

The UK Number One album: Bay City Rollers – Once Upon A Star

Also this week: North Vietnamese troops seize control of Saigon. (30th)

The UK Top 10 singles for the week ending May the 10th

1 Mud — Oh Boy
2 Minnie Riperton — Lovin' You
3 Tammy Wynette — Stand By Your Man
4 Susan Cadogan — Hurt So Good
5 Bobby Goldsboro — Honey
6 Tammy Jones — Let Me Try Again
7 Frankie Valli And The Four Seasons — The Night
8 Bay City Rollers — Bye Bye Baby
9 Three Degrees — Take Good Care Of Yourself
10 Gilbert Becaud — A Little Love And Understanding

The US Number One single: Tony Orlando And Dawn – He Don't Love You (Like I Love You)
The US Number One album: Chicago – Chicago VIII
The UK Number One album: Bay City Rollers – Once Upon A Star
Also this week: The Cambridge 'hooded rapist' claims his seventh victim. (6th)

The UK Top 10 singles for the week ending May the 17th

1 Tammy Wynette — Stand By Your Man
2 Mud — Oh Boy
3 Minnie Riperton — Lovin' You
4 Susan Cadogan — Hurt So Good
5 Tammy Jones — Let Me Try Again
6 Disco Tex And The Sex-O-Lettes — I Wanna Dance Wit Choo
7 The Carpenters — Only Yesterday
8 Bobby Goldsboro — Honey
9 Frankie Valli And The Four Seasons — The Night
10 Gary Glitter — Love Like You And Me

The US Number One single: Tony Orlando And Dawn – He Don't Love You (Like I Love You)
The US Number One album: Earth, Wind & Fire/ Soundtrack – That's The Way Of The World
The UK Number One album: Bay City Rollers – Once Upon A Star
Also this week: Inflation in Britain now exceeds twenty per cent. (13th)

The UK Top 10 singles for the week ending May the 24th

1 Tammy Wynette   Stand By Your Man
2 Windsor Davies/Don Estelle Whispering Grass
3 Mud   Oh Boy
4 Minnie Riperton   Lovin' You
5 Gladys Knight   The Way We Were
6 Stylistics   Sing Baby Sing
7 Tammy Jones   Let Me Try Again
8 Susan Cadogan   Hurt So Good
9 Mac And Katie Kissoon   Don't Do It Baby
10 Carpenters   Only Yesterday

The US Number One single: Earth, Wind & Fire – Shining Star
The US Number One album: Earth, Wind & Fire/ Soundtrack – That's The Way Of The World
The UK Number One album: Stylistics – The Best Of The Stylistics
Also this week: The trial of the Baader-Meinhof terrorist gang begins. (21st)

The UK Top 10 singles for the week ending May the 31st

1 Tammy Wynette   Stand By Your Man
2 Windsor Davies/Don Estelle Whispering Grass
3 Stylistics   Sing Baby Sing
4 Gladys Knight   The Way We Were
5 Showaddywaddy   Three Steps To Heaven
6 Judy Collins   Send In The Clowns
7 Slade   Thanks For The Memory
8 Disco Tex And The Sex-O-Lettes I Wanna Dance Wit Choo
9 Tammy Jones   Let Me Try Again
10 Status Quo   Roll Over Lay Down

The US Number One single: Freddy Fender – Before The Next Teardrop Falls
The US Number One album: Earth, Wind & Fire/ Soundtrack – That's The Way Of The World
The UK Number One album: Stylistics – The Best Of The Stylistics
Also this week: A coach crashes in the Yorkshire Dales, killing thirty-two. (27th)

The song of the month for May 1975

I'm Not In Love by 10cc (peak chart position: No.1)

10cc had been among the most consistent hit-makers in the last few years, having previously climbed onto the UK singles summit with 'Rubber Bullets' in 1973. It therefore came as little surprise when they reached the pop heights again, though the material this time was radically different. 'I'm Not In Love' is a deliciously mellow recording which would have found favour with both young and old. It sounded considerably more mature and sophisticated than their previous Number One and it is undoubtedly one of the highlights of the 1970s.

The UK Top 10 singles for the week ending June the 7th

1	Windsor Davies/Don Estelle	Whispering Grass
2	Tammy Wynette	Stand By Your Man
3	Showaddywaddy	Three Steps To Heaven
4	Stylistics	Sing Baby Sing
5	Gladys Knight	The Way We Were
6	Judy Collins	Send In The Clowns
7	Osmonds	The Proud One
8	10cc	I'm Not In Love
9	Status Quo	Roll Over Lay Down
10	Desmond Dekker	Israelites

The US Number One single: John Denver – Thank God I'm A Country Boy
The US Number One album: Elton John – Captain Fantastic And The Brown Dirt Cowboy
The UK Number One album: Stylistics – The Best Of The Stylistics
Also this week: Britain's Common Market membership is endorsed in a referendum. (6th)

The UK Top 10 singles for the week ending June the 14th

1	Windsor Davies/Don Estelle	Whispering Grass
2	Showaddywaddy	Three Steps To Heaven
3	10cc	I'm Not In Love
4	Stylistics	Sing Baby Sing
5	Tammy Wynette	Stand By Your Man
6	Osmonds	The Proud One
7	Gladys Knight	The Way We Were
8	Judy Collins	Send In The Clowns
9	Van McCoy	The Hustle
10	Wings	Listen To What The Man Said

The US Number One single: America – Sister Golden Hair
The US Number One album: Elton John – Captain Fantastic And The Brown Dirt Cowboy
The UK Number One album: Stylistics – The Best Of The Stylistics
Also this week: Inflation in Britain reaches a staggering twenty-five per cent. (13th)

The UK Top 10 singles for the week ending June the 21st

1	Windsor Davies/Don Estelle	Whispering Grass
2	10cc	I'm Not In Love
3	Showaddywaddy	Three Steps To Heaven
4	Van McCoy	The Hustle
5	Osmonds	The Proud One
6	Wings	Listen To What The Man Said
7	Tammy Wynette	Stand By Your Man
8	Stylistics	Sing Baby Sing
9	Gladys Knight	The Way We Were
10	Hamilton Bohannon	Disco Stomp

The US Number One single: Captain & Tennille – Love Will Keep Us Together
The US Number One album: Elton John – Captain Fantastic And The Brown Dirt Cowboy
The UK Number One album: Stylistics – The Best Of The Stylistics
Also this week: The West Indies win the Lord's cricket world cup final. (21st)

The UK Top 10 singles for the week ending June the 28th

1	10cc	I'm Not In Love
2	Windsor Davies/Don Estelle	Whispering Grass
3	Showaddywaddy	Three Steps To Heaven
4	Van McCoy	The Hustle
5	Johnny Nash	Tears On My Pillow
6	Gary Glitter	Doing All Right With The Boys
7	Osmonds	The Proud One
8	Hamilton Bohannon	Disco Stomp
9	Wings	Listen To What The Man Said
10	Ray Stevens	Misty

The US Number One single: Captain & Tennille – Love Will Keep Us Together
The US Number One album: Elton John – Captain Fantastic And The Brown Dirt Cowboy
The UK Number One album: Wings – Venus And Mars
Also this week: The colony of Mozambique becomes independent of Portugal. (24th)

The song of the month for June 1975

Tears On My Pillow by Johnny Nash (peak chart position: No.1)

American singer Johnny Nash had previously had an association with Bob Marley so it was hardly surprising that he should flirt with reggae music. Yet again the British singles-buyers were clearly feeling sorry for themselves as they took a shine to this tearjerker which enjoyed one week at the 'top of the pops'. This was the sixth time that a Nash release had invaded the UK Top Ten but hereafter the absence of any further successes would have been reason enough for more tears on his pillow.

The UK Top 10 singles for the week ending July the 5th

1	10cc	I'm Not In Love
2	Johnny Nash	Tears On My Pillow
3	Van McCoy	The Hustle
4	Windsor Davies/Don Estelle	Whispering Grass
5	Ray Stevens	Misty
6	Hamilton Bohannon	Disco Stomp
7	Showaddywaddy	Three Steps To Heaven
8	Gary Glitter	Doing All Right With The Boys
9	Chi-Lites	Have You Seen Her/ Oh Girl
10	Mud	Moonshine Sally

The US Number One single: Captain & Tennille – Love Will Keep Us Together
The US Number One album: Elton John – Captain Fantastic And The Brown Dirt Cowboy
The UK Number One album: Carpenters – Horizon
Also this week: Thirteen people are killed when a bomb explodes in Jerusalem. (4th)

The UK Top 10 singles for the week ending July the 12th

1	Johnny Nash	Tears On My Pillow
2	Ray Stevens	Misty
3	Van McCoy	The Hustle
4	10cc	I'm Not In Love
5	Chi-Lites	Have You Seen Her/ Oh Girl
6	Gary Glitter	Doing All Right With The Boys
7	Bay City Rollers	Give A Little Love
8	Hamilton Bohannon	Disco Stomp
9	Windsor Davies/Don Estelle	Whispering Grass
10	Pete Wingfield	Eighteen With A Bullet

The US Number One single: Captain & Tennille – Love Will Keep Us Together
The US Number One album: Elton John – Captain Fantastic And The Brown Dirt Cowboy
The UK Number One album: Carpenters – Horizon
Also this week: Israel's Yitzhak Rabin pays a state visit to West Germany. (8th)

The UK Top 10 singles for the week ending July the 19th

1	Bay City Rollers	Give A Little Love
2	Johnny Nash	Tears On My Pillow
3	Ray Stevens	Misty
4	Van McCoy	The Hustle
5	Typically Tropical	Barbados
6	Chi-Lites	Have You Seen Her/Oh Girl
7	Pete Wingfield	Eighteen With A Bullet
8	10cc	I'm Not In Love
9	Hamilton Bohannon	Disco Stomp
10	Judge Dread	Je T'Aime

The US Number One single: Wings – Listen To What The Man Said
The US Number One album: Wings – Venus And Mars
The UK Number One album: Wings – Venus And Mars
Also this week: Graham Hill announces his retirement from motor racing. (18th)

The UK Top 10 singles for the week ending July the 26th

1	Bay City Rollers	Give A Little Love
2	Typically Tropical	Barbados
3	Johnny Nash	Tears On My Pillow
4	Ray Stevens	Misty
5	David Essex	Rolling Stone
6	Chi-Lites	Have You Seen Her/Oh Girl
7	Van McCoy	The Hustle
8	Pete Wingfield	Eighteen With A Bullet
9	Judge Dread	Je T'Aime
10	Bryan Hyland	Sealed With A Kiss

The US Number One single: Van McCoy – The Hustle
The US Number One album: Eagles – One Of These Nights
The UK Number One album: Carpenters – Horizon
Also this week: British unemployment is at its highest level since 1940. (24th)

The song of the month for July 1975

Barbados by Typically Tropical (peak chart position: No.1)

British music lovers engaged in a flight of fancy as they warmed on that hot summer to the sounds of 'Barbados' which nudged the Bay City Rollers off the Number One perch. The artists responsible were Typically Tropical who can lay a credible claim to having provided one of the best tunes from a 'one hit wonder'. The song includes a mock address from the aeroplane pilot at the start of the 'flight' as the singer shares his excitement at the prospect of travelling to the attractive island in the Caribbean.

The UK Top 10 singles for the week ending August the 2nd

1	Bay City Rollers	Give A Little Love
2	Typically Tropical	Barbados
3	Johnny Nash	Tears On My Pillow
4	Ray Stevens	Misty
5	Bee Gees	Jive Talkin'
6	Smokie	If You Think You Know How To Love Me
7	Bryan Hyland	Sealed With A Kiss
8	Linda Lewis	It's In His Kiss
9	Van McCoy	The Hustle
10	Judge Dread	Je T'Aime

The US Number One single: Eagles – One Of These Nights

The US Number One album: Eagles – One Of These Nights

The UK Number One album: Carpenters – Horizon

Also this week: Three members of Ireland's Miami Showband die in an ambush. (31st)

The UK Top 10 singles for the week ending August the 9th

1 Typically Tropical — Barbados
2 Bay City Rollers — Give A Little Love
3 Stylistics — I Can't Give You Anything (But My Love)
4 Smokie — If You Think You Know How To Love Me
5 Bee Gees — Jive Talkin'
6 Linda Lewis — It's In His Kiss
7 Bryan Hyland — Sealed With A Kiss
8 Sensational Alex Harvey Band — Delilah
9 Judge Dread — Je T'Aime
10 Johnny Nash — Tears On My Pillow

The US Number One single: Bee Gees – Jive Talkin'
The US Number One album: Eagles – One Of These Nights
The UK Number One album: Carpenters – Horizon
Also this week: London melts under a record of thirty-two degrees centigrade. (7th)

The UK Top 10 singles for the week ending August the 16th

1 Stylistics — I Can't Give You Anything (But My Love)
2 Typically Tropical — Barbados
3 Smokie — If You Think You Know How To Love Me
4 Bay City Rollers — Give A Little Love
5 Roger Whittaker — The Last Farewell
6 Bee Gees — Jive Talkin'
7 Sensational Alex Harvey Band — Delilah
8 George McCrae — It's Been So Long
9 Linda Lewis — It's In His Kiss
10 Adrian Baker — Sherry

The US Number One single: Bee Gees – Jive Talkin'
The US Number One album: Eagles – One Of These Nights
The UK Number One album: Stylistics – The Best Of The Stylistics
Also this week: New Zealand's John Walker sets a new mile world record. (12th)

The UK Top 10 singles for the week ending August the 23rd

1	Stylistics	I Can't Give You Anything (But My Love)
2	Rod Stewart	Sailing
3	Roger Whittaker	The Last Farewell
4	Typically Tropical	Barbados
5	Smokie	If You Think You Know How To Love Me
6	George McCrae	It's Been So Long
7	Billie Jo Spears	Blanket On The Ground
8	K.C. And The Sunshine Band	That's The Way (I Like It)
9	Bee Gees	Jive Talkin'
10	Moments	Dolly My Love

The US Number One single: Hamilton, Joe Frank & Reynolds – Fallin' In Love
The US Number One album: Eagles – One Of These Nights
The UK Number One album: Stylistics – The Best Of The Stylistics
Also this week: A group of protesters vandalise the Headingley test match pitch. (19th)

The UK Top 10 singles for the week ending August the 30th

1	Stylistics	I Can't Give You Anything (But My Love)
2	Rod Stewart	Sailing
3	Roger Whittaker	The Last Farewell
4	George McCrae	It's Been So Long
5	K.C. And The Sunshine Band	That's The Way (I Like It)
6	Billie Jo Spears	Blanket On The Ground
7	Gladys Knight & The Pips	Best Thing That Ever Happened
8	Typically Tropical	Barbados
9	Mike Batt	Summertime City
10	Smokie	If You Think You Know How To Love Me

The US Number One single: KC And The Sunshine Band – Get Down Tonight
The US Number One album: Elton John – Captain Fantastic And The Brown Dirt Cowboy
The UK Number One album: Rod Stewart – Atlantic Crossing
Also this week: Australia's Ian Chappell hits 192 at the Oval against England. (29th)

The song of the month for August 1975

Sailing by Rod Stewart (peak chart position: No.1)

Not a year seemed to go by without Rod Stewart making his presence felt in the world of pop. This time he stepped forth with a song whose popularity probably eclipses his 'Maggie May' offering. This smash hit demonstrated his knack of sourcing a good song from elsewhere – in this instance from the Sutherland brothers. The musical accompaniment is first class as Rod sings from the heart. This is one of the few records that emerge in any era which retains its appeal through the march of time. Its sales figures speak for themselves.

The UK Top 10 singles for the week ending September the 6th

1	Rod Stewart	Sailing
2	Stylistics	I Can't Give You Anything (But My Love)
3	Roger Whittaker	The Last Farewell
4	K.C. And The Sunshine Band	That's The Way (I Like It)
5	George McCrae	It's Been So Long
6	Mike Batt	Summertime City
7	Billie Jo Spears	Blanket On The Ground
8	Hot Chocolate	A Child's Prayer
9	Gladys Knight & The Pips	Best Thing That Ever Happened
10	Jasper Carrott	Funky Moped/Magic Roundabout

The US Number One single: Glen Campbell – Rhinestone Cowboy

The US Number One album: Jefferson Starship – Red Octopus

The UK Number One album: Rod Stewart – Atlantic Crossing

Also this week: A bomb explodes at London's Hilton hotel, killing two people. (5th)

The UK Top 10 singles for the week ending September the 13th

1	Rod Stewart	Sailing
2	Roger Whittaker	The Last Farewell
3	Stylistics	I Can't Give You Anything (But My Love)
4	Leo Sayer	Moonlighting
5	K.C. And The Sunshine Band	That's The Way (I Like It)
6	Mike Batt	Summertime City
7	Hot Chocolate	A Child's Prayer
8	Jasper Carrott	Funky Moped/Magic Roundabout
9	Gladys Knight & The Pips	Best Thing That Ever Happened
10	Kenny	Julie-Ann

The US Number One single: Glen Campbell – Rhinestone Cowboy
The US Number One album: The Isley Brothers – The Heat Is On
The UK Number One album: Rod Stewart – Atlantic Crossing
Also this week: The last Wolseley car rolls off the production line. (14th)

The UK Top 10 singles for the week ending September the 20th

1	Rod Stewart	Sailing
2	Leo Sayer	Moonlighting
3	Roger Whittaker	The Last Farewell
4	Mike Batt	Summertime City
5	Jasper Carrott	Funky Moped/Magic Roundabout
6	5000 Volts	I'm On Fire
7	Showadddywaddy	Heartbeat
8	Hot Chocolate	A Child's Prayer
9	David Essex	Hold Me Close
10	K.C. And The Sunshine Band	That's The Way (I Like It)

The US Number One single: David Bowie – Fame
The US Number One album: Janis Ian – Between The Lines
The UK Number One album: Rod Stewart – Atlantic Crossing
Also this week: Papua New Guinea becomes independent of Australia. (15th)

The UK Top 10 singles for the week ending September the 27th

1	Rod Stewart	Sailing
2	David Essex	Hold Me Close
3	Leo Sayer	Moonlighting
4	5000 Volts	I'm On Fire
5	Jasper Carrott	Funky Moped/Magic Roundabout
6	Roger Whittaker	The Last Farewell
7	Showadddywaddy	Heartbeat
8	Drifters	There Goes My First Love
9	Hot Chocolate	A Child's Prayer
10	Art Garfunkel	I Only Have Eyes For You

The US Number One single: John Denver – Calypso/I'm Sorry

The US Number One album: Jefferson Starship – Red Octopus

The UK Number One album: Rod Stewart – Atlantic Crossing

Also this week: Five convicted Basque terrorists are executed in Madrid. (27th)

The song of the month for September 1975

Shine On You Crazy Diamond Parts 1 to 5 by Pink Floyd (album track)

The album opener to the newly-released 'Wish You Were Here' represents the very best of the Floyd. It evolves in characteristically languid style with a fine contribution from Dave Gilmour's guitar. The 'hero' of the song, one Roger 'Syd' Barrett just happened to venture into the Abbey Road recording studios during its creation for a brief and typically bizarre reunion with his former 'colleagues'. Barrett explained to his horrified (former) friends that his overweight condition was due to the large pork chops that he had in his fridge – a crazy diamond indeed.

The UK Top 10 singles for the week ending October the 4th

1	David Essex	Hold Me Close
2	Rod Stewart	Sailing
3	Drifters	There Goes My First Love
4	Art Garfunkel	I Only Have Eyes For You
5	Leo Sayer	Moonlighting
6	Jasper Carrott	Funky Moped/Magic Roundabout
7	Showadddywaddy	Heartbeat
8	5000 Volts	I'm On Fire
9	Carl Malcom	Fattie Bum Bum
10	Jonathan King	Una Paloma Blanca

The US Number One single: David Bowie – Fame
The US Number One album: Pink Floyd – Wish You Were Here
The UK Number One album: Pink Floyd – Wish You Were Here
Also this week: Muhammad Ali defeats Joe Frazier in the 'thrilla in Manila'. (30th)

The UK Top 10 singles for the week ending October the 11st

1	David Essex	Hold Me Close
2	Art Garfunkel	I Only Have Eyes For You
3	Drifters	There Goes My First Love
4	5000 Volts	I'm On Fire
5	Jonathan King	Una Paloma Blanca
6	Chi-Lites	It's Time For Love
7	Jasper Carrott	Funky Moped/Magic Roundabout
8	Carl Malcom	Fattie Bum Bum
9	Four Seasons	Who Loves You
10	George Baker	Paloma Blanca

The US Number One single: Neil Sedaka – Bad Blood
The US Number One album: Pink Floyd – Wish You Were Here
The UK Number One album: Rod Stewart – Atlantic Crossing
Also this week: Richard Burton and Elizabeth Taylor remarry in Botswana. (10th)

The UK Top 10 singles for the week ending October the 18th

1. David Essex — Hold Me Close
2. Art Garfunkel — I Only Have Eyes For You
3. Drifters — There Goes My First Love
4. Morris Albert — Feelings
5. Chi-Lites — It's Time For Love
6. Four Seasons — Who Loves You
7. Abba — S.O.S.
8. Band Of The Black Watch — Scotch On The Rocks
9. Jonathan King — Una Paloma Blanca
10. Mud — L-L-Lucy

The US Number One single: Neil Sedaka – Bad Blood
The US Number One album: John Denver – Windsong
The UK Number One album: Rod Stewart – Atlantic Crossing
Also this week: King Hassan of Morocco vows to claim the Spanish Sahara. (16th)

The UK Top 10 singles for the week ending October the 25th

1. Art Garfunkel — I Only Have Eyes For You
2. David Essex — Hold Me Close
3. Drifters — There Goes My First Love
4. David Bowie — Space Oddity
5. Morris Albert — Feelings
6. Abba — S.O.S.
7. Chi-Lites — It's Time For Love
8. Smokie — Don't Play Your Rock And Roll To Me
9. Four Seasons — Who Loves You
10. Band Of The Black Watch — Scotch On The Rocks

The US Number One single: Neil Sedaka – Bad Blood
The US Number One album: John Denver – Windsong
The UK Number One album: Jim Reeves – 40 Golden Greats
Also this week: An ailing General Franco suffers a heart attack. (21st)

The song of the month for October 1975

Space Oddity by David Bowie (peak chart position: No.1)

It was indeed something of an oddity that David Bowie's first hit single from six years ago should land once more on planet pop and then soar into orbit – or to Number One to be precise. Such a success for the ever-changing Bowie was overdue, though this 'sixties artefact was a surprise package. Bowie had also previously tasted American charts glory in collaboration with John Lennon on 'Fame' and Bowie's own fame was enhanced by this 'new' success. Bowie remained a chart regular over the next few years in spite of a spiralling drug habit.

The UK Top 10 singles for the week ending November the 1st

1	Art Garfunkel	I Only Have Eyes For You
2	David Bowie	Space Oddity
3	Drifters	There Goes My First Love
4	Morris Albert	Feelings
5	Roxy Music	Love Is The Drug
6	Abba	S.O.S.
7	David Essex	Hold Me Close
8	Esther Phillips	What A Difference A Day Makes
9	Smokie	Don't Play Your Rock And Roll To Me
10	Glen Campbell	Rhinestone Cowboy

The US Number One single: Elton John – Island Girl
The US Number One album: Jefferson Starship – Red Octopus
The UK Number One album: Jim Reeves – 40 Golden Greats
Also this week: Prince Juan Carlos takes temporary charge in Spain. (30th)

The UK Top 10 singles for the week ending November the 8th

1	David Bowie	Space Oddity
2	Roxy Music	Love Is The Drug
3	Art Garfunkel	I Only Have Eyes For You
4	Glen Campbell	Rhinestone Cowboy
5	Trammps	Hold Back The Night
6	Esther Phillips	What A Difference A Day Makes
7	Abba	S.O.S.
8	Morris Albert	Feelings
9	Billy Connolly	D.I.V.O.R.C.E.
10	Justin Hayward & John Lodge	Blue Guitar

The US Number One single: Elton John – Island Girl
The US Number One album: Elton John – Rock Of The Westies
The UK Number One album: Jim Reeves – 40 Golden Greats
Also this week: Britain asks the International Monetary Fund for a loan. (7th)

The UK Top 10 singles for the week ending November the 15th

1	David Bowie	Space Oddity
2	Billy Connolly	D.I.V.O.R.C.E.
3	Roxy Music	Love Is The Drug
4	Glen Campbell	Rhinestone Cowboy
5	Jim Capaldi	Love Hurts
6	John Lennon	Imagine
7	Trammps	Hold Back The Night
8	Justin Hayward & John Lodge	Blue Guitar
9	Hello	New York Groove
10	Hot Chocolate	You Sexy Thing

The US Number One single: Elton John – Island Girl
The US Number One album: Elton John – Rock Of The Westies
The UK Number One album: Max Boyce – We All Had Doctors' Papers
Also this week: Britain 'sacks' Australia's Labour Prime Minister, Gough Whitlam. (11th)

The UK Top 10 singles for the week ending November the 22nd

1	Billy Connolly	D.I.V.O.R.C.E.
2	David Bowie	Space Oddity
3	Hot Chocolate	You Sexy Thing
4	Roxy Music	Love Is The Drug
5	Jim Capaldi	Love Hurts
6	John Lennon	Imagine
7	Glen Campbell	Rhinestone Cowboy
8	Rod Stewart	This Old Heart Of Mine
9	Queen	Bohemian Rhapsody
10	Jigsaw	Sky High

The US Number One single: KC And The Sunshine Band – That's The Way (I Like It)
The US Number One album: Elton John – Rock Of The Westies
The UK Number One album: Perry Como – 40 Greatest Hits
Also this week: Ronald Reagan announces that he wants to be American President. (20th)

The UK Top 10 singles for the week ending November the 29th

1	Queen	Bohemian Rhapsody
2	Hot Chocolate	You Sexy Thing
3	Billy Connolly	D.I.V.O.R.C.E.
4	Jim Capaldi	Love Hurts
5	Bay City Rollers	Money Honey
6	John Lennon	Imagine
7	Rod Stewart	This Old Heart Of Mine
8	Maxine Nightingale	Right Back Where We Started From
9	Jigsaw	Sky High
10	David Bowie	Space Oddity

The US Number One single: Silver Convention – Fly, Robin, Fly
The US Number One album: Jefferson Starship – Red Octopus
The UK Number One album: Perry Como – 40 Greatest Hits
Also this week: King Juan Carlos declares a general amnesty in Spain. (25th)

The song of the month for November 1975
Bohemian Rhapsody by Queen (peak chart position: No.1)

Freddie Mercury and his troops took the British charts by storm at the end of 1975 when 'Bohemian Rhapsody' took up a phenomenal nine-week residence at the top of the pop tree. Not since the 1950s had any single monopolised the lists to such an extent. It was widely accepted that the exposure of the song's video was a major factor in its success. The tune itself typified the eccentric brand of rock that Queen represented, with piano one moment and electric guitar the next, culminating in a gong being hit at the tune's conclusion. This was predictably the lead single from the 'A Night At The Opera' project which is only narrowly defeated by 'Wish You Were Here' for album of the year.

The UK Top 10 singles for the week ending December the 6th

1	Queen	Bohemian Rhapsody
2	Hot Chocolate	You Sexy Thing
3	Bay City Rollers	Money Honey
4	Rod Stewart	This Old Heart Of Mine
5	Steelye Span	All Around My Hat
6	Stylistics	Na Na Is The Saddest Word
7	Billy Connolly	D.I.V.O.R.C.E.
8	Jim Capaldi	Love Hurts
9	Laurel And Hardy	The Trail Of The Lonesome Pine
10	John Lennon	Imagine

The US Number One single: Silver Convention – Fly, Robin, Fly

The US Number One album: Paul Simon – Still Crazy After All These Years

The UK Number One album: Perry Como – 40 Greatest Hits

Also this week: The IRA-instigated Balcombe Street siege begins in London. (6th)

The UK Top 10 singles for the week ending December the 13th

1	Queen	Bohemian Rhapsody
2	Hot Chocolate	You Sexy Thing
3	Laurel And Hardy	The Trail Of The Lonesome Pine
4	Bay City Rollers	Money Honey
5	Stylistics	Na Na Is The Saddest Word
6	Steelye Span	All Around My Hat
7	Rod Stewart	This Old Heart Of Mine
8	Mud	Show Me You're A Woman
9	Chubby Checker	Let's Twist Again/The Twist
10	John Lennon	Imagine

The US Number One single: Silver Convention – Fly, Robin, Fly
The US Number One album: Chicago – Chicago IX:Chicago's Greatest Hits
The UK Number One album: Perry Como – 40 Greatest Hits
Also this week: Malcolm Fraser's Liberal Party win the Australian general election. (13th)

The UK Top 10 singles for the week ending December the 20th

1	Queen	Bohemian Rhapsody
2	Laurel And Hardy	The Trail Of The Lonesome Pine
3	Greg Lake	I Believe In Father Christmas
4	Hot Chocolate	You Sexy Thing
5	Demis Rousos	Happy To Be On An Island In The Sun
6	Chubby Checker	Let's Twist Again/The Twist
7	Stylistics	Na Na Is The Saddest Word
8	David Bowie	Golden Years
9	Steelye Span	All Around My Hat
10	Mud	Show Me You're A Woman

The US Number One single: KC And The Sunshine Band – That's The Way (I Like It)
The US Number One album: Chicago – Chicago IX:Chicago's Greatest Hits
The UK Number One album: Perry Como – 40 Greatest Hits
Also this week: Willy Brandt's former assistant, Gunther Guillaume, is jailed for spying. (15th)

The UK Top 10 singles for the week ending December the 27th

1	Queen	Bohemian Rhapsody
2	Greg Lake	I Believe In Father Christmas
3	Laurel And Hardy	The Trail Of The Lonesome Pine
4	Dana	It's Gonna Be A Cold Cold Christmas
5	Chubby Checker	Let's Twist Again/The Twist
6	Demis Rousos	Happy To Be On An Island In The Sun
7	Hot Chocolate	You Sexy Thing
8	Stylistics	Na Na Is The Saddest Word
9	David Bowie	Golden Years
10	Chris Hill	Renta Santa

The US Number One single: The Staple Singers – Let's Do It Again
The US Number One album: Chicago – Chicago IX:Chicago's Greatest Hits
The UK Number One album: Queen – A Night At The Opera
Also this week: 372 miners die in a huge blast in India. (27th)

The song of the month for December 1975
Mamma Mia by Abba (peak chart position: No.1)

After the triumph of 'Waterloo', Sweden's finest foursome experienced a couple of false starts before their pop career resumed in earnest. It took the success of 'S.O.S' to indicate that Abba had more to offer than merely a 'one-hit wonder'. The next item in the Abba assembly line of smash hits was 'Mamma Mia'. This single mercifully relieved 'Bohemian Rhapsody' of its occupation of the British pop summit whilst laying the foundations for a year of world domination. The song (or at least its title) has since inspired both a musical and a popular film.

Listed Below are the Top 10 Best Selling UK Singles of 1975

1	Bye Bye Baby	The Bay City Rollers
2	Sailing	Rod Stewart
3	Can't Give You Anything (But My Love)	The Stylistics
4	Whispering Grass	Windsor Davies and Don Estelle
5	Stand By Your Man	Tammy Wynette
6	Give A Little Love	The Bay City Rollers
7	Hold Me Close	David Essex
8	I Only Have Eyes For You	Art Garfunkel
9	The Last Farewell	Roger Whittaker
10	I'm Not In Love	10CC

1975's CONCERTS OF THE YEAR

A new rock group called the Sex Pistols shocked audiences in London with an unprecedented display of amateurism and aggression that kick started punk rock in the United Kingdom. Punk was held aloft as the yoof generation's challenge to the rock dinosaurs who had taken live shows away from the intimacy of clubs and concert halls in favour of stadium venues. The biggest culprits were perhaps the Rolling Stones and Led Zeppelin. Both outfits were 'back by popular demand' in the United States as the former introduced their new team member, Ronnie Wood, whilst the latter were trying to market their acclaimed double album, 'Physical Graffiti'. After completing their tenth invasion of Uncle Sam's home, Zeppelin took Earls Court in west London by storm, with five gigs there in the spring. Punk rock and the new wave may have just been around the corner, but they would have to wait until the Zeppelin exited the stage. Meanwhile, Bob Marley and the Wailers entertained the assembled mass at the Lyceum in London, thereby confirming them as one of the hottest acts on planet pop. The accompanying live album provided Robert Nesta with another incursion into the UK album charts, whilst 'No Woman No Cry' (performed live) would be his first British hit single.

1975's ALBUM OF THE YEAR

Wish You Were Here by Pink Floyd
(released in September; reached No.1 in the UK)

Side One:

1. Shine On You Crazy Diamond
   (Parts I-V); 13:31
2. Welcome to the Machine; 7:30

Side Two:

1. Have A Cigar; 5:08
2. Wish You Were Here; 5:26
3. Shine On You Crazy Diamond
   (Parts VI-IX); 12:28

After 'The Dark Side Of The Moon' began to accumulate record sales that were beyond anyone's wildest dreams, the Floyd became victims of their own success. Just how, after all, were they supposed to match or improve upon their 'dark moon' project? Indeed in many quarters, 'Wish You Were Here' was indeed viewed as a case of 'after the Lord Mayor's show', but it is held in high regard by most Pink Floyd aficionados. Once again the group (and Roger Waters in particular) were expressing their negative outlook of how society was evolving, or indeed deteriorating. 'Welcome To The Machine' was the obvious example of a band that was both world-weary and bored with the trappings of 'stardom'. 'Meanwhile 'Have A Cigar' (with lead vocals from Roy Harper) is a more amusing but ironic swipe at the music industry. The title track is simply an exquisite acoustic guitar track. The centre piece of the album is 'Shine On You Crazy Diamond', which is characteristically divided into nine 'parts'. It isn't so much a case of the foursome pining for the impossible return of the unhinged Syd Barrett, but more a case of the quartet offloading their guilt at jettisoning their former friend several years previously when he became something of an 'acid casualty'. 'Wish You Were Here' is not instantly likeable, but it grows in appeal with every listen.

SPORT IN 1975

English Division One football champions: Derby County, runners-up: Liverpool

English FA Cup final: West Ham United 2 Fulham 0

English League Cup Final: Aston Villa 1 Norwich City 0

Scottish Division One football champions: Glasgow Rangers; runners-up: Hibernian

Scottish FA Cup final: Glasgow Celtic 3 Airdrieonians 1

Scottish League Cup final: Glasgow Celtic 6 Hibernian 3

Irish League football champions: Linfield; Irish Cup final: Coleraine 1 Linfield 0 (in a replay)

League Of Ireland football champions: Bohemians; cup winners: Home Farm

European Cup final: Bayern Munich 2 Leeds United 0

European Cup-Winners' Cup final: Dynamo Kiev 3 Ferencvaros 0

UEFA Cup final: Borussia Moenchengladbach beat Twente Enschede 5–1 on aggregate

English county cricket champions: Leicestershire

Five Nations' rugby union champions: Wales (six points)

Formula One world drivers' champion: Niki Lauda (Austria) in a Ferrari car

Gaelic football All-Ireland champions: Kerry; runners-up: Dublin

British Open golf champion: Tom Watson (at Carnoustie)

US Masters golf champion: Jack Nicklaus

US Open golf champion: Lou Graham

USPGA golf champion: Jack Nicklaus

Rugby league Challenge Cup final: Widnes 14 Warrington 7

Wimbledon men's singles tennis final: A Ashe beat J Connors 6–1, 6–1, 5–7, 6–4

Wimbledon ladies' singles tennis final: B-J King beat E Cawley 6–0, 6–1

World snooker final: Ray Reardon (Wales) beat Eddie Charlton (Australia) 31–30

The Aintree Grand National steeplechase winner: L'Escargot; price 13–2

The Epsom Derby winner: Grundy; jockey – Pat Eddery; price 5–1

The Ryder Cup golf contest: United States 21 Great Britain And Ireland 11

1975's DEATHS

February 4th: Louis Jordan (US musician), aged 66

February 14th: Sir Julian Sorell Huxley (British scientist), aged 87

February 14th: Sir Pelham Grenville Wodehouse (British author), aged 93

February 24th: Nikolai Bulganin (Soviet statesman), aged 79

February 28th: Sir John Frederick Neville Cardus (British writer), aged 85

March 14th: Susan Hayward (US actress), aged 56

March 15th: Aristotle Onassis (Greek tycoon), aged 69

March 16th: T-Bone Walker (US musician), aged 64

March 28th: Sir Arthur Edward Drummond Bliss (British composer), aged 83

April 5th: Chiang Kai-shek (Chinese statesman), aged 87

April 12th: Josephine Baker (US entertainer), aged 68

April 15th: Michael Henry Flanders (British actor), aged 53

April 24th: Pete Ham (British musician), aged 27

May 6th: Cardinal Jozsef Mindszenty (from Hungary), aged 83

May 20th: Dame Jocelyn Barbara Hepworth (British sculptor), aged 72

July 2nd: James Robertson Justice (British actor), aged 70

August 9th: Dmitri Shostakovich (Soviet composer), aged 68

August 15th: Sheikh Mujibur Rahman (Bangladesh's President), aged 55

August 27th: Emperor Haile Selassie (of Ethiopia), aged 83

August 29th: Eamon de Valera (ex-Irish Taoiseach), aged 92

October 1st: Al Jackson (US musician), aged 39

October 22nd: Arnold Joseph Toynbee (British historian), aged 86

November 7th: Cardinal Heenan (ex-Archbishop of Westminster), aged 70

November 20th: General Francisco Franco (Spain's dictator), aged 82

November 27th: Ross McWhirter (British journalist), aged 50

November 29th: Norman Graham Hill (British Formula 1 driver), aged 46

December 7th: Thornton Wilder (US author), aged 78

The UK Top 10 singles for the week ending January the 3rd

1	Queen	Bohemian Rhapsody
2	Greg Lake	I Believe In Father Christmas
3	Laurel And Hardy	The Trail Of The Lonesome Pine
4	Dana	It's Gonna Be A Cold Cold Christmas
5	Chubby Checker	Let's Twist Again/The Twist
6	Demis Roussos	Happy To Be On An Island In The Sun
7	Hot Chocolate	You Sexy Thing
8	Stylistics	Na Na Is The Saddest Word
9	David Bowie	Golden Years
10	Chris Hill	Renta Santa

The US Number One single: Bay City Rollers – Saturday Night
The US Number One album: Chicago – Chicago IX:Chicago's Greatest Hits
The UK Number One album: Queen – A Night At The Opera
Also this week: Hurricane-force winds cause havoc in the United Kingdom. (2nd)

The UK Top 10 singles for the week ending January the 10th

1	Queen	Bohemian Rhapsody
2	Laurel And Hardy	The Trail Of The Lonesome Pine
3	Greg Lake	I Believe In Father Christmas
4	Sailor	Glass Of Champagne
5	Chubby Checker	Let's Twist Again/The Twist
6	Andy Fairweather Low	Wide Eyed And Legless
7	10cc	Art For Art's Sake
8	David Bowie	Golden Years
9	Dana	It's Gonna Be A Cold Cold Christmas
10	Drifters	Can I Take You Home Little Girl

The US Number One single: C.W. McCall – Convoy
The US Number One album: Chicago – Chicago IX:Chicago's Greatest
The UK Number One album: Perry Como – 40 Greatest Hits
Also this week: The frigate HMS Andromeda is rammed by an Icelandic gunboat. (10th)

The UK Top 10 singles for the week ending January the 17th

1	Queen	Bohemian Rhapsody
2	Sailor	Glass Of Champagne
3	Abba	Mamma Mia
4	Mike Oldfield	In Dulce Jubilo/On Horseback
5	10cc	Art For Art's Sake
6	Chubby Checker	Let's Twist Again/The Twist
7	Andy Fairweather Low	Wide Eyed And Legless
8	Billy Howard	King Of The Cops
9	Small Faces	Itchycoo Park
10	Demis Roussos	Happy To Be On An Island In The Sun

The US Number One single: Barry Manilow – I Write The Songs
The US Number One album: Earth, Wind & Fire – Gratitude
The UK Number One album: Queen – A Night At The Opera
Also this week: Malaysian Premier, Abdul Razak, dies while visiting London. (14th)

The UK Top 10 singles for the week ending January the 24th

1	Queen	Bohemian Rhapsody
2	Sailor	Glass Of Champagne
3	Abba	Mamma Mia
4	Mike Oldfield	In Dulce Jubilo/On Horseback
5	Miracles	Love Machine (Part 1)
6	Billy Howard	King Of The Cops
7	R & J Stone	We Do It
8	Andy Fairweather Low	Wide Eyed And Legless
9	Barry White	Let The Music Play
10	Paul Davidson	Midnight Rider

The US Number One single: Diana Ross – Theme From Mahogany
The US Number One album: Earth, Wind & Fire – Gratitude
The UK Number One album: Queen – A Night At The Opera
Also this week: The Soviet Union denounces Margaret Thatcher as the 'Iron Lady'. (24th)

The UK Top 10 singles for the week ending January the 31st

1	Abba	Mamma Mia
2	Slik	Forever And Ever
3	Queen	Bohemian Rhapsody
4	Miracles	Love Machine (Part 1)
5	Sailor	Glass Of Champagne
6	Donna Summer	Love To Love You Baby
7	R & J Stone	We Do It
8	Mike Oldfield	In Dulce Jubilo/On Horseback
9	Billy Howard	King Of The Cops
10	E.L.O.	Evil Woman

The US Number One single: The Ohio Players – Love Rollercoaster
The US Number One album: Earth, Wind & Fire – Gratitude
The UK Number One album: Roy Orbison – The Best Of Roy Orbison
Also this week: 128 British mercenaries fly to Angola to join the conflict. (28th)

The song of the month for January 1976
Forever And Ever by Slik (peak chart position: No.1)

Slik were perhaps guilty of attempting to imitate the highly-successful Bay City Rollers, but they did record a single which was superior to much of the teenage pop that had been unleashed in the previous couple of years. 'Forever And Ever' (with lead vocals by a young chap called Midge Ure) surrounds the vows taken at a wedding ceremony. Slik however soon vanished when the next single ('Requiem') failed to sell many copies.

The UK Top 10 singles for the week ending February the 7th

1	Abba	Mamma Mia
2	Slik	Forever And Ever
3	Miracles	Love Machine (Part 1)
4	Donna Summer	Love To Love You Baby
5	R & J Stone	We Do It
6	Queen	Bohemian Rhapsody
7	Sailor	Glass Of Champagne
8	Four Seasons	December, 1963 (Oh, What A Night)
9	Billy Howard	King Of The Cops
10	Mike Oldfield	In Dulce Jubilo/On Horseback

The US Number One single: Paul Simon – 50 Ways To Leave Your Lover
The US Number One album: Bob Dylan – Desire
The UK Number One album: Slim Whitman – The Very Best Of Slim Whitman
Also this week: Hua Kuo-feng becomes the acting Premier in China. (7th)

The UK Top 10 singles for the week ending February the 14th

1	Slik	Forever And Ever
2	Abba	Mamma Mia
3	Four Seasons	December, 1963 (Oh, What A Night)
4	Miracles	Love Machine (Part 1)
5	Donna Summer	Love To Love You Baby
6	R & J Stone	We Do It
7	Walker Brothers	No Regrets
8	Manuel And The Music Of The Mountains	Rodrigo's Guitar Concerto
9	Barbara Dickson	Answer Me
10	David Ruffin	Walk Away From Love

The US Number One single: Paul Simon – 50 Ways To Leave Your Lover
The US Number One album: Bob Dylan – Desire
The UK Number One album: Slim Whitman – The Very Best Of Slim Whitman
Also this week: Birmingham's John Curry wins an Olympic gold for figure skating. (11th)

The UK Top 10 singles for the week ending February the 21st

1	Four Seasons	December, 1963 (Oh, What A Night)
2	Slik	Forever And Ever
3	Tina Charles	I Love To Love
4	Manuel And The Music Of The Mountains	Rodrigo's Guitar Concerto
5	Abba	Mamma Mia
6	Donna Summer	Love To Love You Baby
7	C.W. McCall	Convoy
8	Miracles	Love Machine (Part 1)
9	R & J Stone	We Do It
10	Pluto Shervington	Dat

The US Number One single: Paul Simon – 50 Ways To Leave Your Lover
The US Number One album: Bob Dylan – Desire
The UK Number One album: Slim Whitman – The Very Best Of Slim Whitman
Also this week: Basil Hume is chosen to become the Archbishop of Westminster. (17th)

The UK Top 10 singles for the week ending February the 28th

1	Four Seasons	December, 1963 (Oh, What A Night)
2	Tina Charles	I Love To Love
3	Manuel And The Music Of The Mountains	Rodrigo's Guitar Concerto
4	C.W. McCall	Convoy
5	Slik	Forever And Ever
6	Yvonne Fair	It Should Have Been Me
7	Pluto Shervington	Dat
8	Walker Brothers	No Regrets
9	Status Quo	Rain
10	Who	Squeeze Box

The US Number One single: Rhythm Heritage – Theme From S.W.A.T.
The US Number One album: Bob Dylan – Desire
The UK Number One album: Slim Whitman – The Very Best Of Slim Whitman
Also this week: Britain's Post Office announces the end of Sunday collections. (27th)

The song of the month for February 1976
Convoy by C.W. McCall (peak chart position: No.2)

Every now and then a box office success would yield smash hits and the latest film to inspire a foray into the pop charts was the American 'road movie', 'Convoy', starring the bearded country and western singer Kris Kristofferson. The artist responsible was C.W. McCall who provided a spoken role throughout the tune. The song found favour with a public that was keen on American chase movies such as 'Smokey And The Bandit'. It also inspired a spoof cover version from Laurie Lingo And The Dipsticks, entitled 'Convoy GB'.

The UK Top 10 singles for the week ending March the 6th

1	Tina Charles	I Love To Love
2	Four Seasons	December, 1963 (Oh, What A Night)
3	C.W. McCall	Convoy
4	Manuel And The Music Of The Mountains	Rodrigo's Guitar Concerto
5	Yvonne Fair	It Should Have Been Me
6	Pluto Shervington	Dat
7	Status Quo	Rain
8	Billy Ocean	Love Really Hurts Without You
9	Slik	Forever And Ever
10	Stylistics	Funky Weekend

The US Number One single: The Miracles – Love Machine (Part 1)
The US Number One album: Bob Dylan – Desire
The UK Number One album: Slim Whitman – The Very Best Of Slim Whitman
Also this week: The pound falls below two dollars for the first time. (5th)

The UK Top 10 singles for the week ending March the 13th

1	Tina Charles	I Love To Love
2	Four Seasons	December,1963 (Oh, What A Night)
3	C.W. McCall	Convoy
4	Billy Ocean	Love Really Hurts Without You
5	Manuel And The Music Of The Mountains	Rodrigo's Guitar Concerto
6	Yvonne Fair	It Should Have Been Me
7	Glitter Band	People Like You People Like Me
8	Status Quo	Rain
9	Guys And Dolls	You Don't Have To Say You Love Me
10	Fatback Band	(Do The) Spanish Hustle

The US Number One single: Four Seasons – December, 1963 (Oh, What A Night)
The US Number One album: The Eagles – Their Greatest Hits (1971–1975)
The UK Number One album: Slim Whitman – The Very Best Of Slim Whitman
Also this week: Forty-two skiers die in an Italian cable car tragedy. (9th)

The UK Top 10 singles for the week ending March the 20th

1	Tina Charles	I Love To Love
2	C.W. McCall	Convoy
3	Billy Ocean	Love Really Hurts Without You
4	Brotherhood Of Man	Save Your Kisses For Me
5	Guys And Dolls	You Don't Have To Say You Love Me
6	Barry White	You See The Trouble With Me
7	Glitter Band	People Like You People Like Me
8	Gallagher & Lyle	I Wanna Stay With You
9	Four Seasons	December, 1963 (Oh, What A Night)
10	Yvonne Fair	It Should Have Been Me

The US Number One single: Four Seasons – December, 1963 (Oh, What A Night)
The US Number One album: The Eagles – Their Greatest Hits (1971–1975)
The UK Number One album: Status Quo – Blue For You
Also this week: Harold Wilson announces his resignation as British Prime Minister. (16th)

The UK Top 10 singles for the week ending March the 27th

1	Brotherhood Of Man	Save Your Kisses For Me
2	Billy Ocean	Love Really Hurts Without You
3	Tina Charles	I Love To Love
4	Barry White	You See The Trouble With Me
5	Glitter Band	People Like You People Like Me
6	Guys And Dolls	You Don't Have To Say You Love Me
7	Gallagher & Lyle	I Wanna Stay With You
8	C.W. McCall	Convoy
9	Marmalade	Falling Apart At The Seams
10	Beatles	Yesterday

The US Number One single: Four Seasons – December, 1963 (Oh, What A Night)
The US Number One album: The Eagles – Their Greatest Hits (1971–1975)
The UK Number One album: Status Quo – Blue For You
Also this week: Argentine President, Isabel Peron, is deposed in a bloodless coup. (24th)

The song of the month for March 1976
Music by John Miles (peak chart position: No.3)

John Miles was the spokesperson for millions of people when he sang that "music is my first love and it will be my last". This single spent three weeks at its peak position of Number 3. The song was quite a grandiose recording, assisted by an orchestral accompaniment. It even found its way deservedly on to a subsequent compilation, entitled 'Milestones – 20 Rock Operas', taking its place alongside many other classic recordings.

The UK Top 10 singles for the week ending April the 3rd

1	Brotherhood Of Man	Save Your Kisses For Me
2	Barry White	You See The Trouble With Me
3	Billy Ocean	Love Really Hurts Without You
4	John Miles	Music
5	Tina Charles	I Love To Love
6	Gallagher & Lyle	I Wanna Stay With You
7	Elton John	Pinball Wizard
8	Beatles	Yesterday
9	Marmalade	Falling Apart At The Seams
10	Glitter Band	People Like You People Like Me

The US Number One single: Johnnie Taylor – Disco Lady
The US Number One album: The Eagles – Their Greatest Hits (1971–1975)
The UK Number One album: Status Quo – Blue For You
Also this week: A group of economists predict economic recession beyond the 1970s. (28th)

The UK Top 10 singles for the week ending April the 10th

1	Brotherhood Of Man	Save Your Kisses For Me
2	Barry White	You See The Trouble With Me
3	John Miles	Music
4	Abba	Fernando
5	Billy Ocean	Love Really Hurts Without You
6	10 CC	I'm Mandy Fly Me
7	Hank Mizell	Jungle Rock
8	Elton John	Pinball Wizard
9	Beatles	Yesterday
10	Diana Ross	Theme From Mahogany (Do You Know Where You're Going To)

The US Number One single: Johnnie Taylor – Disco Lady
The US Number One album: Peter Frampton – Frampton Comes Alive!
The UK Number One album: TV Soundtrack – Rock Follies
Also this week: James Callaghan succeeds Harold Wilson as the new Prime Minister. (5th)

The UK Top 10 singles for the week ending April the 17th

1 Brotherhood Of Man — Save Your Kisses For Me
2 Abba — Fernando
3 John Miles — Music
4 Barry White — You See The Trouble With Me
5 Hank Mizell — Jungle Rock
6 10cc — I'm Mandy Fly Me
7 Diana Ross — Theme From Mahogany (Do You Know Where You're Going To)
8 Bay City Rollers — Love Me Like I Love You
9 Sailor — Girls Girls Girls
10 Elton John — Pinball Wizard

The US Number One single: Johnnie Taylor – Disco Lady
The US Number One album: The Eagles – Their Greatest Hits (1971–1975)
The UK Number One album: TV Soundtrack – Rock Follies
Also this week: Andrei Sakharov and his wife are arrested in Moscow. (14th)

The UK Top 10 singles for the week ending April the 24th

1 Brotherhood Of Man — Save Your Kisses For Me
2 Abba — Fernando
3 John Miles — Music
4 Hank Mizell — Jungle Rock
5 Diana Ross — Theme From Mahogany (Do You Know Where You're Going To)
6 10cc — I'm Mandy Fly Me
7 Sailor — Girls Girls Girls
8 Bay City Rollers — Love Me Like I Love You
9 Barry White — You See The Trouble With Me
10 Silver Convention — Get Up And Boogie

The US Number One single: Johnnie Taylor – Disco Lady
The US Number One album: Wings – Wings At The Speed Of Sound
The UK Number One album: Led Zeppelin – Presence
Also this week: Mrs Gandhi proposes to restore diplomatic relations with Pakistan. (19th)

The song of the month for April 1976

No Charge by J.J. Barrie (peak chart position: No.1)

This country and western flavoured novelty release sneaked into the Top Fifty at the end of April before 'charging' its way up the singles chart. J.J. Barrie actually talks his way through this emotional little number in which a small child runs through a bill of chores completed for his mother, after which the mother makes her son aware of her 'services', all performed with no charge. The British public certainly took it to their hearts, whilst Billy Connolly was inspired to perform a spoof entitled 'No Chance'.

The UK Top 10 singles for the week ending May the 1st

1	Brotherhood Of Man	Save Your Kisses For Me
2	Abba	Fernando
3	Hank Mizell	Jungle Rock
4	Bay City Rollers	Love Me Like I Love You
5	Fox	S-S-S-Single Bed
6	Diana Ross	Theme From Mahogany (Do You Know Where You're Going To)
7	Sailor	Girls Girls Girls
8	10cc	I'm Mandy Fly Me
9	Silver Convention	Get Up And Boogie
10	Isaac Hayes	Disco Connection

The US Number One single: Bellamy Brothers – Let Your Love Flow

The US Number One album: Led Zeppelin – Presence

The UK Number One album: TV Soundtrack – Rock Follies

Also this week: Muhammad Ali defeats Jimmy Young to remain World heavyweight champion. (30th)

The UK Top 10 singles for the week ending May the 8th

1	Abba	Fernando
2	Brotherhood Of Man	Save Your Kisses For Me
3	Hank Mizell	Jungle Rock
4	Laurie Lingo & The Dipsticks	Convoy GB
5	Fox	S-S-S-Single Bed
6	Four Seasons	Silver Star
7	Silver Convention	Get Up And Boogie
8	Diana Ross	Theme From Mahogany (Do You Know Where You're Going To)
9	Sheer Elegance	Life Is Too Short Girl
10	Isaac Hayes	Disco Connection

The US Number One single: John Sebastian – Welcome Back
The US Number One album: Led Zeppelin – Presence
The UK Number One album: Abba – Greatest Hits
Also this week: The Conservatives make sweeping gains in Britain's local elections. (6th)

The UK Top 10 singles for the week ending May the 15th

1	Abba	Fernando
2	Brotherhood Of Man	Save Your Kisses For Me
3	Hank Mizell	Jungle Rock
4	Fox	S-S-S-Single Bed
5	Andrea True Connection	More More More
6	Sutherland Brothers And Quiver	Arms Of Mary
7	Laurie Lingo & The Dipsticks	Convoy GB
8	Silver Convention	Get Up And Boogie
9	Four Seasons	Silver Star
10	Stylistics	Can't Help Falling In Love

The US Number One single: The Sylvers – Boogie Fever
The US Number One album: The Rolling Stones – Black And Blue
The UK Number One album: Abba – Greatest Hits
Also this week: Jeremy Thorpe resigns as leader of the British Liberal Party. (10th)

The UK Top 10 singles for the week ending May the 22nd

1	Abba	Fernando
2	J.J. Barrie	No Charge
3	Four Seasons	Silver Star
4	Stylistics	Can't Help Falling In Love
5	Sutherland Brothers And Quiver	Arms Of Mary
6	Andrea True Connection	More More More
7	Rolling Stones	Fool To Cry
8	Brotherhood Of Man	Save Your Kisses For Me
9	Hank Mizell	Jungle Rock
10	Fox	S-S-S-Single Bed

The US Number One single: Wings – Silly Love Songs
The US Number One album: The Rolling Stones – Black And Blue
The UK Number One album: Abba – Greatest Hits
Also this week: Renewed fighting breaks out in Lebanon after another failed truce. (16th)

The UK Top 10 singles for the week ending May the 29th

1	Abba	Fernando
2	J.J. Barrie	No Charge
3	Wurzels	Combine Harvester
4	Robin Sarstedt	My Resistance Is Low
5	Andrea True Connection	More More More
6	Sutherland Brothers And Quiver	Arms Of Mary
7	Wings	Silly Love Songs
8	Rolling Stones	Fool To Cry
9	Bellamy Brothers	Let Your Love Flow
10	Diana Ross	Love Hangover

The US Number One single: Diana Ross – Love Hangover
The US Number One album: Wings – Wings At The Speed Of Sound
The UK Number One album: Abba – Greatest Hits
Also this week: Muhammad Ali defeats Richard Dunn to stay World heavyweight champion. (24th)

The song of the month for May 1976

Midnight Train To Georgia by Gladys Knight And The Pips
(peak chart position: No.10)

This sad composition had previously climbed to the summit of the American singles list three years earlier for Gladys Knight and her Pips. In the British charts, their effort was 'pipped' to the top of the charts but it remains one of the greatest soul singles in the history of popular music. This fabulous story was to provide the act with the third of four UK Top Ten hits in the 1970s, though its peak position of No.10 was an injustice.

The UK Top 10 singles for the week ending June the 5th

1	J.J. Barrie	No Charge
2	Wurzels	Combine Harvester
3	Robin Sarstedt	My Resistance Is Low
4	Abba	Fernando
5	Wings	Silly Love Songs
6	Rolling Stones	Fool To Cry
7	Bellamy Brothers	Let Your Love Flow
8	Sutherland Brothers And Quiver	Arms Of Mary
9	Cliff Richard	Devil Woman
10	Gladys Knight & The Pips	Midnight Train To Georgia

The US Number One single: Diana Ross – Love Hangover
The US Number One album: The Rolling Stones – Black And Blue
The UK Number One album: Abba – Greatest Hits
Also this week: Britain and Iceland agree a truce, ending the 'Cod War'. (1st)

The UK Top 10 singles for the week ending June the 12th

1	Wurzels	Combine Harvester
2	Wings	Silly Love Songs
3	J.J. Barrie	No Charge
4	Abba	Fernando
5	Real Thing	You To Me Are Everything
6	Robin Sarstedt	My Resistance Is Low
7	Rolling Stones	Fool To Cry
8	Bellamy Brothers	Let Your Love Flow
9	Melba Moore	This Is It
10	Sutherland Brothers And Quiver	Arms Of Mary

The US Number One single: Wings – Silly Love Songs

The US Number One album: The Rolling Stones – Black And Blue

The UK Number One album: Abba – Greatest Hits

Also this week: Syrian troops launch attacks against Lebanon's Palestinian guerrillas. (9th)

The UK Top 10 singles for the week ending June the 19th

1	Wurzels	Combine Harvester
2	Real Thing	You To Me Are Everything
3	Wings	Silly Love Songs
4	Our Kid	You Just Might See Me Cry
5	J.J. Barrie	No Charge
6	Gallagher & Lyle	Heart On My Sleeve
7	Dolly Parton	Jolene
8	Rod Stewart	Tonight's The Night
9	Robin Sarstedt	My Resistance Is Low
10	Peter Frampton	Show Me The Way

The US Number One single: Wings – Silly Love Songs

The US Number One album: Wings – Wings At The Speed Of Sound

The UK Number One album: Abba – Greatest Hits

Also this week: Rioting breaks out throughout South Africa's black townships. (16th)

The UK Top 10 singles for the week ending June the 26th

1 Real Thing · You To Me Are Everything
2 Wurzels · Combine Harvester
3 Wings · Silly Love Songs
4 Our Kid · You Just Might See Me Cry
5 Rod Stewart · Tonight's The Night
6 Candi Staton · Young Hearts Run Free
7 Bryan Ferry · Let's Stick Together
8 Gallagher & Lyle · Heart On My Sleeve
9 Dolly Parton · Jolene
10 Thin Lizzy · The Boys Are Back In Town

The US Number One single: Wings – Silly Love Songs
The US Number One album: Wings – Wings At The Speed Of Sound
The UK Number One album: Abba – Greatest Hits
Also this week: Almost three hundred Britons and Americans flee strife-torn Beirut.
(20th)

The song of the month for June 1976
Let's Stick Together by Bryan Ferry (peak chart position: No.4)

Geordie crooner Bryan Ferry continued to cultivate a solo career alongside his association with Roxy Music. In between band projects, Ferry did a commendable re-working of Canned Heat's 'Let's Work Together' which provided the singer with his first Top Ten hit since 'A Hard Rain's Gonna Fall'. Ferry's other half, Jerry Hall, made a contribution to the song's video, before she decided to go off and stick together with Mick Jagger.

The UK Top 10 singles for the week ending July the 3rd

1	Real Thing	You To Me Are Everything
2	Our Kid	You Just Might See Me Cry
3	Candi Staton	Young Hearts Run Free
4	Bryan Ferry	Let's Stick Together
5	Rod Stewart	Tonight's The Night
6	Gallagher & Lyle	Heart On My Sleeve
7	Shangri Las	Leader Of The Pack
8	Thin Lizzy	The Boys Are Back In Town
9	Wurzels	Combine Harvester
10	Wings	Silly Love Songs

The US Number One single: Wings – Silly Love Songs
The US Number One album: Wings – Wings At The Speed Of Sound
The UK Number One album: Abba – Greatest Hits
Also this week: Six Palestinians hijack an Air France Airbus. (27th)

The UK Top 10 singles for the week ending July the 10th

1	Real Thing	You To Me Are Everything
2	Candi Staton	Young Hearts Run Free
3	Demis Roussos	The Roussos Phenomenon
4	Our Kid	You Just Might See Me Cry
5	Bryan Ferry	Let's Stick Together
6	Manhattans	Kiss And Say Goodbye
7	Dr. Hook	A Little Bit More
8	Rod Stewart	Tonight's The Night
9	Elton John & Kiki Dee	Don't Go Breaking My Heart
10	Shangri Las	Leader Of The Pack

The US Number One single: Starland Vocal Band – Afternoon Delight
The US Number One album: Wings – Wings At The Speed Of Sound
The UK Number One album: Rod Stewart – A Night On The Town
Also this week: Israeli commandos rescue the hostages held at Entebbe airport. (4th)

The UK Top 10 singles for the week ending July the 17th

1 Demis Roussos   The Roussos Phenomenon
2 Elton John & Kiki Dee   Don't Go Breaking My Heart
3 Dr. Hook   A Little Bit More
4 Candi Staton   Young Hearts Run Free
5 Manhattans   Kiss And Say Goodbye
6 Real Thing   You To Me Are Everything
7 Queen   You're My Best Friend
8 Bryan Ferry   Let's Stick Together
9 Our Kid   You Just Might See Me Cry
10 Dorothy Moore   Misty Blue

The US Number One single: Starland Vocal Band – Afternoon Delight
The US Number One album: Wings – Wings At The Speed Of Sound
The UK Number One album: Rod Stewart – A Night On The Town
Also this week: Roy Jenkins is appointed President of the European Commisssion. (13th)

The UK Top 10 singles for the week ending July the 24th

1 Elton John & Kiki Dee   Don't Go Breaking My Heart
2 Dr. Hook   A Little Bit More
3 Demis Roussos   The Roussos Phenomenon
4 Candi Staton   Young Hearts Run Free
5 Manhattans   Kiss And Say Goodbye
6 Dorothy Moore   Misty Blue
7 Real Thing   You To Me Are Everything
8 Queen   You're My Best Friend
9 One Hundred Ton And A Feather   It Only Takes A Minute
10 Bryan Ferry   Let's Stick Together

The US Number One single: The Manhattans – Kiss And Say Goodbye
The US Number One album: Peter Frampton – Frampton Comes Alive!
The UK Number One album: The Beach Boys – 20 Golden Greats
Also this week: Britain's ambassador in Dublin, Christopher Ewart-Biggs, is murdered. (21st)

The UK Top 10 singles for the week ending July the 31st

1	Elton John & Kiki Dee	Don't Go Breaking My Heart
2	Dr. Hook	A Little Bit More
3	Demis Roussos	The Roussos Phenomenon
4	Manhattans	Kiss And Say Goodbye
5	Tavares	Heaven Must Be Missing An Angel
6	Candi Staton	Young Hearts Run Free
7	Dorothy Moore	Misty Blue
8	David Dundas	Jeans On
9	One Hundred Ton And A Feather	It Only Takes A Minute
10	Queen	You're My Best Friend

The US Number One single: The Manhattans – Kiss And Say Goodbye
The US Number One album: George Benson – Breezin'.
The UK Number One album: The Beach Boys – 20 Golden Greats
Also this week: Britain severs her diplomatic relations with Uganda. (31st)

The song of the month for July 1976

Don't Go Breaking My Heart by Elton John And Kiki Dee
(peak chart position: No.1)

Elton John was no stranger to the Billboard Number One position, but it took a collaboration with Kiki Dee to earn the popular singer his first UK chart-topper. Not content with reaching the pop summit, Elton and Kiki promptly stayed there for a further five weeks. This excellent pop song would end the year as the second biggest-selling single in the British charts. For four August heatwave weeks, this duet would sit at the top of the pop music lists in both the United States and the United Kingdom.

The UK Top 10 singles for the week ending August the 7th

1	Elton John & Kiki Dee	Don't Go Breaking My Heart
2	Dr. Hook	A Little Bit More
3	David Dundas	Jeans On
4	Demis Roussos	The Roussos Phenomenon
5	Dorothy Moore	Misty Blue
6	Tavares	Heaven Must Be Missing An Angel
7	Manhattans	Kiss And Say Goodbye
8	Jimmy James & The Vagabonds	Now Is The Time
9	Candi Staton	Young Hearts Run Free
10	Isley Brothers	Harvest For The World

The US Number One single: Elton John & Kiki Dee – Don't Go Breaking My Heart
The US Number One album: George Benson – Breezin'
The UK Number One album: The Beach Boys – 20 Golden Greats
Also this week: World champion Niki Lauda is seriously injured at the Nurburgring.
(1st)

The UK Top 10 singles for the week ending August the 14th

1	Elton John & Kiki Dee	Don't Go Breaking My Heart
2	Dr. Hook	A Little Bit More
3	David Dundas	Jeans On
4	Tavares	Heaven Must Be Missing An Angel
5	Jimmy James & The Vagabonds	Now Is The Time
6	Demis Roussos	The Roussos Phenomenon
7	Johnny Wakelin	In Zaire
8	5000 Volts	Dr. Kiss Kiss
9	Dorothy Moore	Misty Blue
10	Bee Gees	You Should Be Dancing

The US Number One single: Elton John & Kiki Dee – Don't Go Breaking My Heart
The US Number One album: Peter Frampton – Frampton Comes Alive!
The UK Number One album: The Beach Boys – 20 Golden Greats
Also this week: Viv Richards hits 291 in an Oval test match. (13th)

The UK Top 10 singles for the week ending August the 21st

1	Elton John & Kiki Dee	Don't Go Breaking My Heart
2	Dr. Hook	A Little Bit More
3	David Dundas	Jeans On
4	Johnny Wakelin	In Zaire
5	Wings	Let 'Em In
6	Tavares	Heaven Must Be Missing An Angel
7	Jimmy James & The Vagabonds	Now Is The Time
8	5000 Volts	Dr. Kiss Kiss
9	Bee Gees	You Should Be Dancing
10	Steve Harley & Cockney Rebel	Here Comes The Sun

The US Number One single: Elton John & Kiki Dee – Don't Go Breaking My Heart
The US Number One album: Peter Frampton – Frampton Comes Alive!
The UK Number One album: The Beach Boys – 20 Golden Greats
Also this week: West Indies defeat England, with Michael Holding taking fourteen wickets. (17th)

The UK Top 10 singles for the week ending August the 28th

1	Elton John & Kiki Dee	Don't Go Breaking My Heart
2	Wings	Let 'Em In
3	Dr. Hook	A Little Bit More
4	David Dundas	Jeans On
5	Johnny Wakelin	In Zaire
6	Bee Gees	You Should Be Dancing
7	Tavares	Heaven Must Be Missing An Angel
8	5000 Volts	Dr. Kiss Kiss
9	Chi-Lites	You Don't Have To Go
10	Jimmy James & The Vagabonds	Now Is The Time

The US Number One single: Elton John & Kiki Dee – Don't Go Breaking My Heart
The US Number One album: Peter Frampton – Frampton Comes Alive!
The UK Number One album: The Beach Boys – 20 Golden Greats
Also this week: Disgraced jailbird John Stonehouse resigns his parliamentary seat. (27th)

The song of the month for August 1976

The Killing Of Georgia by Rod Stewart (peak chart position: No.2)

This outstanding item lived in the shadow of the million-selling 'Sailing' which is quite unjust, considering that it is arguably the better song. Here Rod branches out into a ballad about the murder of a gay friend in New York. Not only does the tragic end of Georgie make for an interesting story but the second half of the song's extended version is most poignant. This tune must surely be a strong contender for the best track of the year.

The UK Top 10 singles for the week ending September the 4th

1	Abba	Dancing Queen
2	Wings	Let 'Em In
3	Elton John & Kiki Dee	Don't Go Breaking My Heart
4	Billie Jo Spears	What I've Got In Mind
5	Dr. Hook	A Little Bit More
6	Johnny Wakelin	In Zaire
7	Bryan Ferry	Extended Play
8	Rod Stewart	The Killing Of Georgie
9	Chi-Lites	You Don't Have To Go
10	David Dundas	Jeans On

The US Number One single: The Bee Gees – You Should Be Dancing
The US Number One album: Fleetwood Mac – Fleetwood Mac
The UK Number One album: The Beach Boys – 20 Golden Greats
Also this week: The Notting Hill carnival descends into riotous street skirmishes. (31st)

The UK Top 10 singles for the week ending September the 11th

1	Abba	Dancing Queen
2	Wings	Let 'Em In
3	Chi-Lites	You Don't Have To Go
4	Elton John & Kiki Dee	Don't Go Breaking My Heart
5	Bee Gees	You Should Be Dancing
6	Rod Stewart	The Killing Of Georgie
7	Stylistics	16 Bars
8	Gheorghe Zamfir	(Light Of Experience) Doina De Jale
9	Billie Jo Spears	What I've Got In Mind
10	Lou Rawls	You'll Never Find Another Love Like Mine

The US Number One single: KC & The Sunshine Band – (Shake, Shake, Shake) Shake Your Booty
The US Number One album: Peter Frampton – Frampton Comes Alive!
The UK Number One album: The Beach Boys – 20 Golden Greats
Also this week: Roy Mason replaces Merlyn Rees as the Northern Ireland Secretary. (10th)

The UK Top 10 singles for the week ending September the 18th

1	Abba	Dancing Queen
2	Rod Stewart	The Killing Of Georgie
3	Real Thing	Can't Get By Without You
4	Gheorghe Zamfir	(Light Of Experience) Doina De Jale
5	Acker Bilk	Aria
6	Wings	Let 'Em In
7	Stylistics	16 Bars
8	Chi-Lites	You Don't Have To Go
9	Wurzels	I Am A Cider Drinker
10	Bay City Rollers	I Only Wanna Be With You

The US Number One single: Wild Cherry – Play That Funky Music
The US Number One album: Peter Frampton – Frampton Comes Alive!
The UK Number One album: The Beach Boys – 20 Golden Greats
Also this week: A massive anti-Apartheid demonstration takes place in Cape Town. (15th)

The UK Top 10 singles for the week ending September the 25th

1	Abba	Dancing Queen
2	Real Thing	Can't Get By Without You
3	Wurzels	I Am A Cider Drinker
4	Bay City Rollers	I Only Wanna Be With You
5	Pussycat	Mississippi
6	Manfred Mann's Earthband	Blinded By The Light
7	Acker Bilk	Aria
8	Rod Stewart	The Killing Of Georgie
9	Tina Charles	Dance Little Lady Dance
10	Gheorghe Zamfir	(Light Of Experience) Doina De Jale

The US Number One single: Wild Cherry – Play That Funky Music
The US Number One album: Peter Frampton – Frampton Comes Alive!
The UK Number One album: The Beach Boys – 20 Golden Greats
Also this week: Patti Hearst is jailed for seven years for armed robbery. (24th)

The song of the month for September 1976

Girl Of My Best Friend by Elvis Presley (peak chart position: No.9)

His health may have been in terminal decline, but for all the personal turmoil, Elvis Presley still enjoyed regular incursions into the British Top Ten. This 'latest' success story was actually a recording that dated back to 1960. The 'Girl Of My Best Friend' was born around the same time as the smash hits 'Are You Lonesome Tonight' and 'It's Now Or Never'. This slice of nostalgia was a reminder of the majesty of the King.

The UK Top 10 singles for the week ending October the 2nd

1 Abba   Dancing Queen
2 Real Thing   Can't Get By Without You
3 Pussycat   Mississippi
4 Wurzels   I Am A Cider Drinker
5 Bay City Rollers   I Only Wanna Be With You
6 Tina Charles   Dance Little Lady Dance
7 Rod Stewart   Sailing
8 Acker Bilk   Aria
9 Manfred Mann's Earthband   Blinded By The Light
10 Rick Dees And His Cast Of Idiots Disco Duck (Part One)

The US Number One single: Wild Cherry – Play That Funky Music
The US Number One album: Peter Frampton – Frampton Comes Alive!
The UK Number One album: The Stylistics – Best Of The Stylistics, Volume 2
Also this week: Britain applies to the International Monetary Fund for a loan. (29th)

The UK Top 10 singles for the week ending October the 9th

1 Abba   Dancing Queen
2 Pussycat   Mississippi
3 Real Thing   Can't Get By Without You
4 Rod Stewart   Sailing
5 Wurzels   I Am A Cider Drinker
6 Rick Dees And His Cast Of Idiots Disco Duck (Part One)
7 Bay City Rollers   I Only Wanna Be With You
8 Tina Charles   Dance Little Lady Dance
9 Manfred Mann's Earthband   Blinded By The Light
10 Acker Bilk   Aria

The US Number One single: Walter Murphy And The Big Apple Band – A Fifth Of Beethoven
The US Number One album: Peter Frampton – Frampton Comes Alive!
The UK Number One album: Dr. Feelgood – Stupidity
Also this week: Bishop Abel Muzorewa returns to Rhodesia, having been in exile. (3rd)

The UK Top 10 singles for the week ending October the 16th

1	Pussycat	Mississippi
2	Abba	Dancing Queen
3	Rod Stewart	Sailing
4	Sherbet	Howzat
5	Demis Roussos	When Forever Has Gone
6	Rick Dees And His Cast Of Idiots	Disco Duck (Part One)
7	Real Thing	Can't Get By Without You
8	Tina Charles	Dance Little Lady Dance
9	Elvis Presley	Girl Of My Best Friend
10	Ritchie Family	The Best Disco In Town

The US Number One single: Rick Dees And His Cast Of Idiots – Disco Duck (Part One)
The US Number One album: Stevie Wonder – Songs In The Key Of Life
The UK Number One album: Abba – Greatest Hits
Also this week: Chairman Mao's widow and three others are arrested in China. (11th)

The UK Top 10 singles for the week ending October the 23rd

1	Pussycat	Mississippi
2	Demis Roussos	When Forever Has Gone
3	Rod Stewart	Sailing
4	Chicago	If You Leave Me Now
5	Manhattans	Hurt
6	Abba	Dancing Queen
7	Simon May	Summer Of My Life
8	Sherbet	Howzat
9	Tavares	Don't Take Away The Music
10	Rick Dees And His Cast Of Idiots	Disco Duck (Part One)

The US Number One single: Chicago – If You Leave Me Now
The US Number One album: Stevie Wonder – Songs In The Key Of Life
The UK Number One album: Abba – Greatest Hits
Also this week: Black September leader, Ali Hassan Salameh, is found dead. (19th)

The UK Top 10 singles for the week ending October the 30th

1 Pussycat   Mississippi
2 Demis Roussos   When Forever Has Gone
3 Chicago   If You Leave Me Now
4 Sherbet   Howzat
5 Manhattans   Hurt
6 Tavares   Don't Take Away The Music
7 Simon May   Summer Of My Life
8 Abba   Dancing Queen
9 Paul Nicholas   Dancing With The Captain
10 Rod Stewart   Sailing

The US Number One single: Chicago – If You Leave Me Now
The US Number One album: Stevie Wonder – Songs In The Key Of Life
The UK Number One album: Various Artist Compilation – Soul Motion
Also this week: China's 'Gang Of Four' are imprisoned for plotting a coup. (23rd)

The song of the month for October 1976

If You Leave Me Now by Chicago (peak chart position: No.1)

Peter Cetera and his Chicago outfit had already enjoyed a two-week stint at the top of the Billboard chart when they emulated this success by securing a three-week sojourn at the summit of the UK singles listings. Here was yet another of those sensitive songs that the British public took a liking to. Chicago hadn't visited the Top Ten for six years and it would be a further 6 years before they returned.

The UK Top 10 singles for the week ending November the 6th

1	Pussycat	Mississippi
2	Chicago	If You Leave Me Now
3	Demis Roussos	When Forever Has Gone
4	Manhattans	Hurt
5	Tavares	Don't Take Away The Music
6	Sherbet	Howzat
7	Simon May	Summer Of My Life
8	Paul Nicholas	Dancing With The Captain
9	Rod Stewart	Sailing
10	Wild Cherry	Play That Funky Music

The US Number One single: The Steve Miller Band – Rock'n Me
The US Number One album: Stevie Wonder – Songs In The Key Of Life
The UK Number One album: Various Artist Compilation – Soul Motion
Also this week: Jimmy Carter defeats Gerald Ford in the American Presidential election. (2nd)

The UK Top 10 singles for the week ending November the 13th

1	Chicago	If You Leave Me Now
2	Pussycat	Mississippi
3	Leo Sayer	You Make Me Feel Like Dancing
4	Tavares	Don't Take Away The Music
5	Demis Roussos	When Forever Has Gone
6	Manhattans	Hurt
7	Wild Cherry	Play That Funky Music
8	Sherbet	Howzat
9	Simon May	Summer Of My Life
10	Joan Armatrading	Love And Affection

The US Number One single: Rod Stewart – Tonight's The Night (Gonna Be Alright)
The US Number One album: Stevie Wonder – Songs In The Key Of Life
The UK Number One album: Led Zeppelin – The Song Remains The Same
Also this week: Callaghan's government is defeated on the Dock Work Regulation Bill. (10th)

The UK Top 10 singles for the week ending November the 20th

1	Chicago	If You Leave Me Now
2	Leo Sayer	You Make Me Feel Like Dancing
3	Showaddywaddy	Under The Moon Of Love
4	Pussycat	Mississippi
5	Dr. Hook	If Not You
6	Manhattans	Hurt
7	Who	Substitute
8	Tavares	Don't Take Away The Music
9	Wild Cherry	Play That Funky Music
10	Climax Blues Band	Couldn't Get It Right

The US Number One single: Rod Stewart – Tonight's The Night (Gonna Be Alright)
The US Number One album: Stevie Wonder – Songs In The Key Of Life
The UK Number One album: Bert Weedon – 22 Golden Guitar Greats
Also this week: Italy beat England 2–0 in a World Cup qualifier. (17th)

The UK Top 10 singles for the week ending November the 27th

1	Chicago	If You Leave Me Now
2	Showaddywaddy	Under The Moon Of Love
3	Leo Sayer	You Make Me Feel Like Dancing
4	Queen	Somebody To Love
5	Dr. Hook	If Not You
6	Pussycat	Mississippi
7	Wild Cherry	Play That Funky Music
8	Yvonne Elliman	Love Me
9	Bonnie Tyler	Lost In France
10	Abba	Money Money Money

The US Number One single: Rod Stewart – Tonight's The Night (Gonna Be Alright)
The US Number One album: Stevie Wonder – Songs In The Key Of Life
The UK Number One album: Glen Campbell – 20 Golden Greats
Also this week: Six thousand are reported dead after an earthquake in Turkey. (24th)

The song of the month for November 1976

Money Money Money by Abba (peak chart position: No.3)

The all-conquering Abba experienced relative failure when 'Money Money Money' could 'only' manage a Number 3 peak position after a hat-trick of chart-toppers in the previous twelve months. This new smash hit still remained one of the most memorable tunes from the quartet's esteemed repertoire. It is after all the kind of lyrics which many gold-digging females could relate to. The single spent four weeks in the Top Three, but was eclipsed by Abba's next three releases which also topped the UK charts.

The UK Top 10 singles for the week ending December the 4th

1	Showaddywaddy	Under The Moon Of Love
2	Chicago	If You Leave Me Now
3	Leo Sayer	You Make Me Feel Like Dancing
4	Queen	Somebody To Love
5	E.L.O.	Livin' Thing
6	Abba	Money Money Money
7	Yvonne Elliman	Love Me
8	Dr. Hook	If Not You
9	Bonnie Tyler	Lost In France
10	Pussycat	Mississippi

The US Number One single: Rod Stewart – Tonight's The Night (Gonna Be Alright)
The US Number One album: Stevie Wonder – Songs In The Key Of Life
The UK Number One album: Glen Campbell – 20 Golden Greats
Also this week: The Sex Pistols utter obscenities on Bill Grundy's 'Today' programme. (3rd)

The UK Top 10 singles for the week ending December the 11th

1	Showaddywaddy	Under The Moon Of Love
2	Queen	Somebody To Love
3	Abba	Money Money Money
4	Chicago	If You Leave Me Now
5	E.L.O.	Livin' Thing
6	Leo Sayer	You Make Me Feel Like Dancing
7	Yvonne Elliman	Love Me
8	Johnny Mathis	When A Child Is Born
9	Dr. Hook	If Not You
10	Bonnie Tyler	Lost In France

The US Number One single: Rod Stewart – Tonight's The Night (Gonna Be Alright)
The US Number One album: Stevie Wonder – Songs In The Key Of Life
The UK Number One album: Glen Campbell – 20 Golden Greats
Also this week: Mairead Corrigan and Betty Williams are awarded Nobel Peace Prizes. (10th)

The UK Top 10 singles for the week ending December the 18th

1	Showaddywaddy	Under The Moon Of Love
2	Johnny Mathis	When A Child Is Born
3	Queen	Somebody To Love
4	E.L.O.	Livin' Thing
5	Abba	Money Money Money
6	Yvonne Elliman	Love Me
7	Mud	Lean On Me
8	Chicago	If You Leave Me Now
9	Mike Oldfield	Portsmouth
10	Leo Sayer	You Make Me Feel Like Dancing

The US Number One single: Rod Stewart – Tonight's The Night (Gonna Be Alright)
The US Number One album: Stevie Wonder – Songs In The Key Of Life
The UK Number One album: Glen Campbell – 20 Golden Greats
Also this week: Ian Trethowan is appointed Director-General of the BBC. (17th)

The UK Top 10 singles for the week ending December the 25th

1	Johnny Mathis	When A Child Is Born
2	Showaddywaddy	Under The Moon Of Love
3	Abba	Money Money Money
4	Queen	Somebody To Love
5	Mike Oldfield	Portsmouth
6	E.L.O.	Livin' Thing
7	Yvonne Elliman	Love Me
8	Tina Charles	Dr. Love
9	Smokie	Living Next Door To Alice
10	Chris Hill	Bionic Santa

The US Number One single: Rod Stewart – Tonight's The Night (Gonna Be Alright)
The US Number One album: Stevie Wonder – Songs In The Key Of Life
The UK Number One album: Glen Campbell – 20 Golden Greats
Also this week: Takeo Fukudu is elected as Japan's Prime Minister. (24th)

The song of the month for December 1976
The Last Resort by The Eagles (album track)

This seven and a half minute epic brought the curtain down on the highly acclaimed 'Hotel California' long player. The song is a critique of the white man's colonisation of North America in the name of God. It is a powerful, thought-provoking grandiose recording which never seemed to acquire the recognition it has merited. Perhaps it has been overshadowed by the album's hit singles, but 'The Last Resort' is a giant album track.

Listed Below are the Top 10 Best Selling UK Singles of 1976

1   Save Your Kisses For Me   Brotherhood of Man
2   Don't Go Breaking My Heart   Elton John and Kiki Dee
3   Mississippi   Pussycat
4   Dancing Queen   Abba
5   A Little Bit More   Dr. Hook
6   If You Leave Me Now   Chicago
7   Fernando   Abba
8   I Love To Love   Tina Charles
9   The Roussos Phenonemon (EP)   Demis Roussos
10 Under The Moon Of Love   Showaddywaddy

1976's CONCERTS OF THE YEAR

The runaway train, otherwise known as the Sex Pistols, took off around England's green and pleasant land, as the 'Anarchy Tour' caused merry mayhem. The Lesser Free Trade Hall in Manchester was one such venue that enjoyed the peculiar pleasures of a Pistols' performance. From this happening began the great Manchester music scene that dominated the new wave and indie genres for the subsequent dozen years. Other punk acts such as the Clash and the Damned were treating the disenfranchised youth to their own particular rocky horror shows. Meanwhile, one slightly less punk outfit, the Brotherhood of Man, were triumphing at the Eurovision Song Contest with the twee 'Save Your Kisses For me'. The reclusive Brian Wilson also stepped out of his bedroom and joined the Beach Boys back on stage for the first time in several years as the group continued to entertain their fans with their 'sixties 'surfin' repertoire. Speaking of 'sixties legends, the Rolling Stones were strutting their stuff at the Knebworth summer festival. Out in the Carribbean, Bob Marley made an astonishing appearance at the Smile Jamaica concert, a few hours after being shot in an assassination attempt at his home. It would be Marley's last outing in Jamaica for 16 months.

1976's ALBUM OF THE YEAR

Hotel California by The Eagles
(released in December;reached No.2 in the UK)

Side One:

1. Hotel California; 6:30
2. New Kid in Town; 5:03
3. Life in the Fast Lane; 4:46
4. Wasted Time; 4:55

Side Two:

1. Wasted Time (Reprise); 1:22
2. Victim of Love; 4:11
3. Pretty Maids All in a Row; 3:58
4. Try and Love Again; 5:10
5. The Last Resort; 7:28

The Eagles were the biggest success story to emerge from North America in the 'seventies. They were loosely described as a rock band, but their own brand of laid back, west coast 'rock' was considerably more accessible than heavy metal whilst their material refreshingly swerved the standard alpha male, macho posturing of the likes of the Rolling Stones and the Who. The group's creative peak was almost certainly 'Hotel California'. Whilst the record is best remembered for its trio of hit singles, 'Life In The Fast Lane', 'The New Kid In Town',and the epic title track, the rest of the long player is anything but 'album filler'. The band's sensitive side was much in evidence on such items as the majestic 'Wasted Time' and the beautiful 'Pretty Maids All In A Row'. 'Try And Love Again' is another impressive 'soft rock' composition, but pride of place must go to 'The Last Resort'. This concluding piece is surely one of the most under-rated tracks in the history of popular music. With such an armoury of quality songs, it is small wonder that 'Hotel California' thrived in the UK and US charts.

SPORT IN 1976

English Division One football champions: Liverpool; runners-up: Queen's Park Rangers

English FA Cup final: Southampton 1 Manchester United 0

English League Cup Final: Manchester City 2 Newcastle United 1

Scottish Premier Division football champions: Glasgow Rangers; runners-up: Glasgow Celtic

Scottish FA Cup final: Glasgow Rangers 3 Hearts 1

Scottish League Cup final: Glasgow Rangers 1 Glasgow Celtic 0

Irish League football champions: Crusaders; Irish Cup final: Carrick Rangers 2 Linfield 1

League Of Ireland football champions: Dundalk; cup winners: Bohemians

European Cup final: Bayern Munich 1 St Etienne 0

European Cup-Winners' Cup final: Anderlecht 4 West Ham United 2

UEFA Cup final: Liverpool beat Bruges 4–3 on aggregate

English county cricket champions: Middlesex

Five Nations' rugby union champions: Wales (the Grand Slam); runners-up: France

Formula One world drivers' champion: James Hunt (United Kingdom) in a McLaren car

Gaelic football All-Ireland champions: Dublin; runners-up: Kerry

British Open golf champion: Johnny Miller (at Royal Birkdale)

US Masters golf champion: Ray Floyd

US Open golf champion: Jerry Pate

USPGA golf champion: Dave Stockton

Rugby league Challenge Cup final: St Helens 20 Widnes 5

Wimbledon men's singles tennis final: B Borg beat I Nastase 6–4, 6–2, 9–7

Wimbledon ladies' singles tennis final: C Evert beat E Cawley 6–3, 4–6, 8–6

World snooker final: Ray Reardon (Wales) beat Alex Higgins (Northern Ireland) 27–16

The Aintree Grand National steeplechase winner: Rag Trade; price 14–1

The Epsom Derby winner: Empery; jockey – Lester Piggott; price 10–1

European Championship final: Czechoslovakia beat West Germany on penalties (2–2 after full time)

1976's DEATHS

January 5th: John Aloysius Costello (Irish ex-Taoiseach), aged 84

January 8th: Chou En-lai (Chinese statesman), aged 77

January 12th: Dame Agatha Christie (British author), aged 85

January 23rd: Paul Robeson (US singer), aged 77

February 22nd: Florence Glenda Ballard Chapman (US singer), aged 32

February 23rd: Laurence Stephen Lowry (British artist), aged 78

March 14th: Busby Berkeley (US choreographer), aged 80

March 19th: Paul Francis Kossoff (British musician), aged 25

March 24th: Field Marshal Montgomery (British soldier), aged 88

April 1st: Max Ernst (French artist), aged 84

April 5th: Howard Hughes (US tycoon), aged 70

April 25th: Sir Carol Reed (British film director), aged 69

April 26th: Sidney James (British actor), aged 62

May 26th: Dame Maggie Teyte (British soprano), aged 88

June 6th: John Paul Getty (US oil tycoon), aged 83

June 9th: Dame Agnes Sybil Thorndike (British actress), aged 93

June 25th: Johnny Mercer (US singer), aged 66

July 22nd: Sir Robert Wheeler (British archaeologist), aged 85

August 2nd: Fritz Lang (German film director), aged 85

August 4th: Baron Thomson of Fleet (British newspaper owner), aged 82

August 19th: Alastair George Bell Sim (British actor), aged 75

August 29th: Jimmy Reed (US musician), aged 50

September 9th: Mao Tse-tung (Chinese dictator), aged 82

September 21st: Sir William Alexander Roy Collins (British publisher), aged 76

October 14th: Dame Edith Evans (British actress), aged 88

October 22nd: Edward John Burra (British artist), aged 71

November 18th: Man Ray (US artist), aged 86

November 19th: Sir Basil Urwin Spence (British architect), aged 69

November 23rd: Andre Malraux (French author), aged 75

December 4th: Tommy Bolin (US musician), aged 25

December 4th: Edward Benjamin Britten (British composer), aged 63

The UK Top 10 singles for the week ending January the 1st

1	Johnny Mathis	When A Child Is Born
2	Showaddywaddy	Under The Moon Of Love
3	Abba	Money Money Money
4	Queen	Somebody To Love
5	Mike Oldfield	Portsmouth
6	E.L.O.	Livin' Thing
7	Yvonne Elliman	Love Me
8	Tina Charles	Dr. Love
9	Smokie	Living Next Door To Alice
10	Chris Hill	Bionic Santa

The US Number One single: Rod Stewart – Tonight's The Night (Gonna Be Alright)
The US Number One album: Stevie Wonder – Songs In The Key Of Life
The UK Number One album: Glen Campbell – 20 Golden Greats
Also this week: Winnie Mandela is released from prison in South Africa. (28th)

The UK Top 10 singles for the week ending January the 8th

1	Johnny Mathis	When A Child Is Born
2	Showaddywaddy	Under The Moon Of Love
3	Mike Oldfield	Portsmouth
4	Abba	Money Money Money
5	Smokie	Living Next Door To Alice
6	Queen	Somebody To Love
7	Tina Charles	Dr. Love
8	David Soul	Don't Give Up On Us
9	Paul Nicholas	Grandma's Party
10	Mud	Lean On Me

The US Number One single: Marilyn McCoo & Billy Davis Jr – You Don't Have To Be A Star
The US Number One album: Stevie Wonder – Songs In The Key Of Life
The UK Number One album: Queen – A Day At The Races
Also this week: Roy Jenkins resigns his parliamentary seat. (5th)

The UK Top 10 singles for the week ending January the 15th

1 David Soul   Don't Give Up On Us
2 Johnny Mathis   When A Child Is Born
3 Abba   Money Money Money
4 Showaddywaddy   Under The Moon Of Love
5 Barry Biggs   Sideshow
6 10cc   Things We Do For Love
7 Julie Covington   Don't Cry For Me Argentina
8 Tina Charles   Dr. Love
9 Mike Oldfield   Portsmouth
10 Smokie   Living Next Door To Alice

The US Number One single: Leo Sayer – You Make Me Feel Like Dancing
The US Number One album: The Eagles – Hotel California
The UK Number One album: Abba – Arrival
Also this week: Black September's Abu Daoud is released from custody in France. (12th)

The UK Top 10 singles for the week ending January the 22nd

1 David Soul   Don't Give Up On Us
2 Julie Covington   Don't Cry For Me Argentina
3 Barry Biggs   Sideshow
4 Tina Charles   Dr. Love
5 Stevie Wonder   I Wish
6 10cc   Things We Do For Love
7 Mike Oldfield   Portsmouth
8 Abba   Money Money Money
9 Status Quo   Wild Side Of Life
10 Smokie   Living Next Door To Alice

The US Number One single: Stevie Wonder – I Wish
The US Number One album: Wings – Wings Over America
The UK Number One album: Slim Whitman – Red River Valley
Also this week: Jimmy Carter is inaugurated as the new American President. (20th)

The UK Top 10 singles for the week ending January the 29th

1	David Soul	Don't Give Up On Us
2	Julie Covington	Don't Cry For Me Argentina
3	Barry Biggs	Sideshow
4	David Parton	Isn't She Lovely
5	Drifters	You're More Than A Number In My Little Red Book
6	Stevie Wonder	I Wish
7	10cc	Things We Do For Love
8	Boney M	Daddy Cool
9	Status Quo	Wild Side Of Life
10	Rose Royce	Car Wash

The US Number One single: Rose Royce – Car Wash

The US Number One album: Stevie Wonder – Songs In The Key Of Life

The UK Number One album: Slim Whitman – Red River Valley

Also this week: Seven IRA bombs explode in London's West End. (29th)

The song of the month for January 1977
Isn't She Lovely by David Parton (peak chart position: No.4)

Not to be confused with Dolly Parton, Mr. David Parton took hold of a Stevie Wonder composition and promptly escorted it into a lofty position in the British singles lists. Wonder had originally recorded the track for his highly acclaimed 1976 album 'Songs In The Key Of Life'. The item was written to celebrate the birth of his daughter, Aisha. Meanwhile David Parton (real name Des Parton) was enjoying his brief flirtation with fame, courtesy of this one-hit wonder. Having said that, he had previously written Sweet Sensation's 'Sad Sweet Dreamer'.

The UK Top 10 singles for the week ending February the 5th

1	David Soul	Don't Give Up On Us
2	Julie Covington	Don't Cry For Me Argentina
3	Barry Biggs	Sideshow
4	David Parton	Isn't She Lovely
5	Leo Sayer	When I Need You
6	Boney M	Daddy Cool
7	Drifters	You're More Than A Number In My Little Red Book
8	10cc	Things We Do For Love
9	Elvis Presley	Suspicion
10	Rose Royce	Car Wash

The US Number One single: Mary MacGregor – Torn Between Two Lovers
The US Number One album: The Eagles – Hotel California
The UK Number One album: Slim Whitman – Red River Valley
Also this week: Police discover an IRA bomb factory in Liverpool. (4th)

The UK Top 10 singles for the week ending February the 12th

1	Julie Covington	Don't Cry For Me Argentina
2	David Soul	Don't Give Up On Us
3	Leo Sayer	When I Need You
4	Barry Biggs	Sideshow
5	David Parton	Isn't She Lovely
6	Harold Melvin And The Blue Notes	Don't Leave Me This Way
7	Boney M	Daddy Cool
8	Moments	Jack In The Box
9	Rose Royce	Car Wash
10	Elvis Presley	Suspicion

The US Number One single: Mary MacGregor – Torn Between Two Lovers
The US Number One album: Barbra Streisand – A Star Is Born (OST)
The UK Number One album: Slim Whitman – Red River Valley
Also this week: The IRA Balcombe Street gang are imprisoned for life. (10th)

The UK Top 10 singles for the week ending February the 19th

1	Leo Sayer	When I Need You
2	Julie Covington	Don't Cry For Me Argentina
3	David Soul	Don't Give Up On Us
4	Barry Biggs	Sideshow
5	David Parton	Isn't She Lovely
6	Heatwave	Boogie Nights
7	Harold Melvin And The Blue Notes	Don't Leave Me This Way
8	Moments	Jack In The Box
9	Boney M	Daddy Cool
10	Elvis Presley	Suspicion

The US Number One single: Manfred Mann's Earth Band – Blinded By The Light
The US Number One album: Barbra Streisand – A Star Is Born (OST)
The UK Number One album: The Shadows – 20 Golden Greats
Also this week: British Foreign Secretary, Tony Crosland, suffers a massive stroke. (13th)

The UK Top 10 singles for the week ending February the 26th

1	Leo Sayer	When I Need You
2	Julie Covington	Don't Cry For Me Argentina
3	David Soul	Don't Give Up On Us
4	Heatwave	Boogie Nights
5	Harold Melvin And The Blue Notes	Don't Leave Me This Way
6	Manhattan Transfer	Chanson D'Amour
7	Moments	Jack In The Box
8	Brothers	Sing Me
9	Barry Biggs	Sideshow
10	Bryan Ferry	This Is Tomorrow

The US Number One single: Eagles – New Kid In Town
The US Number One album: Barbra Streisand – A Star Is Born (OST)
The UK Number One album: The Shadows – 20 Golden Greats
Also this week: Doctor David Owen succeeds the deceased Crosland as Foreign Secretary. (21st)

The song of the month for February 1977

Sound And Vision by David Bowie (peak chart position: No.3)

David Bowie made a welcome return to the UK Top Three, thanks to the repetitive, yet highly infectious 'Sound And Vision', which was a product of his 'Low' project. Bowie at this time had been laid low by substance abuse which had threatened to undermine his renowned creativity. Hence, the Thin White Duke found himself ensconced in Berlin, rather strung out and waiting for the gifts of sound and vision to return to his consciousness. They clearly did, judging by the popularity of this single, decorated by the guitar of Carlos Alomar.

The UK Top 10 singles for the week ending March the 5th

1   Leo Sayer — When I Need You
2   Heatwave — Boogie Nights
3   Manhattan Transfer — Chanson D'Amour
4   Mr. Big — Romeo
5   Julie Covington — Don't Cry For Me Argentina
6   David Soul — Don't Give Up On Us
7   Harold Melvin And The Blue Notes — Don't Leave Me This Way
8   Brothers — Sing Me
9   Moments — Jack In The Box
10 Boz Scaggs — What Can I Say

The US Number One single: Barbra Streisand – Evergreen (Love Theme From A Star Is Born)
The US Number One album: Barbra Streisand – A Star Is Born (OST)
The UK Number One album: The Shadows – 20 Golden Greats
Also this week: Hundreds are feared dead in a massive earthquake in Rumania. (4th)

The UK Top 10 singles for the week ending March the 12th

1	Manhattan Transfer	Chanson D'Amour
2	Leo Sayer	When I Need You
3	Heatwave	Boogie Nights
4	Mary MacGregor	Torn Between Two Lovers
5	Mr. Big	Romeo
6	David Bowie	Sound And Vision
7	Abba	Knowing Me Knowing You
8	Julie Covington	Don't Cry For Me Argentina
9	Bryan Ferry	This Is Tomorrow
10	Harold Melvin And The Blue Notes	Don't Leave Me This Way

The US Number One single: Barbra Streisand – Evergreen (Love Theme From A Star Is Born)
The US Number One album: Barbra Streisand – A Star Is Born (OST)
The UK Number One album: The Shadows – 20 Golden Greats
Also this week: Ali Bhutto wins the parliamentary elections in Pakistan. (7th)

The UK Top 10 singles for the week ending March the 19th

1	Manhattan Transfer	Chanson D'Amour
2	Abba	Knowing Me Knowing You
3	Heatwave	Boogie Nights
4	Mr. Big	Romeo
5	David Bowie	Sound And Vision
6	Showaddywaddy	When
7	Leo Sayer	When I Need You
8	Mary MacGregor	Torn Between Two Lovers
9	E.L.O	Rockaria
10	Rubettes	Baby I Know

The US Number One single: Barbra Streisand – Evergreen (Love Theme From A Star Is Born)
The US Number One album: Barbra Streisand – A Star Is Born (OST)
The UK Number One album: The Shadows – 20 Golden Greats
Also this week: Australia narrowly defeat England in the Centenary test in Melbourne. (17th)

The UK Top 10 singles for the week ending March the 26th

1 Manhattan Transfer — Chanson D'Amour
2 Abba — Knowing Me Knowing You
3 David Bowie — Sound And Vision
4 Showaddywaddy — When
5 David Soul — Going In With My Eyes Open
6 Mary MacGregor — Torn Between Two Lovers
7 Heatwave — Boogie Nights
8 Elvis Presley — Moody Blue
9 Mr. Big — Romeo
10 E.L.O. — Rockaria

The US Number One single: Daryl Hall And John Oates – Rich Girl
The US Number One album: Eagles – Hotel California
The UK Number One album: The Shadows – 20 Golden Greats
Also this week: Mrs Gandhi is emphatically beaten in the Indian general election. (22nd)

The song of the month for March 1977
Nightclubbing by Iggy Pop (album track)

Iggy Pop was yet another artist to benefit from the assistance of David Bowie. The artist formerly known as Ziggy Stardust took on the role of producer for Iggy Pop's album, 'The Idiot', which was released in March 1977. The wacky Mr.Pop proved himself no idiot with the cool yet delightfully sleazy 'Nightclubbing' recording. The item would later be used in the opening sequence of the film 'D.O.A.' which recounted the Sex Pistols' ill-fated tour of North America. Iggy and Bowie were very much a mutual appreciation society and the latter would later cover the former's 'China Girl' with considerable success in 1983 as well as produce his next long player, 'Lust For Life'.

The UK Top 10 singles for the week ending April the 2nd

1 Abba — Knowing Me Knowing You
2 David Soul — Going In With My Eyes Open
3 Manhattan Transfer — Chanson D'Amour
4 Showaddywaddy — When
5 David Bowie — Sound And Vision
6 Elvis Presley — Moody Blue
7 Boney M — Sunny
8 Berni Flint — I Don't Want To Put A Hold On You
9 Mary MacGregor — Torn Between Two Lovers
10 Heatwave — Boogie Nights

The US Number One single: Daryl Hall And John Oates – Rich Girl
The US Number One album: Fleetwood Mac – Rumours
The UK Number One album: Frank Sinatra – Portrait Of Sinatra
Also this week: An airport runway disaster in the Canary Islands kills 574. (27th)

The UK Top 10 singles for the week ending April the 9th

1 Abba — Knowing Me Knowing You
2 David Soul — Going In With My Eyes Open
3 Showaddywaddy — When
4 David Bowie — Sound And Vision
5 Manhattan Transfer — Chanson D'Amour
6 Berni Flint — I Don't Want To Put A Hold On You
7 Elvis Presley — Moody Blue
8 Billy Ocean — Red Light Spells Danger
9 Boney M — Sunny
10 Brotherhood Of Man — Oh Boy

The US Number One single: Abba – Dancing Queen
The US Number One album: Fleetwood Mac – Rumours
The UK Number One album: Frank Sinatra – Portrait Of Sinatra
Also this week: Zaire breaks off diplomatic relations with Cuba. (4th)

The UK Top 10 singles for the week ending April the 16th

1 Abba — Knowing Me Knowing You
2 David Soul — Going In With My Eyes Open
3 Boney M — Sunny
4 Showaddywaddy — When
5 Berni Flint — I Don't Want To Put A Hold On You
6 Billy Ocean — Red Light Spells Danger
7 Elvis Presley — Moody Blue
8 Brotherhood Of Man — Oh Boy
9 David Bowie — Sound And Vision
10 Marilyn McCoo & Billy Davis Jr — You Don't Have To Be A Star

The US Number One single: David Soul – Don't Give Up On Us
The US Number One album: The Eagles – Hotel California
The UK Number One album: Abba – Arrival
Also this week: Foreign Secretary David Owen has talks with Rhodesia's Ian Smith. (14th)

The UK Top 10 singles for the week ending April the 23rd

1 Abba — Knowing Me Knowing You
2 Billy Ocean — Red Light Spells Danger
3 Berni Flint — I Don't Want To Put A Hold On You
4 Deniece Williams — Free
5 David Soul — Going In With My Eyes Open
6 Showaddywaddy — When
7 Dead End Kids — Have I The Right
8 Boney M — Sunny
9 Stevie Wonder — Sir Duke
10 Marilyn McCoo & Billy Davis Jr — You Don't Have To Be A Star

The US Number One single: Thelma Houston – Don't Leave Me This Way
The US Number One album: The Eagles – Hotel California
The UK Number One album: Abba – Arrival
Also this week: Shimon Peres succeeds Yitzhak Rabin as Israel's Prime Minister. (22nd)

The UK Top 10 singles for the week ending April the 30th

1 Abba   Knowing Me Knowing You
2 Billy Ocean   Red Light Spells Danger
3 Deniece Williams   Free
4 Stevie Wonder   Sir Duke
5 Berni Flint   I Don't Want To Put A Hold On You
6 Dead End Kids   Have I The Right
7 Marilyn McCoo & Billy Davis Jr   You Don't Have To Be A Star
8 David Soul   Going In With My Eyes Open
9 Elkie Brooks   Pearl's A Singer
10 Boney M   Sunny

The US Number One single: Glen Campbell – Southern Nights
The US Number One album: The Eagles – Hotel California
The UK Number One album: Abba – Arrival
Also this week: British Aerospace is established. (29th)

The song of the month for April 1977
Police And Thieves by The Clash (album track)

Whenever the Sex Pistols kicked down the door of rock and pop, their fellow west London punk rockers, the Clash were among the first to rush in. This formidable foursome were acknowledged as arguably the most talented of the new wave of working class three minute heroes. Their first album surfaced in April 1977, having been recorded with much haste and little expense. The frantic material with an anti-capitalist agenda contained a decent reggae cover version of Junior Murvin's 'Police And Thieves', sang by the late Joe Strummer.

The UK Top 10 singles for the week ending May the 7th

1	Deniece Williams	Free
2	Stevie Wonder	Sir Duke
3	Billy Ocean	Red Light Spells Danger
4	Rod Stewart	I Don't Want To Talk About It/
		First Cut Is The Deepest
5	Tavares	Whodunit
6	Dead End Kids	Have I The Right
7	Abba	Knowing Me Knowing You
8	Elkie Brooks	Pearl's A Singer
9	Berni Flint	I Don't Want To Put A Hold On You
10	Leo Sayer	How Much Love

The US Number One single: The Eagles – Hotel California
The US Number One album: The Eagles – Hotel California
The UK Number One album: Abba – Arrival
Also this week: A loyalist general strike takes place in Northern Ireland. (2nd)

The UK Top 10 singles for the week ending May the 14th

1	Deniece Williams	Free
2	Rod Stewart	I Don't Want To Talk About It/
		First Cut Is The Deepest
3	Stevie Wonder	Sir Duke
4	Joe Tex	Ain't Gonna Bump No More
5	Tavares	Whodunit
6	Van McCoy	The Shuffle
7	Dead End Kids	Have I The Right
8	Eagles	Hotel California
9	10cc	Good Morning Judge
10	Elkie Brooks	Pearl's A Singer

The US Number One single: Leo Sayer – When I Need You
The US Number One album: The Eagles – Hotel California
The UK Number One album: Abba – Arrival
Also this week: Patty Hearst is released from prison on five years' probation. (9th)

The UK Top 10 singles for the week ending May the 21st

1	Rod Stewart	I Don't Want To Talk About It/
		First Cut Is The Deepest
2	Deniece Williams	Free
3	Joe Tex	Ain't Gonna Bump No More
4	Van McCoy	The Shuffle
5	Kenny Rogers	Lucille
6	Barbra Streisand	Evergreen
7	Tavares	Whodunit
8	Stevie Wonder	Sir Duke
9	Eagles	Hotel California
10	10cc	Good Morning Judge

The US Number One single: Stevie Wonder – Sir Duke
The US Number One album: Fleetwood Mac – Rumours
The UK Number One album: Abba – Arrival
Also this week: Menachem Begin's Likud Party wins the Israeli general election. (18th)

The UK Top 10 singles for the week ending May the 28th

1	Rod Stewart	I Don't Want To Talk About It/
		First Cut Is The Deepest
2	Joe Tex	Ain't Gonna Bump No More
3	Barbra Streisand	Evergreen
4	Kenny Rogers	Lucille
5	10cc	Good Morning Judge
6	Van McCoy	The Shuffle
7	Deniece Williams	Free
8	Piero Umiliani	Mah Na Mah Na
9	Marvin Gaye	Got To Give It Up
10	Eagles	Hotel California

The US Number One single: Stevie Wonder – Sir Duke
The US Number One album: Fleetwood Mac – Rumours
The UK Number One album: Abba – Arrival
Also this week: Pierre and Margaret Trudeau announce their formal separation. (27th)

The song of the month for May 1977

Peaches by The Stranglers (peak chart position: No.8)

The Stranglers were another new wave act that were able to successfully cash in on the punk explosion. They were denounced by that nice Johnny Rotten as "short-haired hippies", but the Stranglers found favour with the teenage punk audience when their single 'Peaches' ventured into the British Top Ten. Hugh Cornwell and the gang had a sound that was reminiscent of the Doors and they were able to enjoy chart success much longer than their peers and contemporaries. The quirky 'Peaches' was responsible for laying such foundations.

The UK Top 10 singles for the week ending June the 4th

1	Rod Stewart	I Don't Want To Talk About It/ First Cut Is The Deepest
2	Kenny Rogers	Lucille
3	Joe Tex	Ain't Gonna Bump No More
4	Barbra Streisand	Evergreen
5	Van McCoy	The Shuffle
6	10cc	Good Morning Judge
7	Marvin Gaye	Got To Give It Up
8	Muppets	Halfway Down The Stairs
9	Piero Umiliani	Mah Na Mah Na
10	Rock Follies	O.K.

The US Number One single: Stevie Wonder – Sir Duke
The US Number One album: Fleetwood Mac – Rumours
The UK Number One album: Abba – Arrival
Also this week: Jubilant Scottish soccer fans help themselves to the Wembley turf. (4th)

The UK Top 10 singles for the week ending June the 11th

1	Rod Stewart	I Don't Want To Talk About It/ First Cut Is The Deepest
2	Sex Pistols	God Save The Queen
3	Kenny Rogers	Lucille
4	Barbra Streisand	Evergreen
5	Joe Tex	Ain't Gonna Bump No More
6	Jacksons	Show You The Way To Go
7	Carole Bayer Sager	You're Moving Out Today
8	Van McCoy	The Shuffle
9	10cc	Good Morning Judge
10	Muppets	Halfway Down The Stairs

The US Number One single: KC And The Sunshine Band – I'm Your Boogie Man
The US Number One album: Fleetwood Mac – Rumours
The UK Number One album: Abba – Arrival
Also this week: Martin Luther King's killer, James Earl Ray, escapes from prison. (10th)

The UK Top 10 singles for the week ending June the 18th

1	Kenny Rogers	Lucille
2	Rod Stewart	I Don't Want To Talk About It/ First Cut Is The Deepest
3	Jacksons	Show You The Way To Go
4	Sex Pistols	God Save The Queen
5	Barbra Streisand	Evergreen
6	Carole Bayer Sager	You're Moving Out Today
7	Muppets	Halfway Down The Stairs
8	E.L.O.	Telephone Line
9	Joe Tex	Ain't Gonna Bump No More
10	Van McCoy	The Shuffle

The US Number One single: Fleetwood Mac – Dreams
The US Number One album: Fleetwood Mac – Rumours
The UK Number One album: The Beatles – The Beatles Live At The Hollywood Bowl
Also this week: Jack Lynch's Fianna Fail win the Irish general election. (17th)

The UK Top 10 singles for the week ending June the 25th

1	Jacksons	Show You The Way To Go
2	Kenny Rogers	Lucille
3	Hot Chocolate	So You Win Again
4	Barbra Streisand	Evergreen
5	Rod Stewart	I Don't Want To Talk About It/ First Cut Is The Deepest
6	Carole Bayer Sager	You're Moving Out Today
7	Gladys Knight & The Pips	Baby Don't Change Your Mind
8	Emerson Lake And Palmer	Fanfare For The Common Man
9	Sex Pistols	God Save The Queen
10	E.L.O.	Telephone Line

The US Number One single: Marvin Gaye – Got To Give It Up

The US Number One album: Fleetwood Mac – Rumours

The UK Number One album: The Muppets – The Muppet Show

Also this week: Violence escalates between pickets and police at the Grunwick strike. (20th)

The song of the month for June 1977

God Save The Queen by The Sex Pistols (peak chart position: No.2)

The mischievous Malcolm McLaren always had a nose for publicity and he jumped at the opportunity to seize upon the Silver Jubilee of Queen Elizabeth II to issue what would be regarded as the most controversial single to hit the airwaves. Johnny Rotten had originally intended for this raucous composition to be entitled 'No Future' (a summation of his view of life in Britain for the disenfranchised youth), but he acquiesced in the change of song title. This recording did have a future in the hit parade though it is commonly believed that it was denied a place at Number One in a deliberate attempt to spare her Royal Lowness (or "moron") any embarrassment.

The UK Top 10 singles for the week ending July the 2nd

1	Hot Chocolate	So You Win Again
2	Jacksons	Show You The Way To Go
3	Emerson Lake And Palmer	Fanfare For The Common Man
4	Kenny Rogers	Lucille
5	Gladys Knight & The Pips	Baby Don't Change Your Mind
6	Carole Bayer Sager	You're Moving Out Today
7	Barbra Streisand	Evergreen
8	E.L.O.	Telephone Line
9	Olivia Newton-John	Sam
10	Stranglers	Peaches

The US Number One single: Bill Conti – Gonna Fly Now (Theme From Rocky)
The US Number One album: Fleetwood Mac – Rumours
The UK Number One album: Barbra Streisand – A Star Is Born (OST)
Also this week: Djibouti, France's last African colony, becomes independent. (26th)

The UK Top 10 singles for the week ending July the 9th

1	Hot Chocolate	So You Win Again
2	Jacksons	Show You The Way To Go
3	Emerson Lake And Palmer	Fanfare For The Common Man
4	Gladys Knight & The Pips	Baby Don't Change Your Mind
5	Boney M	Ma Baker
6	Olivia Newton-John	Sam
7	Kenny Rogers	Lucille
8	Stranglers	Peaches
9	Carole Bayer Sager	You're Moving Out Today
10	Barbra Streisand	Evergreen

The US Number One single: Alan O'Day – Undercover Angel
The US Number One album: Fleetwood Mac – Rumours
The UK Number One album: Barbra Streisand – A Star Is Born (OST)
Also this week: General Zia deposes Ali Bhutto who is also arrested. (5th)

The UK Top 10 singles for the week ending July the 16th

1 Hot Chocolate   So You Win Again
2 Emerson Lake And Palmer   Fanfare For The Common Man
3 Donna Summer   I Feel Love
4 Boney M   Ma Baker
5 Gladys Knight & The Pips   Baby Don't Change Your Mind
6 Jacksons   Show You The Way To Go
7 Sex Pistols   Pretty Vacant
8 Olivia Newton-John   Sam
9 Stranglers   Peaches
10 Brotherhood Of Man   Angelo

The US Number One single: Shaun Cassidy – Da Doo Ron Ron
The US Number One album: Barry Manilow – Barry Manilow Live
The UK Number One album: Johnny Mathis – The Johnny Mathis Collection
Also this week: England trounce Australia in an Ashes test at Old Trafford. (12th)

The UK Top 10 singles for the week ending July the 23rd

1 Donna Summer   I Feel Love
2 Hot Chocolate   So You Win Again
3 Boney M   Ma Baker
4 Emerson Lake And Palmer   Fanfare For The Common Man
5 Brotherhood Of Man   Angelo
6 Gladys Knight & The Pips   Baby Don't Change Your Mind
7 Sex Pistols   Pretty Vacant
8 Olivia Newton-John   Sam
9 Alessi   Oh Lori
10 John Miles   Slow Down

The US Number One single: Barry Manilow – Looks Like We Made It
The US Number One album: Fleetwood Mac – Rumours
The UK Number One album: Johnny Mathis – The Johnny Mathis Collection
Also this week: Mrs Bandaranaike loses the Sri Lankan general election. (21st)

The UK Top 10 singles for the week ending July the 30th

1	Donna Summer	I Feel Love
2	Boney M	Ma Baker
3	Emerson Lake And Palmer	Fanfare For The Common Man
4	Brotherhood Of Man	Angelo
5	Hot Chocolate	So You Win Again
6	Sex Pistols	Pretty Vacant
7	Gladys Knight & The Pips	Baby Don't Change Your Mind
8	Alessi	Oh Lori
9	Rita Coolidge	We're All Alone
10	Commodores	Easy

The US Number One single: Andy Gibb – I Just Want To Be Your Everything
The US Number One album: Fleetwood Mac – Rumours
The UK Number One album: Johnny Mathis – The Johnny Mathis Collection
Also this week: The Spanish democratic government requests to join the EEC. (28th)

The song of the month for July 1977

I Feel Love by Donna Summer (peak chart position: No.1)

The disco genre was now fighting off the challenge of punk rock for the attentions of the teenage pop market. However, one new release soon towered over all its competitors when Donna Summer finally sailed to the top of the British singles list with the dancefloor favourite, 'I Feel Love'. This smash hit showcased the synthesizer sound as Giorgio Moroder supervised the creation of this modern pop classic. Summer's semi-orgasmic vocals are a key component in an item which must be a candidate for the best chart-topper of the decade.

The UK Top 10 singles for the week ending August the 6th

1	Donna Summer	I Feel Love
2	Brotherhood Of Man	Angelo
3	Boney M	Ma Baker
4	Hot Chocolate	So You Win Again
5	Emerson Lake And Palmer	Fanfare For The Common Man
6	Rita Coolidge	We're All Alone
7	Smokie	It's Your Life
8	Sex Pistols	Pretty Vacant
9	Showaddywaddy	You Got What It Takes
10	Alessi	Oh Lori

The US Number One single: Andy Gibb – I Just Want To Be Your Everything
The US Number One album: Fleetwood Mac – Rumours
The UK Number One album: Johnny Mathis – The Johnny Mathis Collection
Also this week: Kerry Packer takes the English cricket authorities to court. (3rd)

The UK Top 10 singles for the week ending August the 13th

1	Donna Summer	I Feel Love
2	Brotherhood Of Man	Angelo
3	Showaddywaddy	You Got What It Takes
4	Floaters	Float On
5	Boney M	Ma Baker
6	Rita Coolidge	We're All Alone
7	Rah Band	The Crunch
8	Emerson Lake And Palmer	Fanfare For The Common Man
9	Commodores	Easy
10	Smokie	It's Your Life

The US Number One single: Andy Gibb – I Just Want To Be Your Everything
The US Number One album: Fleetwood Mac – Rumours
The UK Number One album: Yes – Going For The One
Also this week: Geoff Boycott hits 191 against Australia at Headingley. (12th)

The UK Top 10 singles for the week ending August the 20th

1	Brotherhood Of Man	Angelo
2	Showaddywaddy	You Got What It Takes
3	Donna Summer	I Feel Love
4	Floaters	Float On
5	Smokie	It's Your Life
6	Rah Band	The Crunch
7	Boney M	Ma Baker
8	Rita Coolidge	We're All Alone
9	Stranglers	Something Better Change
10	Deniece Williams	That's What Friends Are For

The US Number One single: The Emotions – Best Of My Love
The US Number One album: Fleetwood Mac – Rumours
The UK Number One album: Yes – Going For The One
Also this week: England reclaim the Ashes after an innings victory in Leeds. (15th)

The UK Top 10 singles for the week ending August the 27th

1	Floaters	Float On
2	Brotherhood Of Man	Angelo
3	Showaddywaddy	You Got What It Takes
4	Elvis Presley	Way Down
5	Donna Summer	I Feel Love
6	Rah Band	The Crunch
7	Rita Coolidge	We're All Alone
8	Deniece Williams	That's What Friends Are For
9	Candi Staton	Nights On Broadway
10	Carly Simon	Nobody Does It Better

The US Number One single: The Emotions – Best Of My Love
The US Number One album: Fleetwood Mac – Rumours
The UK Number One album: Connie Francis – 20 All Time Greats
Also this week: New smaller one pound notes are introduced in Britain. (23rd)

The song of the month for August 1977

Nobody Does It Better by Carly Simon (peak chart position: No.7)

American songbird, Carly Simon, had previously tasted chart-topping success in the United States with the excellent 'You're So Vain'. She eventually stepped forth with another commendable single when 'Nobody Does It Better' journeyed into the UK Top Ten in the late summer of 1977. This release was the signature tune for the latest James Bond movie, 'The Spy Who Loved Me' (starring Roger Moore and Barbara Bach). Carly Simon was not a regular visitor to the hit parade but when she did appear, the song was worth writing about.

The UK Top 10 singles for the week ending September the 3rd

1	Elvis Presley	Way Down
2	Floaters	Float On
3	Brotherhood Of Man	Angelo
4	Showaddywaddy	You Got What It Takes
5	Space	Magic Fly
6	Candi Staton	Nights On Broadway
7	Rah Band	The Crunch
8	Deniece Williams	That's What Friends Are For
9	Carly Simon	Nobody Does It Better
10	David Soul	Silver Lady

The US Number One single: The Emotions – Best Of My Love
The US Number One album: Fleetwood Mac – Rumours
The UK Number One album: Connie Francis – 20 All Time Greats
Also this week: Britain's inflation rate falls to eleven per cent. (2nd)

The UK Top 10 singles for the week ending September the 10th

1 Elvis Presley   Way Down
2 Space   Magic Fly
3 Floaters   Float On
4 Jean Michel Jarre   Oxygene Part 4
5 Donna Summer   Down Deep Inside
6 Brotherhood Of Man   Angelo
7 Candi Staton   Nights On Broadway
8 David Soul   Silver Lady
9 Deniece Williams   That's What Friends Are For
10 Carly Simon   Nobody Does It Better

The US Number One single: The Emotions – Best Of My Love
The US Number One album: Fleetwood Mac – Rumours
The UK Number One album: Elvis Presley – Elvis Presley's 40 Greatest Hits
Also this week: An agreement decides the future of the Panama Canal. (6th)

The UK Top 10 singles for the week ending September the 17th

1 Elvis Presley   Way Down
2 Space   Magic Fly
3 David Soul   Silver Lady
4 Jean Michel Jarre   Oxygene Part 4
5 Donna Summer   Down Deep Inside
6 Floaters   Float On
7 Carly Simon   Nobody Does It Better
8 Candi Staton   Nights On Broadway
9 Brotherhood Of Man   Angelo
10 Meri Wilson   Telephone Man

The US Number One single: Andy Gibb – I Just Want To Be Your Everything
The US Number One album: Fleetwood Mac – Rumours
The UK Number One album: Diana Ross & The Supremes – 20 Golden Greats
Also this week: Many students assemble in South Africa to mourn Steve Biko. (15th)

The UK Top 10 singles for the week ending September the 24th

1	Elvis Presley	Way Down
2	Space	Magic Fly
3	David Soul	Silver Lady
4	Jean Michel Jarre	Oxygene Part 4
5	Donna Summer	Down Deep Inside
6	Meri Wilson	Telephone Man
7	Carly Simon	Nobody Does It Better
8	Emotions	Best Of My Love
9	Eddie And The Hot Rods	Do Anything You Wanna Do
10	Deniece Williams	That's What Friends Are For

The US Number One single: The Emotions – Best Of My Love

The US Number One album: Fleetwood Mac – Rumours

The UK Number One album: Diana Ross & The Supremes – 20 Golden Greats

Also this week: Roman Polanski is imprisoned for under-age sex. (19th)

The song of the month for September 1977

Yes Sir I Can Boogie by Baccara (peak chart position: No.1)

Baccara scored another notable success for disco music with the hugely likeable 'Yes Sir I Can Boogie'. The artists in question hailed from Spain and were a female duo called Mayte Mateos and Maria Mendiola. This eye-catching pair eventually evicted David Soul from the British chart summit in late October, but their triumph proved to be short-lived and they failed to find anything to match this smash hit, although their follow-up single, 'Sorry I'm A Lady' did sneak into the UK Top Ten in early 1978.

The UK Top 10 singles for the week ending October the 1st

1	Elvis Presley	Way Down
2	David Soul	Silver Lady
3	Space	Magic Fly
4	Jean Michel Jarre	Oxygene Part 4
5	Donna Summer	Down Deep Inside
6	Meri Wilson	Telephone Man
7	Emotions	Best Of My Love
8	La Belle Epoque	Black Is Black
9	Patsy Gallant	From New York To LA
10	Elkie Brooks	Sunshine After The Rain

The US Number One single: Meco – Star Wars Theme/Cantina Band
The US Number One album: Fleetwood Mac – Rumours
The UK Number One album: Diana Ross & The Supremes – 20 Golden Greats
Also this week: Freddie Laker's first Skytrain flies from Gatwick to New York. (26th)

The UK Top 10 singles for the week ending October the 8th

1	David Soul	Silver Lady
2	Elvis Presley	Way Down
3	La Belle Epoque	Black Is Black
4	Emotions	Best Of My Love
5	Space	Magic Fly
6	Patsy Gallant	From New York To LA
7	Yes	Wondrous Stories
8	Danny Mirror	I Remember Elvis Presley
9	Meri Wilson	Telephone Man
10	Donna Summer	Down Deep Inside

The US Number One single: Meco – Star Wars Theme/Cantina Band
The US Number One album: Fleetwood Mac – Rumours
The UK Number One album: Diana Ross & The Supremes – 20 Golden Greats
Also this week: Many British undertakers go on strike. (8th)

The UK Top 10 singles for the week ending October the 15th

1 David Soul   Silver Lady
2 La Belle Epoque   Black Is Black
3 Baccara   Yes Sir I Can Boogie
4 Danny Mirror   I Remember Elvis Presley
5 Emotions   Best Of My Love
6 Elvis Presley   Way Down
7 Rod Stewart   You're In My Heart
8 Patsy Gallant   From New York To LA
9 Stranglers   No More Heroes
10 Meri Wilson   Telephone Man

The US Number One single: Debby Boone – You Light Up My Life
The US Number One album: Fleetwood Mac – Rumours
The UK Number One album: Diana Ross & The Supremes – 20 Golden Greats
Also this week: George Best plays his last match for Northern Ireland. (12th)

The UK Top 10 singles for the week ending October the 22nd

1 David Soul   Silver Lady
2 La Belle Epoque   Black Is Black
3 Baccara   Yes Sir I Can Boogie
4 Rod Stewart   You're In My Heart
5 Danny Mirror   I Remember Elvis Presley
6 Emotions   Best Of My Love
7 Meco   Star Wars Theme
8 Stranglers   No More Heroes
9 Ram Jam   Black Betty
10 Elvis Presley   Way Down

The US Number One single: Debby Boone – You Light Up My Life
The US Number One album: Fleetwood Mac – Rumours
The UK Number One album: Diana Ross & The Supremes – 20 Golden Greats
Also this week: Hostages are rescued after Palestinians hijack an aeroplane in Somalia. (18th)

The UK Top 10 singles for the week ending October the 29th

1	Baccara	Yes Sir I Can Boogie
2	La Belle Epoque	Black Is Black
3	Rod Stewart	You're In My Heart
4	David Soul	Silver Lady
5	Abba	Name Of The Game
6	Status Quo	Rockin' All Over The World
7	Ram Jam	Black Betty
8	Sex Pistols	Holidays In The Sun
9	Danny Mirror	I Remember Elvis Presley
10	Meco	Star Wars Theme

The US Number One single: Debby Boone – You Light Up My Life
The US Number One album: Fleetwood Mac – Rumours
The UK Number One album: Diana Ross & The Supremes – 20 Golden Greats
Also this week: Jeremy Thorpe denies having an affair with Norman Scott. (27th)

The song of the month for October 1977

You Make Loving Fun by Fleetwood Mac (peak chart position: No.45)

Singer-songwriter and keyboardist Christine McVie was responsible for arguably the best track of 1977, yet when 'You Make Loving Fun' was issued as a single in the autumn of this year, it failed to make a splash in the UK. McVie's soft rock masterpiece features a fine guitar contribution from Lindsey Buckingham as Christine pays tribute to a current boyfriend. The harmonies are of the highest quality, as indeed is the magnificent rhythm. Why this release did not achieve more airplay and subsequent sales is beyond all understanding.

The UK Top 10 singles for the week ending November the 5th

1	Abba	Name Of The Game
2	Baccara	Yes Sir I Can Boogie
3	Rod Stewart	You're In My Heart
4	La Belle Epoque	Black Is Black
5	Status Quo	Rockin' All Over The World
6	Queen	We Are The Champions / We Will Rock You
7	David Soul	Silver Lady
8	Tom Robinson Band	2–4–6–8 Motorway
9	Sex Pistols	Holidays In The Sun
10	Carpenters	Calling Occupants Of Interplanetary Craft

The US Number One single: Debby Boone – You Light Up My Life
The US Number One album: Fleetwood Mac – Rumours
The UK Number One album: Cliff Richard & The Shadows – 40 Golden Greats
Also this week: The United Nations bans arms sales to South Africa. (4th)

The UK Top 10 singles for the week ending November the 12th

1	Abba	Name Of The Game
2	Baccara	Yes Sir I Can Boogie
3	Rod Stewart	You're In My Heart
4	Status Quo	Rockin' All Over The World
5	Tom Robinson Band	2–4–6–8 Motorway
6	Queen	We Are The Champions / We Will Rock You
7	La Belle Epoque	Black Is Black
8	Ram Jam	Black Betty
9	Carpenters	Calling Occupants Of Interplanetary Craft
10	Smokie	Needles And Pins

The US Number One single: Debby Boone – You Light Up My Life
The US Number One album: Fleetwood Mac – Rumours
The UK Number One album: The Sex Pistols – Never Mind The Bollocks, Here's
The Sex Pistols
Also this week: Ingrid Schubert, from the Baader-Meinhof gang, kills herself. (12th)

The UK Top 10 singles for the week ending November the 19th

1	Abba	Name Of The Game
2	Queen	We Are The Champions/We Will Rock You
3	Status Quo	Rockin' All Over The World
4	Baccara	Yes Sir I Can Boogie
5	Tom Robinson	2–4–6–8 Motorway
6	Rod Stewart	You're In My Heart
7	Barron Knights	Live In Trouble
8	Showaddywaddy	Dancin' Party
9	Bee Gees	How Deep Is Your Love
10	Carpenters	Calling Occupants Of Interplanetary Craft

The US Number One single: Debby Boone – You Light Up My Life

The US Number One album: Fleetwood Mac – Rumours

The UK Number One album: The Sex Pistols – Never Mind The Bollocks, Here's The Sex Pistols

Also this week: Anwar Sadat becomes the first Arab leader to visit Israel. (18th)

The UK Top 10 singles for the week ending November the 26th

1	Abba	Name Of The Game
2	Queen	We Are The Champions/We Will Rock You
3	Status Quo	Rockin' All Over The World
4	Showaddywaddy	Dancin' Party
5	Wings	Mull Of Kintyre/Girls' School
6	Bee Gees	How Deep Is Your Love
7	Darts	Daddy Cool
8	Tom Robinson	2–4–6–8 Motorway
9	Baccara	Yes Sir I Can Boogie
10	Barron Knights	Live In Trouble

The US Number One single: Debby Boone – You Light Up My Life

The US Number One album: Fleetwood Mac – Rumours

The UK Number One album: Bread – The Sound Of Bread

Also this week: A High Court decrees that Packer's cricketers cannot be banned. (25th)

The song of the month for November 1977

White Punks On Dope by The Tubes (peak chart position: No.28)

This remarkably eccentric recording is described as a punk song, by virtue of the word punk in the title, but quite frankly this gem of a single simply occupies its very own planet. The Tubes sing of poor little Californian rich kids desperately in search of street credibility, and if the fusion of guitars and piano seldom works better than here, the social comment lyrics are equally worthy of note, with such pearls as "Sounds real classy living in a chateau/ So lonely all the other kids will never know." This is one of pop music's finest five minutes.

The UK Top 10 singles for the week ending December the 3rd

1	Wings	Mull Of Kintyre/Girls' School
2	Queen	We Are The Champions/We Will Rock You
3	Status Quo	Rockin' All Over The World
4	Abba	Name Of The Game
5	Bee Gees	How Deep Is Your Love
6	Showaddywaddy	Dancin' Party
7	Darts	Daddy Cool
8	Ruby Winters	I Will
9	Brighouse And Rastrick Brass Band	The Floral Dance
10	Barron Knights	Live In Trouble

The US Number One single: Debby Boone – You Light Up My Life
The US Number One album: Linda Ronstadt – Simple Dreams
The UK Number One album: Bread – The Sound Of Bread
Also this week: Menachem Begin pays a visit to Britain. (2nd)

The UK Top 10 singles for the week ending December the 10th

1	Wings	Mull Of Kintyre/Girls' School
2	Brighouse And Rastrick Brass Band	The Floral Dance
3	Bee Gees	How Deep Is Your Love
4	Showaddywaddy	Dancin' Party
5	Ruby Winters	I Will
6	Darts	Daddy Cool
7	Queen	We Are The Champions/We Will Rock You
8	Status Quo	Rockin' All Over The World
9	Jonathan Richman	Egyptian Reggae
10	Boney M	Belfast

The US Number One single: Debby Boone – You Light Up My Life
The US Number One album: Linda Ronstadt – Simple Dreams
The UK Number One album: Various Artist Compilation – Disco Fever
Also this week: Amnesty International is awarded the Nobel Peace Prize. (10th)

The UK Top 10 singles for the week ending December the 17th

1	Wings	Mull Of Kintyre/Girls' School
2	Brighouse And Rastrick Brass Band	The Floral Dance
3	Bee Gees	How Deep Is Your Love
4	Ruby Winters	I Will
5	Jonathan Richman	Egyptian Reggae
6	Darts	Daddy Cool
7	Showaddywaddy	Dancin' Party
8	Boney M	Belfast
9	Dooleys	Love Of My Life
10	Queen	We Are The Champions/We Will Rock You

The US Number One single: Debby Boone – You Light Up My Life
The US Number One album: Linda Ronstadt – Simple Dreams
The UK Number One album: Various Artist Compilation – Disco Fever
Also this week: Menachem Begin has talks in Washington with President Carter. (16th)

The UK Top 10 singles for the week ending December the 24th

1	Wings	Mull Of Kintyre/Girls' School
2	Brighouse And Rastrick Brass Band	The Floral Dance
3	Bee Gees	How Deep Is Your Love
4	Ruby Winters	I Will
5	Bing Crosby	White Christmas
6	Donna Summer	Love's Unkind
7	Bonnie Tyler	It's A Heartache
8	Darts	Daddy Cool
9	Jonathan Richman	Egyptian Reggae
10	Hot Chocolate	Put Your Love In Me

The US Number One single: Bee Gees – How Deep Is Your Love
The US Number One album: Linda Ronstadt – Simple Dreams
The UK Number One album: Various Artist Compilation – Disco Fever
Also this week: The Trades Union Congress approves the government's wages policy. (21st)

The UK Top 10 singles for the week ending December the 31st

1	Wings	Mull Of Kintyre/Girls' School
2	Brighouse And Rastrick Brass Band	The Floral Dance
3	Bee Gees	How Deep Is Your Love
4	Ruby Winters	I Will
5	Bing Crosby	White Christmas
6	Donna Summer	Love's Unkind
7	Bonnie Tyler	It's A Heartache
8	Darts	Daddy Cool
9	Jonathan Richman	Egyptian Reggae
10	Hot Chocolate	Put Your Love In Me

The US Number One single: Bee Gees – How Deep Is Your Love
The US Number One album: Linda Ronstadt – Simple Dreams
The UK Number One album: Various Artist Compilation – Disco Fever
Also this week: President Carter offers to negotiate an Arab-Israeli peace pact. (30th)

The song of the month for December 1977

Jamming by Bob Marley And The Wailers
(peak chart position: No.9)

Bob Marley had been a regular on the Caribbean music scene since the mid-sixties but he eventually began to conquer Babylon when the 'Exodus' album enjoyed critical acclaim and decent record sales in 1977. One of the tracks from the album would yield Marley his first British Top Ten single when 'Jamming' coupled with 'Punky Reggae Party' was released towards the end of the year. Although this third item to be issued as a single from 'Exodus' has its merits, it is a bit peculiar that it proved more popular than its predecessor, 'Waiting In Vain', which seemed more likely chart material. Anyhow, British audiences were now beginning to warm to the charming Robert Nesta.

Listed Below are the Top 10 Best Selling UK Singles of 1977

1	Mull of Kintyre	Wings
2	Don't Give Up On Us	David Soul
3	Don't Cry For Me Argentina	Julie Covington
4	When I Need You	Leo Sayer
5	Silver Lady	David Soul
6	Knowing Me Knowing You	Abba
7	I Feel Love	Donna Summer
8	Way Down	Elvis Presley
9	So You Win Again	Hot Chocolate
10	Angelo	Brotherhood of Man

1977's CONCERTS OF THE YEAR

Now firmly established as Public Enemy Number One, the loveable Sex Pistols found their concert ambitions curtailed by numerous local councils who all got stage fright at the prospect of entertaining the fearsome foursome in their town centres. This didn't stop the likes of the Clash, Joy Division, and the Stranglers acting as punk missionaries, bringing their anthems of doomed youth to youngsters throughout the UK. Speaking of missionaries, Bob Marley was back in London town, enchanting the assembled masses at the Rainbow Theatre in Finsbury Park. Marley and his Wailers were displaying new tracks from the aptly-titled 'Exodus' album, including 'Jamming' and an awesome rendition of 'The Heathen'. On the subject of jamming heathen, Led Zeppelin were conquering the United States for an eleventh time. A record-breaking seventy-six thousand attended their treat at the Pontiac Silverdome on the 30th of April; yet three months later their performance at Oakland would prove to be their last on American soil, as personal tragedies took centre stage instead. Back in London, the River Thames was the unlikely host of the decade's most peculiar public performance, when those oh so patriotic Pistols performed their very own 'God Save The Queen' to commemorate the Silver Jubilee of her Royal Lowness.

1977's ALBUM OF THE YEAR

Rumours by Fleetwood Mac

(released in February; reached No.1 in the UK)

Side One:

1. Second Hand News; 2:43
2. Dreams; 4:14
3. Never Going Back Again; 2:14
4. Don't Stop; 3:11
5. Go Your Own Way; 3:38
6. Songbird; 3:20

Side Two:

1. The Chain; 4:28
2. You Make Loving Fun; 3:31
3. I Don't Want to Know; 3:11
4. Oh Daddy; 3:54
5. Gold Dust Woman; 4:51

By the mid-seventies Fleetwood Mac had become more renowned for changes in personnel than for their music. However, the recruitment of Lindsey Buckingham and his partner, Stevie Nicks, transformed the fortunes of the group. The new Anglo-American quintet made an impressive start with their first album together in 1975, but it was the follow-up, 'Rumours', which launched the band into the superstardom stratosphere. Ironically, the new project (or at least some of its material) was a product of emotional strife amongst the five protagonists. Amongst other things, the love affairs between Christine and John McVie, and between Buckingham and Nicks came to an end, as the behind-the-scenes 'proceedings' resembled a soap opera. For all the apparent tension, the music was of the highest quality. 'Go Your Own Way' is the obvious example of the angst that circulated both inside and outside the recording studio. Nevertheless, with such foundations as the under-rated guitar work of Lindsey, the splendid vocals and songwriting of Christine and Stevie, underpinned by the tried and trusted rhythm section of John and Mick, the recipe for a tremendously durable commercial success was in existence. That said, it is almost inconceivable that the resulting long player should sit in the UK album charts for the best part of the ensuing decade! There again, just listen to 'Dreams', 'The Chain', 'Songbird', and 'Gold Dust Woman', and suddenly the record's phenomenal triumph makes perfect sense.

SPORT IN 1977

English Division One football champions: Liverpool; runners-up: Manchester City

English FA Cup final: Manchester United 2 Liverpool 1

English League Cup Final: Aston Villa 3 Everton 2 (after extra time, in a replay)

Scottish Premier Division football champions: Glasgow Celtic; runners-up: Glasgow Rangers

Scottish FA Cup final: Glasgow Celtic 1 Glasgow Rangers 0

Scottish League Cup final: Aberdeen 2 Glasgow Celtic 1

Irish League football champions: Glentoran; Irish Cup final: Coleraine 4 Linfield 1

League Of Ireland football champions: Sligo Rovers; cup winners: Dundalk

European Cup final: Liverpool 3 Borussia Moenchengladbach 1

European Cup-Winners' Cup final: Hamburg 2 Anderlecht 0

UEFA Cup final: Juventus beat Athletico Bilbao on away goals rule (2–2 on aggregate)

English county cricket champions: Kent shared with Middlesex

Five Nations' rugby union champions: France (the Grand Slam); runners-up: Wales

Formula One world drivers' champion: Niki Lauda (Austria) in a Ferrari car

Gaelic football All-Ireland champions: Dublin; runners-up: Armagh

British Open golf champion: Tom Watson (at Turnberry)

US Masters golf champion: Tom Watson

US Open golf champion: Hubert Green

USPGA golf champion: Lanny Wadkins

Rugby league Challenge Cup final: Leeds 16 Widnes 7

Wimbledon men's singles tennis final: B Borg beat J Connors 3–6, 6–2, 6–1, 5–7, 6–4

Wimbledon ladies' singles tennis final: V Wade beat B Stove 4–6, 6–3, 6–1

World snooker final: John Spencer (England) beat Cliff Thorburn (Canada) 25–21

The Aintree Grand National steeplechase winner: Red Rum; price 9–1

The Epsom Derby winner: The Minstrel; jockey – Lester Piggott; price 5–1

The Ryder Cup golf contest: Great Britain And Ireland 7.5 United States 12.5

1977's DEATHS

January 14th: Robert Anthony Eden (ex-British Prime Minister), aged 79

January 14th: Peter Finch (British actor), aged 60

January 14th: Anais Nin (US author), aged 69

January 17th: Gary Gilmore (US murderer), aged 36

February 19th: Charles Anthony Raven Crosland (British Foreign Secretary), aged 58

March 20th: Peter Houseman (British footballer), aged 31

April 11th: Jacques Prevert (French poet), aged 77

May 10th: Joan Crawford (US actress), aged 69

June 3rd: Roberto Rossellini (Italian film director), aged 71

June 16th: Wernher von Braun (German scientist), aged 65

July 2nd: Vladimir Nabokov (Russian writer), aged 78

August 3rd: Archbishop Makarios (Cypriot President), aged 63

August 16th: Elvis Aaron Presley (US singer), aged 42

August 19th: Julius 'Groucho' Marx (US actor), aged 86

September 4th: Ernst Friedrich Schumacher (German economist), aged 65

September 12th: Steve Biko (South African political activist), aged 30

September 13th: Leopold Stokowski (British conductor), aged 95

September 16th: Marc Bolan (British musician), aged 29

September 16th: Maria Callas (Greek soprano), aged 53

October 14th: Harry 'Bing' Crosby (US actor), aged 73

October 20th: Ronnie Van Zant (US musician), aged 29

November 18th: Kurt von Schuschnigg (ex-Austrian Chancellor), aged 79

November 30th: Sir Terence Mervyn Rattigan (British playwright), aged 66

December 12th: Clementine Ogilvy Spencer Churchill (Winston Churchill's wife), aged 92

December 25th: Sir Charles Spencer Chaplin (British actor), aged 88

The UK Top 10 singles for the week ending January the 7th

1	Wings	Mull Of Kintyre/Girls' School
2	Brighouse And Rastrick Brass Band	The Floral Dance
3	Bee Gees	How Deep Is Your Love
4	Donna Summer	Love's Unkind
5	Ruby Winters	I Will
6	Bonnie Tyler	It's A Heartache
7	Darts	Daddy Cool
8	Crystal Gayle	Don't It Make My Brown Eyes Blue
9	Elvis Presley	My Way
10	Chic	Dance Dance Dance

The US Number One single: Bee Gees – How Deep Is Your Love

The US Number One album: Fleetwood Mac – Rumours

The UK Number One album: Various Artist Compilation – Disco Fever

Also this week: Mrs Gandhi is expelled from the Indian Congress Party. (3rd)

The UK Top 10 singles for the week ending January the 14th

1	Wings	Mull Of Kintyre/Girls' School
2	Brighouse And Rastrick Brass Band	The Floral Dance
3	Donna Summer	Love's Unkind
4	Bonnie Tyler	It's A Heartache
5	Crystal Gayle	Don't It Make My Brown Eyes Blue
6	Chic	Dance Dance Dance
7	Bee Gees	How Deep Is Your Love
8	David Soul	Let's Have A Quiet Night In
9	Ruby Winters	I Will
10	Donna Summer	I Love You

The US Number One single: Player – Baby Come Back

The US Number One album: Fleetwood Mac – Rumours

The UK Number One album: Various Artist Compilation – Disco Fever

Also this week: Anti-Shah protests occur in the Iranian city of Qom. (9th)

The UK Top 10 singles for the week ending January the 21st

1	Wings	Mull Of Kintyre/Girls' School
2	Althea And Donna	Uptown Top Ranking
3	Donna Summer	Love's Unkind
4	Bonnie Tyler	It's A Heartache
5	Brighouse And Rastrick Brass Band	The Floral Dance
6	Crystal Gayle	Don't It Make My Brown Eyes Blue
7	Bee Gees	How Deep Is Your Love
8	Odyssey	Native New Yorker
9	Chic	Dance Dance Dance
10	David Soul	Let's Have A Quiet Night In

The US Number One single: Player – Baby Come Back
The US Number One album: Original Soundtrack – Saturday Night Fever
The UK Number One album: Bread – The Sound Of Bread
Also this week: Geoff Boycott captains England's test team for the first time. (18th)

The UK Top 10 singles for the week ending January the 28th

1	Wings	Mull Of Kintyre/Girls' School
2	Althea And Donna	Uptown Top Ranking
3	Donna Summer	Love's Unkind
4	Brotherhood Of Man	Figaro
5	Odyssey	Native New Yorker
6	Bonnie Tyler	It's A Heartache
7	Crystal Gayle	Don't It Make My Brown Eyes Blue
8	Bill Withers	Lovely Day
9	Chic	Dance Dance Dance
10	Scott Fitzgerald & Yvonne Keeley	If I Had Words

The US Number One single: Player – Baby Come Back
The US Number One album: Original Soundtrack – Saturday Night Fever
The UK Number One album: Fleetwood Mac – Rumours
Also this week: Fighting resumes between Ethiopia and Somalia in the Ogaden Desert. (23rd)

The song of the month for January 1978

Mr Blue Sky by E.L.O. (peak chart position: No.6)

Here is another giant of a song which belongs in any 'best of the 'seventies' collections. The track had formed part of the segment of items entitled 'Concerto For A Rainy Day' which featured on E.L.O.'s album, 'Out Of The Blue'. 'Mr Blue Sky' was the perfect embodiment of E.L.O.'s desire to fuse rock music with input from the more classical source of an orchestra. Such a formula had been flirted with since Sergeant Pepper, though I question whether any of the contents of Pepper stand comparison with this five-minute wonder.

The UK Top 10 singles for the week ending February the 4th

1	Althea And Donna	Uptown Top Ranking
2	Wings	Mull Of Kintyre/Girls' School
3	Brotherhood Of Man	Figaro
4	Scott Fitzgerald & Yvonne Keeley	If I Had Words
5	Odyssey	Native New Yorker
6	Donna Summer	Love's Unkind
7	Bill Withers	Lovely Day
8	Bonnie Tyler	It's A Heartache
9	Bob Marley & The Wailers	Jamming/Punky Reggae Party
10	Abba	Take A Chance On Me

The US Number One single: Bee Gees – Stayin' Alive
The US Number One album: Original Soundtrack – Saturday Night Fever
The UK Number One album: Abba – The Album
Also this week: Anwar Sadat arrives in Washington for talks. (3rd)

The UK Top 10 singles for the week ending February the 11st

1 Brotherhood Of Man — Figaro
2 Abba — Take A Chance On Me
3 Althea And Donna — Uptown Top Ranking
4 Scott Fitzgerald & Yvonne Keeley — If I Had Words
5 Wings — Mull Of Kintyre/Girls' School
6 Odyssey — Native New Yorker
7 Bill Withers — Lovely Day
8 Baccara — Sorry I'm A Lady
9 Donna Summer — Love's Unkind
10 Bob Marley & The Wailers — Jamming/Punky Reggae Party

The US Number One single: Bee Gees – Stayin' Alive
The US Number One album: Original Soundtrack – Saturday Night Fever
The UK Number One album: Abba – The Album
Also this week: A state of emergency is declared in Somalia. (9th)

The UK Top 10 singles for the week ending February the 18th

1 Abba — Take A Chance On Me
2 Brotherhood Of Man — Figaro
3 Scott Fitzgerald & Yvonne Keeley — If I Had Words
4 Darts — Come Back My Love
5 Rod Stewart — Hot Legs/I Was Only Joking
6 Rose Royce — Wishing On A Star
7 Althea And Donna — Uptown Top Ranking
8 E.L.O. — Mr Blue Sky
9 Sweet — Love Is Like Oxygen
10 Baccara — Sorry I'm A Lady

The US Number One single: Bee Gees – Stayin' Alive
The US Number One album: Original Soundtrack – Saturday Night Fever
The UK Number One album: Abba – The Album
Also this week: A bomb at Belfast's La Mon hotel kills fourteen people. (17th)

The UK Top 10 singles for the week ending February the 25th

1	Abba	Take A Chance On Me
2	Brotherhood Of Man	Figaro
3	Darts	Come Back My Love
4	Rose Royce	Wishing On A Star
5	Scott Fitzgerald & Yvonne Keeley	If I Had Words
6	E.L.O.	Mr Blue Sky
7	Rod Stewart	Hot Legs/I Was Only Joking
8	Baccara	Sorry I'm A Lady
9	Yellow Dog	Just One More Night
10	Sweet	Love Is Like Oxygen

The US Number One single: Bee Gees – Stayin' Alive
The US Number One album: Original Soundtrack – Saturday Night Fever
The UK Number One album: Abba – The Album
Also this week: South-west England suffers its worst blizzards in years. (20th)

The song of the month for February 1978
Baker Street by Gerry Rafferty (peak chart position: No.3)

Did the 1970s produce a better recording than this epic? Come to think of it, has any decade done so? Gerry Rafferty's album 'City To City' largely owes its success to the appeal of this issued track. The saxophone contribution is truly unforgettable while the guitar outro is also a musical treat as Rafferty narrates the plight of a drifter who never seems to settle down, still chasing elusive dreams. The subject matter is poignant and a lofty position on the UK and US charts was the very least that this extraordinary single deserved.

The UK Top 10 singles for the week ending March the 4th

1	Abba	Take A Chance On Me
2	Darts	Come Back My Love
3	Rose Royce	Wishing On A Star
4	Bee Gees	Stayin' Alive
5	Kate Bush	Wuthering Heights
6	Brotherhood Of Man	Figaro
7	E.L.O.	Mr Blue Sky
8	Yellow Dog	Just One More Night
9	Sweet	Love Is Like Oxygen
10	Scott Fitzgerald & Yvonne Keeley	If I Had Words

The US Number One single: Andy Gibb – (Love Is) Thicker Than Water
The US Number One album: Original Soundtrack – Saturday Night Fever
The UK Number One album: Abba – The Album
Also this week: Ian Smith signs an agreement to end Rhodesia's minority rule. (3rd)

The UK Top 10 singles for the week ending March the 11th

1	Kate Bush	Wuthering Heights
2	Abba	Take A Chance On Me
3	Darts	Come Back My Love
4	Rose Royce	Wishing On A Star
5	Blondie	Denis
6	Bee Gees	Stayin' Alive
7	Eruption	I Can't Stand The Rain
8	Gerry Rafferty	Baker Street
9	E.L.O.	Mr Blue Sky
10	Yellow Dog	Just One More Night

The US Number One single: Andy Gibb – (Love Is) Thicker Than Water
The US Number One album: Original Soundtrack – Saturday Night Fever
The UK Number One album: Abba – The Album
Also this week: Arab terrorists murder 37 Israelis in a bus ambush. (11th)

The UK Top 10 singles for the week ending March the 18th

1	Kate Bush	Wuthering Heights
2	Abba	Take A Chance On Me
3	Blondie	Denis
4	Darts	Come Back My Love
5	Rose Royce	Wishing On A Star
6	Gerry Rafferty	Baker Street
7	Eruption	I Can't Stand The Rain
8	Bee Gees	Stayin' Alive
9	E.L.O.	Mr Blue Sky
10	Brian And Michael	Matchstalk Men And Matchstalk Cats And Dogs

The US Number One single: Bee Gees – Night Fever
The US Number One album: Original Soundtrack – Saturday Night Fever
The UK Number One album: Abba – The Album
Also this week: Ali Bhutto, Pakistan's deposed Prime Minister, is sentenced to death. (18th)

The UK Top 10 singles for the week ending March the 25th

1	Kate Bush	Wuthering Heights
2	Blondie	Denis
3	Brian And Michael	Matchstalk Men And Matchstalk Cats And Dogs
4	Gerry Rafferty	Baker Street
5	Eruption	I Can't Stand The Rain
6	Rose Royce	Wishing On A Star
7	Darts	Come Back My Love
8	Abba	Take A Chance On Me
9	Bee Gees	Stayin' Alive
10	Nick Lowe	I Love The Sound Of Breaking Glass

The US Number One single: Bee Gees – Night Fever
The US Number One album: Original Soundtrack – Saturday Night Fever
The UK Number One album: Buddy Holly & The Crickets – 20 Golden Greats
Also this week: Rhodesia's first three black ministers are sworn in. (21st)

The song of the month for March 1978

Rhiannon by Fleetwood Mac (peak chart position: No.46)

When Mick Fleetwood invited Lindsey Buckingham the opportunity to become Fleetwood Mac's latest guitar hero, Stevie Nicks was not part of the deal. However, Buckingham insisted that she be recruited too, as he and she were a package, both musically and romantically. Buckingham's faith in the female singer was vindicated by her majestic composition, 'Rhiannon', which was a highlight of the group's 'debut album' in 1975. However, when it was issued as a single in early 1978 it shockingly failed to make much impact in the UK.

The UK Top 10 singles for the week ending April the 1st

1	Kate Bush	Wuthering Heights
2	Blondie	Denis
3	Gerry Rafferty	Baker Street
4	Brian And Michael	Matchstalk Men And Matchstalk Cats And Dogs
5	Eruption	I Can't Stand The Rain
6	Andy Cameron	Ally's Tartan Army
7	Nick Lowe	I Love The Sound Of Breaking Glass
8	Darts	Come Back My Love
9	Bob Marley And The Wailers	Is This Love?
10	Suzi Quatro	If You Can't Give Me Love

The US Number One single: Bee Gees – Night Fever

The US Number One album: Original Soundtrack – Saturday Night Fever

The UK Number One album: Buddy Holly & The Crickets – 20 Golden Greats

Also this week: United Nations peace-keeping troops occupy Lebanon. (28th)

The UK Top 10 singles for the week ending April the 8th

1 Brian And Michael   Matchstalk Men And Matchstalk Cats And Dogs
2 Blondie   Denis
3 Kate Bush   Wuthering Heights
4 Gerry Rafferty   Baker Street
5 Showaddywaddy   I Wonder Why
6 Suzi Quatro   If You Can't Give Me Love
7 Eruption   I Can't Stand The Rain
8 Genesis   Follow You Follow Me
9 Andy Cameron   Ally's Tartan Army
10 Nick Lowe   I Love The Sound Of Breaking Glass

The US Number One single: Bee Gees – Night Fever
The US Number One album: Original Soundtrack – Saturday Night Fever
The UK Number One album: Buddy Holly & The Crickets – 20 Golden Greats
Also this week: Jimmy Carter decides to postpone production of the neutron bomb. (7th)

The UK Top 10 singles for the week ending April the 15th

1 Brian And Michael   Matchstalk Men And Matchstalk Cats And Dogs
2 Showaddywaddy   I Wonder Why
3 Gerry Rafferty   Baker Street
4 Suzi Quatro   If You Can't Give Me Love
5 Blondie   Denis
6 Andrew Gold   Never Let Her Slip Away
7 Genesis   Follow You Follow Me
8 Kate Bush   Wuthering Heights
9 Wings   With A Little Luck
10 Johnny Mathis And
   Deniece Williams   Too Much, Too Little, Too Late

The US Number One single: Bee Gees – Night Fever
The US Number One album: Original Soundtrack – Saturday Night Fever
The UK Number One album: Nat 'King' Cole – 20 Golden Greats
Also this week: Dozens die when two trains collide between Bologna and Florence. (15th)

The UK Top 10 singles for the week ending April the 22nd

1 Brian And Michael	Matchstalk Men And Matchstalk Cats And Dogs
2 Bee Gees	Night Fever
3 Showaddywaddy	I Wonder Why
4 Suzi Quatro	If You Can't Give Me Love
5 Wings	With A Little Luck
6 Andrew Gold	Never Let Her Slip Away
7 Johnny Mathis And Deniece Williams	Too Much, Too Little, Too Late
8 Gerry Rafferty	Baker Street
9 Genesis	Follow You Follow Me
10 Blondie	Denis

The US Number One single: Bee Gees – Night Fever
The US Number One album: Original Soundtrack – Saturday Night Fever
The UK Number One album: Nat 'King' Cole – 20 Golden Greats
Also this week: The Senate approves the Carter-Torrijos treaty on Panama's future. (18th)

The UK Top 10 singles for the week ending April the 29th

1 Bee Gees	Night Fever
2 Brian And Michael	Matchstalk Men And Matchstalk Cats And Dogs
3 Showaddywaddy	I Wonder Why
4 Suzi Quatro	If You Can't Give Me Love
5 Johnny Mathis And Deniece Williams	Too Much, Too Little, Too Late
6 Andrew Gold	Never Let Her Slip Away
7 Genesis	Follow You Follow Me
8 Wings	With A Little Luck
9 Gerry Rafferty	Baker Street
10 The Michael Zager Band	Let's All Chant

The US Number One single: Bee Gees – Night Fever
The US Number One album: Original Soundtrack – Saturday Night Fever
The UK Number One album: Nat 'King' Cole – 20 Golden Greats
Also this week: 'Upstairs Downstairs' wins top American television award, the Peabody. (24th)

The song of the month for April 1978

Night Fever by The Bee Gees (peak chart position: No.1)

The dancefloor was the happening place to be in the spring of 1978 as the popularity of the 'Saturday Night Fever' film prompted folk to put on their dancing shoes and get dizzy. The song which was most inspirational was the Bee Gees' 'Night Fever'. With the aid of a delicious strings accompaniment, this item took the American charts by storm, as it dwelt at Number One for a mere 8 weeks. British music lovers were equally appreciative as they stuck this 45 on their record players and started gyrating around their living room floors.

The UK Top 10 singles for the week ending May the 6th

1	Bee Gees	Night Fever
2	Boney M	Rivers Of Babylon
3	Brian And Michael	Matchstalk Men And Matchstalk Cats And Dogs
4	Johnny Mathis And Deniece Williams	Too Much, Too Little, Too Late
5	Andrew Gold	Never Let Her Slip Away
6	Dee D. Jackson	Automatic Lover
7	Showaddywaddy	I Wonder Why
8	Suzi Quatro	If You Can't Give Me Love
9	Wings	With A Little Luck
10	The Michael Zager Band	Let's All Chant

The US Number One single: Bee Gees – Night Fever
The US Number One album: Original Soundtrack – Saturday Night Fever
The UK Number One album: Original Soundtrack – Saturday Night Fever
Also this week: Menachem Begin arrives in Washington for talks with President Carter. (30th)

The UK Top 10 singles for the week ending May the 13th

1	Boney M	Rivers Of Babylon
2	Bee Gees	Night Fever
3	Johnny Mathis And Deniece Williams	Too Much, Too Little, Too Late
4	Dee D. Jackson	Automatic Lover
5	Andrew Gold	Never Let Her Slip Away
6	Brian And Michael	Matchstalk Men And Matchstalk Cats And Dogs
7	Patti Smith	Because The Night
8	The Michael Zager Band	Let's All Chant
9	Chic	Everybody Dance
10	Darts	Boy From New York City

The US Number One single: Yvonne Elliman – If I Can't Have You

The US Number One album: Original Soundtrack – Saturday Night Fever

The UK Number One album: Original Soundtrack – Saturday Night Fever

Also this week: Demonstrators march through Tehran, shouting "Down with the Shah." (11th)

The UK Top 10 singles for the week ending May the 20th

1	Boney M	Rivers Of Babylon
2	Bee Gees	Night Fever
3	Darts	Boy From New York City
4	Johnny Mathis And Deniece Williams	Too Much, Too Little, Too Late
5	Dee D. Jackson	Automatic Lover
6	Patti Smith	Because The Night
7	Andrew Gold	Never Let Her Slip Away
8	John Paul Young	Love Is In The Air
9	The Michael Zager Band	Let's All Chant
10	Yvonne Elliman	If I Can't Have You

The US Number One single: Wings – With A Little Luck

The US Number One album: Original Soundtrack – Saturday Night Fever

The UK Number One album: Original Soundtrack – Saturday Night Fever

Also this week: Three terrorists are shot dead at Orly airport, near Paris. (20th)

The UK Top 10 singles for the week ending May the 27th

1	Boney M	Rivers Of Babylon
2	Bee Gees	Night Fever
3	Darts	Boy From New York City
4	Yvonne Elliman	If I Can't Have You
5	Patti Smith	Because The Night
6	Johnny Mathis And Deniece Williams	Too Much, Too Little, Too Late
7	Tavares	More Than A Woamn
8	John Paul Young	Love Is In The Air
9	Raffaella	Do It Again
10	Blondie	(I'm Always Touched By Your) Presence Dear

The US Number One single: Wings – With A Little Luck
The US Number One album: Original Soundtrack – Saturday Night Fever
The UK Number One album: Original Soundtrack – Saturday Night Fever
Also this week: Trudeau announces that Canada will end its nuclear weapons capability. (26th)

The song of the month for May 1978

You're The One That I Want by John Travolta & Olivia Newton-John (peak chart position: No.1)

With the phenomenal box office success of both 'Saturday Night Fever' and 'Grease', John Travolta was the flavour of the month. He reaped the rewards of his popularity when this duet with Australian chanteuse Olivia Newton-John resided at the top perch of the British singles list for a staggering nine weeks, emulating both Queen and Wings who had enjoyed similar supremacy in recent years. This offering from 'Grease' clearly struck a chord with the teenage market, enabling it to become the second biggest-selling UK single of 1978.

The UK Top 10 singles for the week ending June the 3rd

1	Boney M	Rivers Of Babylon
2	Darts	Boy From New York City
3	Bee Gees	Night Fever
4	Yvonne Elliman	If I Can't Have You
5	John Paul Young	Love Is In The Air
6	John Travolta & Olivia Newton-John	You're The One That I Want
7	Patti Smith	Because The Night
8	Tavares	More Than A Woman
9	Ian Dury And The Blockheads	What A Waste
10	Plastic Bertrand	Ca Plane Pour Moi

The US Number One single: Johnny Mathis & Deniece Williams – Too Much, Too Little, Too Late

The US Number One album: Original Soundtrack – Saturday Night Fever

The UK Number One album: Original Soundtrack – Saturday Night Fever

Also this week: Former Liberal leader, Jeremy Thorpe, is interviewed by detectives. (3rd)

The UK Top 10 singles for the week ending June the 10th

1	Boney M	Rivers Of Babylon
2	John Travolta & Olivia Newton-John	You're The One That I Want
3	Darts	Boy From New York City
4	Rod Stewart	Ole Ola
5	Yvonne Elliman	If I Can't Have You
6	Bee Gees	Night Fever
7	Tavares	More Than A Woman
8	John Paul Young	Love Is In The Air
9	Patti Smith	Because The Night
10	Plastic Bertrand	Ca Plane Pour Moi

The US Number One single: John Travolta & Olivia Newton-John – You're The One That I Want

The US Number One album: Original Soundtrack – Saturday Night Fever

The UK Number One album: Original Soundtrack – Saturday Night Fever

Also this week: Scotland draw 1–1 with Iran in the World Cup. (7th)

The UK Top 10 singles for the week ending June the 17th

1 John Travolta & Olivia Newton-John   You're The One That I Want
2 Boney M   Rivers Of Babylon
3 Rolling Stones   Miss You
4 Darts   Boy From New York City
5 Smokie   Oh Carol
6 Manfred Mann's Earth Band   Davy's On The Road Again
7 James Galway   Annie's Song
8 Yvonne Elliman   If I Can't Have You
9 Plastic Bertrand   Ca Plane Pour Moi
10 Father Abraham And The Smurfs   The Smurfs

The US Number One single: Andy Gibb – Shadow Dancing
The US Number One album: Original Soundtrack – Saturday Night Fever
The UK Number One album: Original Soundtrack – Saturday Night Fever
Also this week: Scotland defeat Holland 3–2 in the World Cup finals. (11th)

The UK Top 10 singles for the week ending June the 24th

1 John Travolta & Olivia Newton-John   You're The One That I Want
2 Father Abraham And The Smurfs   The Smurf Song
3 Boney M   Rivers Of Babylon
4 Rolling Stones   Miss You
5 James Galway   Annie's Song
6 Manfred Mann's Earth Band   Davy's On The Road Again
7 Goldie   Making Up Again
8 Plastic Bertrand   Ca Plane Pour Moi
9 Darts   Boy From New York City
10 Smokie   Oh Carol

The US Number One single: Andy Gibb – Shadow Dancing
The US Number One album: Original Soundtrack – Saturday Night Fever
The UK Number One album: Original Soundtrack – Saturday Night Fever
Also this week: 29 Italian Red Brigade terrorists are sentenced to prison. (23rd)

The song of the month for June 1978

The Man With The Child In His Eyes by Kate Bush
(peak chart position: No.6)

Kate Bush had no intention of living off the acclaim that poured forth from her debut smash hit, 'Wuthering Heights'. She advanced into the British Top Ten once more with the fascinating 'The Man With The Child In His Eyes'. This enchanting yet slightly disturbing piece was another commercial for the highly original talent that was Kate Bush. By the end of the year she would have no fewer than two impressive albums in the public domain. The only drawback for the teenage wonder was her failure to impact upon the USA.

The UK Top 10 singles for the week ending July the 1st

1	John Travolta & Olivia Newton-John	You're The One That I Want
2	Father Abraham And The Smurfs	The Smurf Song
3	James Galway	Annie's Song
4	Rolling Stones	Miss You
5	The Motors	Airport
6	Boney M	Rivers Of Babylon
7	Kate Bush	The Man With The Child In His Eyes
8	Marshall Hain	Dancing In The City
9	Manfred Mann's Earth Band	Davy's On The Road Again
10	Goldie	Making Up Again

The US Number One single: Andy Gibb – Shadow Dancing
The US Number One album: Original Soundtrack – Saturday Night Fever
The UK Number One album: Original Soundtrack – Saturday Night Fever
Also this week: Host nation Argentina beat Holland in the World Cup Final. (25th)

The UK Top 10 singles for the week ending July the 8th

1 John Travolta & Olivia Newton-John   You're The One That I Want
2 Father Abraham And The Smurfs   The Smurf Song
3 James Galway   Annie's Song
4 The Motors   Airport
5 Marshall Hain   Dancing In The City
6 Kate Bush   The Man With The Child In His Eyes
7 Rolling Stones   Miss You
8 Boomtown Rats   Like Clockwork
9 Goldie   Making Up Again
10 Boney M   Rivers Of Babylon

The US Number One single: Andy Gibb – Shadow Dancing
The US Number One album: Gerry Rafferty – City To City
The UK Number One album: Original Soundtrack – Saturday Night Fever
Also this week: Sandro Pertini is elected as Italy's first Socialist President. (8th)

The UK Top 10 singles for the week ending July the 15th

1 John Travolta & Olivia Newton-John   You're The One That I Want
2 Father Abraham And The Smurfs   The Smurf Song
3 Marshall Hain   Dancing In The City
4 James Galway   Annie's Song
5 The Motors   Airport
6 Boomtown Rats   Like Clockwork
7 Sex Pistols   No One Is Innocent/My Way
8 Showaddywaddy   A Little Bit Of Soap
9 Kate Bush   The Man With The Child In His Eyes
10 Rolling Stones   Miss You

The US Number One single: Andy Gibb – Shadow Dancing
The US Number One album: The Rolling Stones – Some Girls
The UK Number One album: Original Soundtrack – Saturday Night Fever
Also this week: An explosion at a Spanish campsite kills almost two hundred. (11th)

The UK Top 10 singles for the week ending July the 22nd

1 John Travolta & Olivia Newton-John   You're The One That I Want
2 Father Abraham And The Smurfs   The Smurf Song
3 Marshall Hain   Dancing In The City
4 Clout   Substitute
5 Showaddywaddy   A Little Bit Of Soap
6 Boomtown Rats   Like Clockwork
7 E.L.O.   Wild West Hero
8 The Motors   Airport
9 Kate Bush   The Man With The Child In His Eyes
10 A Taste Of Honey   Boogie Oogie Oogie

The US Number One single: Andy Gibb – Shadow Dancing
The US Number One album: The Rolling Stones – Some Girls
The UK Number One album: Original Soundtrack – Saturday Night Fever
Also this week: Nelson Mandela is denied access to his sixtieth birthday cards. (18th)

The UK Top 10 singles for the week ending July the 29th

1 John Travolta & Olivia Newton-John   You're The One That I Want
2 Father Abraham And The Smurfs   The Smurf Song
3 Clout   Substitute
4 Marshall Hain   Dancing In The City
5 A Taste Of Honey   Boogie Oogie Oogie
6 Boomtown Rats   Like Clockwork
7 Showaddywaddy   A Little Bit Of Soap
8 E.L.O.   Wild West Hero
9 The Motors   Airport
10 Lindisfarne   Run For Home

The US Number One single: Andy Gibb – Shadow Dancing
The US Number One album: Original Soundtrack – Grease
The UK Number One album: Original Soundtrack – Saturday Night Fever
Also this week: The world's first test-tube baby, Louise Brown, is born. (26th)

The song of the month for July 1978

No-One Is Innocent by The Sex Pistols (peak chart position: No.7)

When the charming Sex Pistols imploded back in January, Steve Jones and his best buddy Paul Cook flew south to Rio De Janeiro for a bizarre musical collaboration with the escaped great train robber, Ronnie Biggs. This meeting of criminal minds resulted in the tasteless 'Belsen Was A Gas', but they still contrived to deliver a new single in which that great vocalist Ronnie Biggs lends his singing expertise to 'No-One Is Innocent' (alternatively known as 'A Punk Prayer'). Reference is made to Martin Bormann and Nazis on the run and to Bill Grundy who had a television altercation with the Pistols. This anything but dull rocker also contained the lines: "God save Myra Hindley and God save Ian Brady/Even though he's horrible and she ain't what you call a lady." Amen to that.

The UK Top 10 singles for the week ending August the 5th

1	John Travolta & Olivia Newton-John	You're The One That I Want
2	Clout	Substitute
3	Father Abraham And The Smurfs	The Smurf Song
4	Marshall Hain	Dancing In The City
5	A Taste Of Honey	Boogie Oogie Oogie
6	E.L.O.	Wild West Hero
7	Showaddywaddy	A Little Bit Of Soap
8	Boomtown Rats	Like Clockwork
9	City Boy	5-7-0-5
10	Boney M	Brown Girl In The Ring

The US Number One single: Rolling Stones – Miss You

The US Number One album: Original Soundtrack – Grease

The UK Number One album: Original Soundtrack – Saturday Night Fever

Also this week: The Queen opens the Commonwealth Games in Edmonton, Canada. (3rd)

The UK Top 10 singles for the week ending August the 12th

1 John Travolta & Olivia Newton-John   You're The One That I Want
2 Clout   Substitute
3 A Taste Of Honey   Boogie Oogie Oogie
4 Father Abraham And The Smurfs   The Smurf Song
5 Commodores   Three Times A Lady
6 Boney M   Brown Girl In The Ring
7 Justin Hayward   Forever Autumn
8 Marshall Hain   Dancing In The City
9 Sham 69   If The Kids Are United
10 E.L.O.   Wild West Hero

The US Number One single: Commodores – Three Times A Lady
The US Number One album: Original Soundtrack – Grease
The UK Number One album: Original Soundtrack – Saturday Night Fever
Also this week: Two hundred thousand people attend Pope Paul's funeral in Rome. (12th)

The UK Top 10 singles for the week ending August the 19th

1 Commodores   Three Times A Lady
2 John Travolta & Olivia Newton-John   You're The One That I Want
3 Clout   Substitute
4 Darts   It's Raining
5 Boney M   Brown Girl In the Ring
6 Justin Hayward   Forever Autumn
7 A Taste Of Honey   Boogie Oogie Oogie
8 City Boy   5–7–0–5
9 Sham 69   If The Kids Are United
10 Renaissance   Northern Lights

The US Number One single: Commodores – Three Times A Lady
The US Number One album: Original Soundtrack – Grease
The UK Number One album: Original Soundtrack – Saturday Night Fever
Also this week: Three Americans achieve the first balloon crossing of the Atlantic. (19th)

The UK Top 10 singles for the week ending August the 26th

1 Commodores	Three Times A Lady
2 John Travolta & Olivia Newton-John	You're The One That I Want
3 Darts	It's Raining
4 Boney M	Brown Girl In The Ring
5 Justin Hayward	Forever Autumn
6 10cc	Dreadlock Holiday
7 Clout	Substitute
8 Cerrone	Supernature
9 A Taste Of Honey	Boogie Oogie Oogie
10 Jilted John	Jilted John

The US Number One single: Frankie Valli – Grease

The US Number One album: Original Soundtrack – Grease

The UK Number One album: Original Soundtrack – Saturday Night Fever

Also this week: The shroud of Turin goes back on public display. (25th)

The song of the month for August 1978

Jilted John by Jilted John (peak chart position: No.4)

There is a mistaken belief that punk rock was merely an outlet for anarchy and angst, but this new wave of music also facilitated one or two amusing one-off tunes. The most notable instance was when poor old Jilted John bemoaned his way into the British Top Ten. At least the Queen was not alone in being labelled a moron, as the dastardly Gordon is called precisely that for hitching up with John's ex-lover Julie. John (whose real name was Graham Fellows) may have been romantically out of luck but he compensated with this entertaining little teenage soap opera. It was the new wave's most noteworthy one-hit wonder.

The UK Top 10 singles for the week ending September the 2nd

1 Commodores	Three Times A Lady
2 Darts	It's Raining
3 Boney M	Brown Girl In The Ring
4 10cc	Dreadlock Holiday
5 John Travolta & Olivia Newton-John	You're The One That I Want
6 David Essex	Oh What A Circus
7 Jilted John	Jilted John
8 Cerrone	Supernature
9 Justin Hayward	Forever Autumn
10 Child	It's Only Make Believe

The US Number One single: Frankie Valli – Grease
The US Number One album: Original Soundtrack – Grease
The UK Number One album: Original Soundtrack – Saturday Night Fever
Also this week: Prince Charles ignores Idi Amin at Jomo Kenyatta's funeral. (31st)

The UK Top 10 singles for the week ending September the 9th

1 Commodores	Three Times A Lady
2 Boney M	Brown Girl In The Ring
3 Darts	It's Raining
4 10cc	Dreadlock Holiday
5 David Essex	Oh What A Circus
6 Jilted John	Jilted John
7 John Travolta & Olivia Newton-John	You're The One That I Want
8 Cerrone	Supernature
9 Hi Tension	British Hustle/Peace On Earth
10 Andy Gibb	An Everlasting Love

The US Number One single: A Taste Of Honey – Boogie Oogie Oogie
The US Number One album: Original Soundtrack – Grease
The UK Number One album: Boney M – Night Flight To Venus
Also this week: The Shah of Iran imposes martial law. (8th)

The UK Top 10 singles for the week ending September the 16th

1 Commodores	Three Times A Lady
2 10cc	Dreadlock Holiday
3 Boney M	Brown Girl In The Ring
4 Darts	It's Raining
5 David Essex	Oh What A Circus
6 Jilted John	Jilted John
7 Siouxsie And The Banshees	Hong Kong Garden
8 Hi Tension	British Hustle/Peace On Earth
9 Cerrone	Supernature
10 Exile	Kiss You All Over

The US Number One single: A Taste Of Honey – Boogie Oogie Oogie
The US Number One album: Boston – Don't Look Back
The UK Number One album: Boney M – Night Flight To Venus
Also this week: A brief earthquake in Iran kills almost twenty thousand. (16th)

The UK Top 10 singles for the week ending September the 23rd

1 10cc	Dreadlock Holiday
2 Commodores	Three Times A Lady
3 David Essex	Oh What A Circus
4 Jilted John	Jilted John
5 Boney M	Brown Girl In The Ring
6 Exile	Kiss You All Over
7 Abba	Summer Night City
8 Darts	It's Raining
9 Frankie Valli	Grease
10 Siouxsie And The Banshees	Hong Kong Garden

The US Number One single: A Taste Of Honey – Boogie Oogie Oogie
The US Number One album: Original Soundtrack – Grease
The UK Number One album: Boney M – Night Flight To Venus
Also this week: Newspaper boy Carl Bridgewater is murdered. (20th)

The UK Top 10 singles for the week ending September the 30th

1 John Travolta & Olivia Newton-John   Summer Nights
2 10cc   Dreadlock Holiday
3 Frankie Valli   Grease
4 Rose Royce   Love Don't Live Here Anymore
5 Commodores   Three Times A Lady
6 David Essex   Oh What A Circus
7 Exile   Kiss You All Over
8 Abba   Summer Night City
9 Jilted John   Jilted John
10 Boney M   Brown Girl In The Ring

The US Number One single: Exile – Kiss You All Over
The US Number One album: Original Soundtrack – Grease
The UK Number One album: Boney M – Night Flight To Venus
Also this week: Pieter Willem Botha is elected South Africa's new Prime Minister. (28th)

The song of the month for September 1978

Now That We've Found Love by Third World
(peak chart position: No.10)

Now that Bob Marley And The Wailers were firmly putting Jamaican music back on the world map, other acts were able to profit from this development. The likes of Inner Circle and Third World did precisely that, although their own brand of reggae appeared closer in sound to disco. Third World for example released 'Now That We've Found Love' which seemed to bear a closer relation to Motown and Philadelphia than Trench Town, Kingston. As a consequence, this reggae-funk-disco crossover sneaked into the UK Top Ten in the autumn of 1978.

The UK Top 10 singles for the week ending October the 7th

1 John Travolta & Olivia Newton-John   Summer Nights
2 Rose Royce   Love Don't Live Here Anymore
3 Frankie Valli   Grease
4 10cc   Dreadlock Holiday
5 Abba   Summer Night City
6 Dean Friedman   Lucky Stars
7 Leo Sayer   I Can't Stop Lovin' You
8 Sylvester   You Make Me Feel Mighty Real
9 Boney M   Rasputin
10 Exile   Kiss You All Over

The US Number One single: Exile – Kiss You All Over
The US Number One album: Boston – Don't Look Back
The UK Number One album: Original Soundtrack – Grease
Also this week: Emily and William Harris are jailed for kidnapping Patty Hearst. (4th)

The UK Top 10 singles for the week ending October the 14th

1 John Travolta & Olivia Newton-John   Summer Nights
2 Rose Royce   Love Don't Live Here Anymore
3 Boney M   Rasputin
4 Dean Friedman   Lucky Stars
5 Frankie Valli   Grease
6 Leo Sayer   I Can't Stop Lovin' You
7 E.L.O.   Sweet Talkin' Woman
8 John Travolta   Sandy
9 Sylvester   You Make Me Feel Mighty Real
10 Third World   Now That We've Found Love

The US Number One single: Exile – Kiss You All Over
The US Number One album: Original Soundtrack – Grease
The UK Number One album: Original Soundtrack – Grease
Also this week: Sid Vicious is arrested after the death of Nancy Spungen. (12th)

The UK Top 10 singles for the week ending October the 21st

1 John Travolta & Olivia Newton-John	Summer Nights
2 Boney M	Rasputin
3 Dean Friedman	Lucky Stars
4 John Travolta	Sandy
5 Rose Royce	Love Don't Live Here Anymore
6 E.L.O.	Sweet Talkin' Woman
7 Leo Sayer	I Can't Stop Lovin' You
8 Frankie Valli	Grease
9 Boomtown Rats	Rat Trap
10 Sylvester	You Make Me Feel Mighty Real

The US Number One single: Exile – Kiss You All Over
The US Number One album: Original Soundtrack – Grease
The UK Number One album: Original Soundtrack – Grease
Also this week: Poland's Karol Wojtyla is elected Pope John Paul II. (16th)

The UK Top 10 singles for the week ending October the 28th

1 John Travolta & Olivia Newton-John	Summer Nights
2 Boney M	Rasputin
3 John Travolta	Sandy
4 Dean Friedman	Lucky Stars
5 Donna Summer	MacArthur Park
6 E.L.O.	Sweet Talkin' Woman
7 Boomtown Rats	Rat Trap
8 Rose Royce	Love Don't Live Here Anymore
9 Jacksons	Blame It On The Boogie
10 Leo Sayer	I Can't Stop Lovin' You

The US Number One single: Nick Gilder – Hot Child In The City
The US Number One album: Original Soundtrack – Grease
The UK Number One album: Original Soundtrack – Grease
Also this week: Begin and Sadat are jointly awarded the Nobel Peace Prize. (27th)

The song of the month for October 1978

Rat Trap by The Boomtown Rats (peak chart position: No.1)

Bob Geldof and his musically gifted rodents made history when they became the first new wave act to climb to the top of the British pop summit with the impressive 'Rat Trap'. This single contained memorable cameos from the saxophone and from the piano of Johnny Fingers. This was the first UK Number One since Dana in 1970 that had its origins in the Emerald Isle. For all the gathering gloom north of the border, the island of Ireland was making its own contribution to new wave music, courtesy of the Undertones and Stiff Little Fingers.

The UK Top 10 singles for the week ending November the 4th

1 John Travolta & Olivia Newton-John   Summer Nights
2 John Travolta   Sandy
3 Boomtown Rats   Rat Trap
4 Boney M   Rasputin
5 Donna Summer   MacArthur Park
6 E.L.O.   Sweet Talkin' Woman
7 Dean Friedman   Lucky Stars
8 Jacksons   Blame It On The Boogie
9 Public Image Limited   Public Image
10 Sham 69   Hurry Up Harry

The US Number One single: Anne Murray – You Needed Me
The US Number One album: Linda Ronstadt – Living In The USA
The UK Number One album: Original Soundtrack – Grease
Also this week: Bread rationing is likely as British bakers go on strike. (4th)

The UK Top 10 singles for the week ending November the 11th

1   John Travolta & Olivia Newton-John   Summer Nights
2   Boomtown Rats   Rat Trap
3   John Travolta   Sandy
4   Olivia Newton-John   Hopelessly Devoted To You
5   Donna Summer   MacArthur Park
6   Frankie Miller   Darlin'
7   Boney M   Rasputin
8   Jacksons   Blame It On The Boogie
9   E.L.O.   Sweet Talkin' Woman
10 Cars   My Best Friend's Girl

The US Number One single: Donna Summer – MacArthur Park
The US Number One album: Donna Summer – Live And More
The UK Number One album: Original Soundtrack – Grease
Also this week: The Shah appoints General Azhari as Iran's new Prime Minister. (6th)

The UK Top 10 singles for the week ending November the 18th

1   Boomtown Rats   Rat Trap
2   Olivia Newton-John   Hopelessly Devoted To You
3   John Travolta & Olivia Newton-John   Summer Nights
4   John Travolta   Sandy
5   Cars   My Best Friend's Girl
6   Frankie Miller   Darlin'
7   Showaddywaddy   Pretty Little Angel Eyes
8   Dan Hartman   Instant Replay
9   Donna Summer   MacArthur Park
10 Jacksons   Blame It On The Boogie

The US Number One single: Donna Summer – MacArthur Park
The US Number One album: Billy Joel – 52nd Street
The UK Number One album: Original Soundtrack – Grease
Also this week: Two hundred die when an aeroplane crashes in Sri Lanka. (16th)

The UK Top 10 singles for the week ending November the 25th

1	Boomtown Rats	Rat Trap
2	Olivia Newton-John	Hopelessly Devoted To You
3	Cars	My Best Friend's Girl
4	Rod Stewart	Da Ya Think I'm Sexy?
5	Showaddywaddy	Pretty Little Angel Eyes
6	Frankie Miller	Darlin'
7	John Travolta & Olivia Newton-John	Summer Nights
8	Dan Hartman	Instant Replay
9	Blondie	Hanging On The Telephone
10	John Travolta	Sandy

The US Number One single: Donna Summer – MacArthur Park
The US Number One album: Billy Joel – 52nd Street
The UK Number One album: Original Soundtrack – Grease
Also this week: Committal proceedings begin against Jeremy Thorpe MP. (20th)

The song of the month for November 1978

Hanging On The Telephone by Blondie (peak chart position: No.5)

Deborah Harry and her merry men were the latest pop sensation who helped themselves to four hit smashes in 1978, the last of which was the fast-paced 'Hanging On The Telephone'. This was the second item to be issued from the hugely popular 'Parallel Lines' album and it found a deserved place in the British Top Five. Although the song is overshadowed by the success of Blondie's next two singles, it is surely an infinitely more worthy candidate for new wave and punk compilations than the fluffy pop of 'Denis'. Rod Stewart was suggesting that blondes have more fun, and judging by the success of the eye-catching Debbie Harry, he may have been right.

The UK Top 10 singles for the week ending December the 2nd

1	Rod Stewart	Da Ya Think I'm Sexy?
2	Boomtown Rats	Rat Trap
3	Olivia Newton-John	Hopelessly Devoted To You
4	Cars	My Best Friend's Girl
5	Blondie	Hanging On The Telephone
6	Showaddywaddy	Pretty Little Angel Eyes
7	Boney M	Mary's Boy Child/Oh My Lord
8	Dan Hartman	Instant Replay
9	Sarah Brightman & Hot Gossip	I Lost My Heart To A Starship Trooper
10	Frankie Miller	Darlin'

The US Number One single: Barbra Streisand & Neil Diamond – You Don't Bring Me Flowers

The US Number One album: Billy Joel – 52nd Street

The UK Number One album: Original Soundtrack – Grease

Also this week: Terrorists murder the deputy governor of the Maze Prison. (26th)

The UK Top 10 singles for the week ending December the 9th

1	Boney M	Mary's Boy Child/Oh My Lord
2	Rod Stewart	Da Ya Think I'm Sexy?
3	Bee Gees	Too Much Heaven
4	Barron Knights	A Taste Of Aggro
5	Boomtown Rats	Rat Trap
6	Sarah Brightman & Hot Gossip	I Lost My Heart To A Starship Trooper
7	Blondie	Hanging On The Telephone
8	Chic	Le Freak
9	Heatwave	Always And Forever/Mind Blowing Decisions
10	Olivia Newton-John	Hopelessly Devoted To You

The US Number One single: Chic – Le Freak

The US Number One album: Billy Joel – 52nd Street

The UK Number One album: Original Soundtrack – Grease

Also this week: The Soviet Union signs a treaty of friendship with Afghanistan. (5th)

The UK Top 10 singles for the week ending December the 16th

1	Boney M	Mary's Boy Child/Oh My Lord
2	Village People	YMCA
3	Rod Stewart	Da Ya Think I'm Sexy?
4	Barron Knights	A Taste Of Aggro
5	Bee Gees	Too Much Heaven
6	Sarah Brightman & Hot Gossip	I Lost My Heart To A Starship Trooper
7	Chic	Le Freak
8	Barbra Streisand & Neil Diamond	You Don't Bring Me Flowers
9	Heatwave	Always And Forever/ Mind Blowing Decisions
10	Blondie	Hanging On The Telephone

The US Number One single: Barbra Streisand & Neil Diamond – You Don't Bring Me Flowers

The US Number One album: Billy Joel – 52nd Street

The UK Number One album: Original Soundtrack – Grease

Also this week: David Gower hits a century against Australia in Perth. (15th)

The UK Top 10 singles for the week ending December the 23rd

1	Boney M	Mary's Boy Child/Oh My Lord
2	Village People	YMCA
3	Barron Knights	A Taste Of Aggro
4	Bee Gees	Too Much Heaven
5	Barbra Streisand & Neil Diamond	You Don't Bring Me Flowers
6	Racey	Lay Your Love On Me
7	Sarah Brightman & Hot Gossip	I Lost My Heart To A Starship Trooper
8	Rod Stewart	Da Ya Think I'm Sexy?
9	Chic	Le Freak
10	Elton John	Song For Guy

The US Number One single: Chic – Le Freak

The US Number One album: Billy Joel – 52nd Street

The UK Number One album: Original Soundtrack – Grease

Also this week: England trounce Australia for the second successive Ashes test. (20th)

The UK Top 10 singles for the week ending December the 30th

1   Boney M   Mary's Boy Child/Oh My Lord
2   Village People   YMCA
3   Barron Knights   A Taste Of Aggro
4   Bee Gees   Too Much Heaven
5   Barbra Streisand & Neil Diamond   You Don't Bring Me Flowers
6   Racey   Lay Your Love On Me
7   Sarah Brightman & Hot Gossip   I Lost My Heart To A Starship Trooper
8   Rod Stewart   Da Ya Think I'm Sexy?
9   Chic   Le Freak
10 Elton John   Song For Guy

The US Number One single: Chic – Le Freak
The US Number One album: Billy Joel – 52nd Street
The UK Number One album: Original Soundtrack – Grease
Also this week: Opposition leader Shahpur Bakhtiar becomes Iran's new premier.
(29th)

The song of the month for December 1978
Song For Guy by Elton John

This mouthwatering semi-instrumental owes its existence to the tragic end to the existence of Guy Burchett who was killed in a motorcycle accident. Elton shifts between piano and synthesizer as he offers the spoken line "Life isn't everything". This 'funeral for a friend' took Elton John back to the British Top Ten where he had lived on numerous occasions since 1971. 'Song For Guy' rates as one of the decade's best instrumentals alongside 'Pick Up The Pieces', 'The Hustle', and 'Oxygene'.

Listed Below are the Top 10 Best Selling UK Singles of 1978

1	Rivers Of Babylon/ Brown Girl In The Ring	Boney M
2	You're The One That I Want	John Travolta & Olivia Newton-John
3	Summer Nights	John Travolta & Olivia Newton-John
4	Three Times A Lady	The Commodores
5	Night Fever	The Bee Gees
6	Smurf Song	Father Abraham
7	Take A Chance On Me	Abba
8	Matchstalk Men And Matchstalk Cats And Dogs	Brian and Michael
9	Rat Trap	The Boomtown Rats
10	Wuthering Heights	Kate Bush

1978's CONCERTS OF THE YEAR

The shy, retiring Malcolm McLaren referred to the Pistols' North American tour in January as "taking civilisation to the barbarians" in the subsequent film, 'The Great Rock 'n' Roll Swindle'. However, it all ended sourly in San Francisco's Winterland ballroom when Johnny Rotten clocked out with the unforgettable words: "Ever had the feeling you're being cheated?" It was the mother of all ironies that both the Beatles and the Sex Pistols played their last gigs in the same Californian city. However, the event of the year was almost certainly Bob Marley's triumphal return to Jamaica where he performed at the One Love peace concert in April. This event witnessed Marley uniting Jamaica's political opposites, Edward Seaga and Michael Manley in a gesture of peace and unity, which was absurdly described by Marley's associate Neville Garrick "as Christ upon the cross between the two thieves."

1978's ALBUM OF THE YEAR

The Kick Inside by Kate Bush
(released in February; reached No.3 in the UK)

Side One:

1. Moving; 3:01
2. The Saxophone Song; 3:51
3. Strange Phenomena; 2:57
4. Kite; 2:56
5. The Man with the Child in His Eyes; 2:39
6. Wuthering Heights; 4:28

Side Two:

1. James and the Cold Gun; 3:34
2. Feel It; 3:02
3. Oh to Be in Love; 3:18
4. L'Amour Looks Something Like You; 2:27
5. Them Heavy People; 3:04
6. Room for the Life; 4:03
7. The Kick Inside; :30

The music scene of the 'seventies could be characterised as one of disco and rock (be it glam, progressive, or punk). Therefore, the arrival of the teenage Kate Bush represented something completely different to occupy its own niche on planet pop. 'The Kick Inside' clearly cashed in on the success of the chart-topper,'Wuthering Heights', but the quality of the record suggested that Miss Bush was not a novelty act, nor likely to be a one-hit wonder. Laying a credible claim to be the best debut album of the decade, 'The Kick Inside' possessed all the features that would typify the music of Kate Bush, namely orchestral arrangements, high-pitched vocals and quirky lyrics and subject matter. 'The Man With The Child In His Eyes' was a commendable follow-up to the 'heights' of the first 45, whilst 'Room For The Life', 'Moving', and 'Kite' were among the best offerings from this delightful LP. Remarkably, Kate Bush remained a well-kept secret in the United States, but 'The Kick Inside' did lay the foundations for a lengthy stint on the airwaves for the inimitable singer-songwriter.

SPORT IN 1978

English Division One football champions: Nottingham Forest; runners-up: Liverpool

English FA Cup final: Ipswich Town 1 Arsenal 0

English League Cup Final: Nottingham Forest 1 Liverpool 0 (in a replay)

Scottish Division One football champions: Glasgow Rangers; runners-up: Aberdeen

Scottish FA Cup final: Glasgow Rangers 2 Aberdeen 1

Scottish League Cup final: Glasgow Rangers 2 Glasgow Celtic 1

Irish League football champions: Linfield; Irish Cup final: Linfield 3 Ballymena United 1

League Of Ireland football champions: Bohemians; cup winners: Shamrock Rovers

European Cup final: Liverpool 1 FC Bruges 0

European Cup-Winners' Cup final: Anderlecht 4 Austria/WAC 0

UEFA Cup final: PSV Eindhoven beat Bastia 3–0 on aggregate

English county cricket champions: Kent

Five Nations' rugby union champions: Wales (the Grand Slam); runners-up: France

Formula One world drivers' champion: Mario Andretti (United States) in a Lotus car

Gaelic football All-Ireland champions: Kerry; runners-up: Dublin

British Open golf champion: Jack Nicklaus (at St Andrews)

US Masters golf champion: Gary Player

US Open golf champion: Andy North

USPGA golf champion: John Mahaffey

Rugby league Challenge Cup final: Leeds 14 St Helens 12

Wimbledon men's singles tennis final: B Borg beat J Connors 6–2, 6–2, 6–3

Wimbledon ladies' singles tennis final: M Navratilova beat C Evert 2–6, 6–4, 7–5

World snooker final: Ray Reardon (Wales) beat Perrie Mans (South Africa) 25–18

The Aintree Grand National steeplechase winner: Lucius; price 14–1

The Epsom Derby winner: Shirley Heights; jockey – Greville Starkey; price 8–1

Football World Cup final: Argentina 3 Holland 1 (after extra time)

1978's DEATHS

January 13th: Hubert Humphrey (US politician), aged 66

January 22nd: Herbert William Sutcliffe (English cricketer), aged 83

April 21st: Sandy Denny (British singer), aged 31

May 9th: Aldo Moro (Italian statesman), aged 61

May 15th: Sir Robert Gordon Menzies (ex-Australian Prime Minister), aged 83

August 6th: Pope Paul VI (born Giovanni Battista Montini), aged 80

August 14th: Nicolas Clerihew Bentley (British cartoonist), aged 71

August 26th: Charles Boyer (French actor), aged 80

September 7th: Keith Moon (British musician), aged 32

September 15th: Willy Messerschmitt (German aircraft engineer), aged 80

September 30th: Pope John Paul (born Albino Luciani), aged 65

October 9th: Jacques Brel (Belgian singer), aged 49

October 21st: Anastas Mikoyan (Soviet politician), aged 82

November 15th: Margaret Mead (US anthropologist), aged 76

November 20th: Giorgio de Chirico (Greek painter), aged 90

December 8th: Golda Meir (ex-Israeli Prime Minister), aged 80

December 27th: Houari Boumedienne (President of Algeria), aged 46

The UK Top 10 singles for the week ending January the 6th

1 Village People — YMCA
2 Boney M — Mary's Boy Child/Oh My Lord
3 Racey — Lay Your Love On Me
4 Barron Knights — A Taste Of Aggro
5 Elton John — Song For Guy
6 Ian Dury And The Blockheads — Hit Me With Your Rhythm Stick
7 Barbra Streisand & Neil Diamond — You Don't Bring Me Flowers
8 Bee Gees — Too Much Heaven
9 Sarah Brightman & Hot Gossip — I Lost My Heart To A Starship Trooper
10 Chic — Le Freak

The US Number One single: Bee Gees – Too Much Heaven
The US Number One album: Barbra Streisand – Barbra Streisand's Greatest Hits, Volume 2
The UK Number One album: Showaddywaddy – Greatest Hits
Also this week: Australia win the third Ashes test in Melbourne. (3rd)

The UK Top 10 singles for the week ending January the 13th

1 Village People — YMCA
2 Ian Dury And The Blockheads — Hit Me With Your Rhythm Stick
3 Racey — Lay Your Love On Me
4 Elton John — Song For Guy
5 Earth Wind And Fire — September
6 Barron Knights — A Taste Of Aggro
7 Boney M — Mary's Boy Child/Oh My Lord
8 Barbra Streisand & Neil Diamond — You Don't Bring Me Flowers
9 Chic — Le Freak
10 Bee Gees — Too Much Heaven

The US Number One single: Bee Gees – Too Much Heaven
The US Number One album: Barbra Streisand – Barbra Streisand's Greatest Hits, Volume 2
The UK Number One album: Showaddywaddy – Greatest Hits
Also this week: England win the fourth Ashes test in Sydney. (11th)

The UK Top 10 singles for the week ending January the 20th

1	Village People	YMCA
2	Ian Dury And The Blockheads	Hit Me With Your Rhythm Stick
3	Racey	Lay Your Love On Me
4	Earth Wind And Fire	September
5	Olivia Newton-John	A Little More Love
6	Paul Evans	Hello This Is Joannie
7	Chic	Le Freak
8	Elton John	Song For Guy
9	Funkadelic	One Nation Under A Groove
10	Driver 67	Car 67

The US Number One single: Chic – Le Freak

The US Number One album: Barbra Streisand – Barbra Streisand's Greatest Hits, Volume 2

The UK Number One album: Various Artist Compilation – Don't Walk-Boogie

Also this week: The beleaguered Shah of Iran goes into exile. (16th)

The UK Top 10 singles for the week ending January the 27th

1	Ian Dury And The Blockheads	Hit Me With Your Rhythm Stick
2	Village People	YMCA
3	Earth Wind And Fire	September
4	Olivia Newton-John	A Little More Love
5	Three Degrees	Woman In Love
6	Blondie	Heart Of Glass
7	Racey	Lay Your Love On Me
8	Paul Evans	Hello This Is Joannie
9	Shadows	Don't Cry For Me Argentina
10	Chic	Le Freak

The US Number One single: Chic – Le Freak

The US Number One album: Billy Joel – 52nd Street

The UK Number One album: Various Artist Compilation – Don't Walk-Boogie

Also this week: A public employees' strike hits Britain's hospitals and schools. (22nd)

The song of the month for January 1979

Heart Of Glass by Blondie (peak chart position: No.1)

Experienced pop music producer Mike Chapman dragged the Blondie group kicking and screaming away from their punk origins and into the mainstream where their own brand of new wave rock would be sufficiently attractive to ensure commercial success. The group's finest triumph indeed came courtesy of a disco-influenced track which could be used as dancefloor material. 'Heart Of Glass' wasn't a typical Blondie tune, but as the group started to branch out into new sounds, there became no such thing as a typical Blondie tune.

The UK Top 10 singles for the week ending February the 3rd

1	Blondie	Heart Of Glass
2	Ian Dury And The Blockheads	Hit Me With Your Rhythm Stick
3	Three Degrees	Woman In Love
4	Village People	YMCA
5	Earth Wind And Fire	September
6	Olivia Newton-John	A Little More Love
7	Driver 67	Car 67
8	Abba	Chiquitita
9	Racey	Lay Your Love On Me
10	Shadows	Don't Cry For Me Argentina

The US Number One single: Chic – Le Freak

The US Number One album: The Blues Brothers – Briefcase Full Of Blues

The UK Number One album: Various Artist Compilation – Don't Walk-Boogie

Also this week: The Ayatollah Khomeini returns to Iran, after being in exile. (1st)

The UK Top 10 singles for the week ending February the 10th

1	Blondie	Heart Of Glass
2	Abba	Chiquitita
3	Three Degrees	Woman In Love
4	Ian Dury And The Blockheads	Hit Me With Your Rhythm Stick
5	Shadows	Don't Cry For Me Argentina
6	Village People	YMCA
7	Leif Garrett	I Was Made For Dancing
8	Earth Wind And Fire	September
9	Driver 67	Car 67
10	Olivia Newton-John	A Little More Love

The US Number One single: Rod Stewart – Da Ya Think I'm Sexy?
The US Number One album: Rod Stewart – Blondes Have More Fun
The UK Number One album: Various Artist Compilation – Action Replay
Also this week: General Zia announces the introduction of Islamic laws in Pakistan. (10th)

The UK Top 10 singles for the week ending February the 17th

1	Blondie	Heart Of Glass
2	Abba	Chiquitita
3	Three Degrees	Woman In Love
4	Leif Garrett	I Was Made For Dancing
5	Shadows	Don't Cry For Me Argentina
6	Edwin Starr	Contact
7	Bee Gees	Tragedy
8	Ian Dury And The Blockheads	Hit Me With Your Rhythm Stick
9	Dr. Feelgood	Milk And Alcohol
10	Driver 67	Car 67

The US Number One single: Rod Stewart – Da Ya Think I'm Sexy?
The US Number One album: Rod Stewart – Blondes Have More Fun
The UK Number One album: Blondie – Parallel Lines
Also this week: Four of the Shah of Iran's generals are executed. (16th)

The UK Top 10 singles for the week ending February the 24th

1	Blondie	Heart Of Glass
2	Bee Gees	Tragedy
3	Abba	Chiquitita
4	Three Degrees	Woman In Love
5	Elvis Costello	Oliver's Army
6	Leif Garrett	I Was Made For Dancing
7	Gloria Gaynor	I Will Survive
8	Edwin Starr	Contact
9	Shadows	Don't Cry For Me Argentina
10	Dr. Feelgood	Milk And Alcohol

The US Number One single: Rod Stewart – Da Ya Think I'm Sexy?
The US Number One album: Rod Stewart – Blondes Have More Fun
The UK Number One album: Blondie – Parallel Lines
Also this week: St. Lucia becomes independent of Britain. (23rd)

The song of the month for February 1979

Chiquitita by Abba (peak chart position: No.2)

By Abba's very high standards, 'Chiquitita' was an abysmal failure, only managing to reach a dismal Number Two in the British singles lists! In fact, pop charts are rarely an accurate barometer of quality so it is possible to argue that this marvellous melodrama is actually superior to some of the fab four's chart-toppers. The tragic 'Chiquitita' would at least provide extra funds for UNICEF as the group donated its royalties to this children's charity. The talented quartet remained regular visitors to the top of the pops for another 2 years.

The UK Top 10 singles for the week ending March the 3rd

1	Bee Gees	Tragedy
2	Blondie	Heart Of Glass
3	Elvis Costello	Oliver's Army
4	Gloria Gaynor	I Will Survive
5	Abba	Chiquitita
6	Edwin Starr	Contact
7	Leif Garrett	I Was Made For Dancing
8	Lene Lovich	Lucky Number
9	Three Degrees	Woman In Love
10	Darts	Get It

The US Number One single: Rod Stewart – Da Ya Think I'm Sexy?
The US Number One album: Bee Gees – Spirits Having Flown
The UK Number One album: Blondie – Parallel Lines
Also this week: Welsh and Scottish voters prove lukewarm about self-government. (2nd)

The UK Top 10 singles for the week ending March the 10th

1	Bee Gees	Tragedy
2	Elvis Costello	Oliver's Army
3	Gloria Gaynor	I Will Survive
4	Lene Lovich	Lucky Number
5	Real Thing	Can You Feel The Force
6	Blondie	Heart Of Glass
7	Sex Pistols	Something Else/Friggin' In The Riggin'
8	Edwin Starr	Contact
9	Abba	Chiquitita
10	Boney M	Painter Man

The US Number One single: Gloria Gaynor – I Will Survive
The US Number One album: Bee Gees – Spirits Having Flown
The UK Number One album: Blondie – Parallel Lines
Also this week: Tanzanian forces advance upon the Ugandan capital of Kampala. (4th)

The UK Top 10 singles for the week ending March the 17th

1 Gloria Gaynor — I Will Survive
2 Elvis Costello — Oliver's Army
3 Bee Gees — Tragedy
4 Lene Lovich — Lucky Number
5 Real Thing — Can You Feel The Force
6 Sex Pistols — Something Else/Friggin' In The Riggin'
7 Chic — I Want Your Love
8 Blondie — Heart Of Glass
9 Gary's Gang — Keep On Dancing
10 Edwin Starr — Contact

The US Number One single: Gloria Gaynor – I Will Survive
The US Number One album: Bee Gees – Spirits Having Flown
The UK Number One album: Bee Gees – Spirits Having Flown
Also this week: Libyan forces arrive in Uganda to assist Idi Amin. (11th)

The UK Top 10 singles for the week ending March the 24th

1 Gloria Gaynor — I Will Survive
2 Elvis Costello — Oliver's Army
3 Lene Lovich — Lucky Number
4 Sex Pistols — Something Else/Friggin' In The Riggin'
5 Real Thing — Can You Feel The Force
6 Bee Gees — Tragedy
7 Chic — I Want Your Love
8 Gary's Gang — Keep On Dancing
9 Thin Lizzy — Waiting For An Alibi
10 Skids — Into The Valley

The US Number One single: Bee Gees – Tragedy
The US Number One album: Bee Gees – Spirits Having Flown
The UK Number One album: Bee Gees – Spirits Having Flown
Also this week: Israel's Knesset parliament approves the Camp David peace accord. (22nd)

The UK Top 10 singles for the week ending March the 31st

1	Gloria Gaynor	I Will Survive
2	Village People	In The Navy
3	Sex Pistols	Something Else/Friggin' In The Riggin'
4	Elvis Costello	Oliver's Army
5	Lene Lovich	Lucky Number
6	Chic	I Want Your Love
7	Real Thing	Can You Feel The Force
8	Players Association	Turn The Music Up
9	Queen	Don't Stop Me Now
10	Gary's Gang	Keep On Dancing

The US Number One single: Bee Gees – Tragedy

The US Number One album: Bee Gees – Spirits Having Flown

The UK Number One album: Barbra Streisand – Barbra Streisand's Greatest Hits, Volume 2

Also this week: James Callaghan is obliged to call a general election. (29th)

The song of the month for March 1979
Bright Eyes by Art Garfunkel (peak chart position: No.1)

The man with the supremely beautiful voice proved that there was life after Simon when he enjoyed two British Number One successes in the 1970s. Whilst 'I Only Have Eyes For You' is a superb love song, 'Bright Eyes' was a mini-epic which finished the year as the UK's biggest-selling single. Composed by the songwriter Mike Batt, this single was associated with the animated 'Watership Down' movie. The music was first class, the singing was of the highest quality and the video with the rabbits was compulsive viewing. It was scarcely a surprise therefore that this recording occupied the British pop summit for six weeks in the spring of 1979.

The UK Top 10 singles for the week ending April the 7th

1 Gloria Gaynor — I Will Survive
2 Village People — In The Navy
3 Art Garfunkel — Bright Eyes
4 Chic — I Want Your Love
5 Sex Pistols — Something Else/Friggin' In The Riggin'
6 Squeeze — Cool For Cats
7 Lene Lovich — Lucky Number
8 Dire Straits — Sultans Of Swing
9 Players Association — Turn The Music Up
10 Elvis Costello — Oliver's Army

The US Number One single: Gloria Gaynor – I Will Survive
The US Number One album: The Doobie Brothers – Minute By Minute
The UK Number One album: Barbra Streisand – Barbra Streisand's Greatest Hits, Volume 2
Also this week: Begin becomes the first Israeli Prime Minister to visit Egypt. (2nd)

The UK Top 10 singles for the week ending April the 14th

1 Art Garfunkel — Bright Eyes
2 Squeeze — Cool For Cats
3 Racey — Some Girls
4 Village People — In The Navy
5 Gloria Gaynor — I Will Survive
6 Sister Sledge — He's The Greatest Dancer
7 Sex Pistols — Silly Thing/Who Killed Bambi
8 Dire Straits — Sultans Of Swing
9 Jacksons — Shake Your Body (Down To The Ground)
10 Three Degrees — The Runner

The US Number One single: The Doobie Brothers – What A Fool Believes
The US Number One album: The Doobie Brothers – Minute By Minute
The UK Number One album: Barbra Streisand – Barbra Streisand's Greatest Hits, Volume 2
Also this week: Yusuf Lule succeeds Idi Amin as Uganda's president. (13th)

The UK Top 10 singles for the week ending April the 21st

1	Art Garfunkel	Bright Eyes
2	Racey	Some Girls
3	Squeeze	Cool For Cats
4	Jacksons	Shake Your Body (Down To The Ground)
5	Milk & Honey	Hallelujah
6	Sex Pistols	Silly Thing/Who Killed Bambi
7	Sister Sledge	He's The Greatest Dancer
8	Village People	In The Navy
9	Gloria Gaynor	I Will Survive
10	Three Degrees	The Runner

The US Number One single: Amii Stewart – Knock On Wood

The US Number One album: Bee Gees – Spirits Having Flown

The UK Number One album: Barbra Streisand – Barbra Streisand's Greatest Hits, Volume 2

Also this week: Lee Marvin is ordered to pay palimony to Michelle Marvin. (18th)

The UK Top 10 singles for the week ending April the 28th

1	Art Garfunkel	Bright Eyes
2	Racey	Some Girls
3	Squeeze	Cool For Cats
4	Jacksons	Shake Your Body (Down To The Ground)
5	M	Pop Muzik
6	Milk & Honey	Hallelujah
7	Supertramp	The Logical Song
8	Sex Pistols	Silly Thing/Who Killed Bambi
9	Wings	Goodnight Tonight
10	Three Degrees	The Runner

The US Number One single: Blondie – Heart Of Glass

The US Number One album: The Doobie Brothers – Minute By Minute

The UK Number One album: Leo Sayer – The Very Best Of Leo Sayer

Also this week: Police and protesters clash at a Southall National Front rally. (23rd)

The song of the month for April 1979

Dance Away by Roxy Music (peak chart position: No.2)

Whilst Britain coped with another general election campaign on the back of a 'winter of discontent', Roxy Music returned to form with their very own 'Manifesto'. The 'Manifesto' included the Top Five smashes 'Angel Eyes' and the outstanding 'Dance Away'. The latter was sung from the point of view of a poor soul who finds no alternative but to close his "eyes and dance 'til dawn" as a means of escaping personal heartache. This hit ought to be short-listed for the song of the year, while Roxy Music's 'Manifesto' would have won my vote.

The UK Top 10 singles for the week ending May the 5th

1	Art Garfunkel	Bright Eyes
2	Racey	Some Girls
3	M	Pop Muzik
4	Boney M	Hooray Hooray It's A Holi Holiday
5	Wings	Goodnight Tonight
6	Jacksons	Shake Your Body (Down To The Ground)
7	Milk & Honey	Hallelujah
8	Squeeze	Cool For Cats
9	Supertramp	The Logical Song
10	Amii Stewart	Knock On Wood

The US Number One single: Peaches And Herb – Reunited

The US Number One album: The Doobie Brothers – Minute By Minute

The UK Number One album: Leo Sayer – The Very Best Of Leo Sayer

Also this week: Mrs Thatcher's Conservative Party wins the British general election. (4th)

The UK Top 10 singles for the week ending May the 12th

1 Art Garfunkel   Bright Eyes
2 M   Pop Muzik
3 Boney M   Hooray Hooray It's A Holi Holiday
4 Abba   Does Your Mother Know
5 Racey   Some Girls
6 Peaches And Herb   Reunited
7 Dickies   Banana Splits
8 Wings   Goodnight Tonight
9 Amii Stewart   Knock On Wood
10 Supertramp   The Logical Song

The US Number One single: Peaches And Herb – Reunited
The US Number One album: The Doobie Brothers – Minute By Minute
The UK Number One album: Leo Sayer – The Very Best Of Leo Sayer
Also this week: Armed forces kill 24 people in San Salvador. (8th)

The UK Top 10 singles for the week ending May the 19th

1 Art Garfunkel   Bright Eyes
2 M   Pop Muzik
3 Boney M   Hooray Hooray It's A Holi Holiday
4 Abba   Does Your Mother Know
5 Peaches And Herb   Reunited
6 Amii Stewart   Knock On Wood
7 Roxy Music   Dance Away
8 Gary Moore   Parisienne Walkways
9 Eruption   One Way Ticket
10 Blondie   Sunday Girl

The US Number One single: Peaches And Herb – Reunited
The US Number One album: Supertramp – Breakfast In America
The UK Number One album: Abba – Voulez-Vous
Also this week: Norman Scott claims that Jeremy Thorpe had twice seduced him. (18th)

The UK Top 10 singles for the week ending May the 26th

1	Blondie	Sunday Girl
2	Roxy Music	Dance Away
3	M	Pop Muzik
4	Abba	Does Your Mother Know
5	Peaches And Herb	Reunited
6	Art Garfunkel	Bright Eyes
7	Boney M	Hooray Hooray It's A Holi Holiday
8	Earth Wind And Fire & The Emotions	Boogie Wonderland
9	David Bowie	Boys Keep Swingin'
10	Eruption	One Way Ticket

The US Number One single: Peaches And Herb – Reunited

The US Number One album: Supertramp – Breakfast In America

The UK Number One album: Abba – Voulez-Vous

Also this week: Joe Clark's Progressive Conservatives win Canada's general election. (23rd)

The song of the month for May 1979
I Fought The Law by The Clash (peak chart position: No.22)

Bracing themselves for the harsh medicine of the new Thatcher administration, the Clash released the 'Cost Of Living' extended player. The song which was afforded most exposure from this 45 was the band's cover of 'I Fought The Law', performed originally by Bobby Fuller. They may not have had to break rocks in the hot sun, but the anti-establishment Clash had fallen foul of the law at various times, so the song title was apt. 1979 culminated in the group's release of the 'London Calling' double album to universal acclaim.

The UK Top 10 singles for the week ending June the 2nd

1	Blondie	Sunday Girl
2	Roxy Music	Dance Away
3	M	Pop Muzik
4	Peaches And Herb	Reunited
5	Earth Wind And Fire & The Emotions	Boogie Wonderland
6	Abba	Does Your Mother Know
7	David Bowie	Boys Keep Swingin'
8	Art Garfunkel	Bright Eyes
9	Shadows	Theme From The Deer Hunter (Cavatina)
10	Gary Moore	Parisienne Walkways

The US Number One single: Donna Summer – Hot Stuff
The US Number One album: Supertramp – Breakfast In America
The UK Number One album: Abba – Voulez-Vous
Also this week: Bishop Muzorewa is sworn in as Rhodesia's first black premier. (29th)

The UK Top 10 singles for the week ending June the 9th

1	Blondie	Sunday Girl
2	Roxy Music	Dance Away
3	Anita Ward	Ring My Bell
4	Earth Wind And Fire & The Emotions	Boogie Wonderland
5	Peaches And Herb	Reunited
6	E.L.O.	Shine A Little Love
7	M	Pop Muzik
8	McFadden & Whitehead	Ain't No Stoppin' Us Now
9	David Bowie	Boys Keep Swingin'
10	Shadows	Theme From The Deer Hunter (Cavatina)

The US Number One single: Bee Gees – Love You Inside Out
The US Number One album: Supertramp – Breakfast In America
The UK Number One album: Abba – Voulez-Vous
Also this week: The first European parliament elections are held. (7th)

The UK Top 10 singles for the week ending June the 16th

1	Anita Ward	Ring My Bell
2	Blondie	Sunday Girl
3	Roxy Music	Dance Away
4	Earth Wind And Fire & The Emotions	Boogie Wonderland
5	McFadden & Whitehead	Ain't No Stoppin' Us Now
6	E.L.O.	Shine A Little Love
7	Tubeway Army	Are Friends Electric
8	Sister Sledge	We Are Family
9	Shadows	Theme From The Deer Hunter (Cavatina)
10	Edwin Starr	H.A.P.P.Y Radio

The US Number One single: Donna Summer – Hot Stuff
The US Number One album: Donna Summer – Bad Girls
The UK Number One album: E.L.O. – Discovery
Also this week: Geoffrey Howe cuts income tax in his first budget. (12th)

The UK Top 10 singles for the week ending June the 23rd

1	Anita Ward	Ring My Bell
2	Tubeway Army	Are Friends Electric
3	Roxy Music	Dance Away
4	Blondie	Sunday Girl
5	Earth Wind And Fire & The Emotions	Boogie Wonderland
6	Squeeze	Up The Junction
7	McFadden & Whitehead	Ain't No Stoppin' Us Now
8	Quantum Jump	The Lone Ranger
9	Sister Sledge	We Are Family
10	Shadows	Theme From The Deer Hunter (Cavatina)

The US Number One single: Donna Summer – Hot Stuff
The US Number One album: Supertramp – Breakfast In America
The UK Number One album: E.L.O. – Discovery
Also this week: Jeremy Thorpe is found not guilty of plotting to murder. (22nd)

The UK Top 10 singles for the week ending June the 30th

1	Tubeway Army	Are Friends Electric
2	Anita Ward	Ring My Bell
3	Squeeze	Up The Junction
4	Earth Wind And Fire & The Emotions	Boogie Wonderland
5	Quantum Jump	The Lone Ranger
6	Roxy Music	Dance Away
7	Blondie	Sunday Girl
8	McFadden & Whitehead	Ain't No Stoppin' Us Now
9	Edwin Starr	H.A.P.P.Y Radio
10	Gerry Rafferty	Night Owl

The US Number One single: Anita Ward – Ring My Bell

The US Number One album: Supertramp – Breakfast In America

The UK Number One album: E.L.O. – Discovery

Also this week: America's General Haig escapes assassination by a car bomb. (25th)

The song of the month for June 1979

C'mon Everybody by The Sex Pistols (peak chart position: No.3)

Once his mate Johnny sloped off to form his own Public Image Limited, the loose cannon that was Sid Vicious was left to his own self-destructive devices. Before long he would be accused of having murdered his girlfriend, Nancy Spungen, and then the tragic fool died of a drugs overdose. In loving memory of Sid (or more likely to capitalise on 'The Great Rock 'N' Roll Swindle' movie), a number of Sid karaoke classics climbed the British charts. Chief among them was a terrific rendition of Eddie Cochran's 'C'mon Everybody'.

The UK Top 10 singles for the week ending July the 7th

1	Tubeway Army	Are Friends Electric
2	Squeeze	Up The Junction
3	Janet Kay	Silly Games
4	Anita Ward	Ring My Bell
5	Gerry Rafferty	Night Owl
6	Amii Stewart	Light My Fire/137 Disco Heaven
7	Quantum Jump	The Lone Ranger
8	Earth Wind And Fire & The Emotions	Boogie Wonderland
9	Sex Pistols	C'mon Everybody
10	Roxy Music	Dance Away

The US Number One single: Anita Ward – Ring My Bell

The US Number One album: Donna Summer – Bad Girls

The UK Number One album: E.L.O. – Discovery

Also this week: Ex-Algerian President, Ahmed Ben Bella, is released from captivity. (4th)

The UK Top 10 singles for the week ending July the 14th

1	Tubeway Army	Are Friends Electric
2	Janet Kay	Silly Games
3	Sex Pistols	C'mon Everybody
4	Squeeze	Up The Junction
5	Amii Stewart	Light My Fire/137 Disco Heaven
6	Gerry Rafferty	Night Owl
7	Ruts	Babylon's Burning
8	Beach Boys	Lady Lynda
9	Quantum Jump	The Lone Ranger
10	Anita Ward	Ring My Bell

The US Number One single: Donna Summer – Bad Girls

The US Number One album: Donna Summer – Bad Girls

The UK Number One album: E.L.O. – Discovery

Also this week: David Gower hits 200 against India at Edgbaston. (13th)

The UK Top 10 singles for the week ending July the 21st

1	Tubeway Army	Are Friends Electric
2	Janet Kay	Silly Games
3	Sex Pistols	C'mon Everybody
4	Dave Edmunds	Girls Talk
5	Chic	Good Times
6	Beach Boys	Lady Lynda
7	Gerry Rafferty	Night Owl
8	Amii Stewart	Light My Fire/137 Disco Heaven
9	Squeeze	Up The Junction
10	Dooleys	Wanted

The US Number One single: Donna Summer – Bad Girls
The US Number One album: Donna Summer – Bad Girls
The UK Number One album: Tubeway Army – Replicas
Also this week: Nicaragua's General Somoza resigns and goes into exile. (20th)

The UK Top 10 singles for the week ending July the 28th

1	Boomtown Rats	I Don't Like Mondays
2	Tubeway Army	Are Friends Electric
3	Janet Kay	Silly Games
4	Dave Edmunds	Girls Talk
5	Dooleys	Wanted
6	Knack	My Sharona
7	Chic	Good Times
8	Sex Pistols	C'mon Everybody
9	Beach Boys	Lady Lynda
10	Supertramp	Breakfast In America

The US Number One single: Donna Summer – Bad Girls
The US Number One album: Donna Summer – Bad Girls
The UK Number One album: Various Artist Compilation – The Best Disco Album In The World
Also this week: The Queen pays a visit to Zambia. (27th)

The song of the month for July 1979

Gangsters by The Specials (peak chart position: No.6)

As punk rock subsided, a new multi-racial dance craze from the English Midlands filled the vacuum. The main protagonists were the special septet, the Specials. Coventry's finest hit the ground running when their first release on their own 'Two Tone' record label advanced into the UK Top Ten. The group had previously toured as support for the Clash, so they were familiar with the machinations of Clash manager, Bernie Rhodes. As a result, 'Gangsters' contained the tongue-in-cheek lyrics of "Bernie Rhodes knows; don't argue."

The UK Top 10 singles for the week ending August the 4th

1	Boomtown Rats	I Don't Like Mondays
2	Police	Can't Stand Losing You
3	Dooleys	Wanted
4	Dave Edmunds	Girls Talk
5	Abba	Angel Eyes / Voulez Vous
6	Janet Kay	Silly Games
7	Tubeway Army	Are Friends Electric
8	Knack	My Sharona
9	Supertramp	Breakfast In America
10	Sparks	Beat The Clock

The US Number One single: Donna Summer – Bad Girls

The US Number One album: Donna Summer – Bad Girls

The UK Number One album: Various Artist Compilation – The Best Disco Album In The World

Also this week: The new Cambodian regime accuses Pol Pot of genocide. (30th)

The UK Top 10 singles for the week ending August the 11th

1	Boomtown Rats	I Don't Like Mondays
2	Cliff Richard	We Don't Talk Anymore
3	Abba	Angel Eyes / Voulez Vous
4	Police	Can't Stand Losing You
5	Dooleys	Wanted
6	Ian Dury And The Blockheads	Reasons To Be Cheerful
7	Sham 69	Hersham Boys
8	E.L.O.	The Diary Of Horace Wimp
9	Dave Edmunds	Girls Talk
10	Patrick Hernandez	Born To Be Alive

The US Number One single: Donna Summer – Bad Girls

The US Number One album: The Knack – Get The Knack

The UK Number One album: Various Artist Compilation – The Best Disco Album In The World

Also this week: Ku Klux Klansmen begin a fifty-mile 'white rights' march. (9th)

The UK Top 10 singles for the week ending August the 18th

1	Boomtown Rats	I Don't Like Mondays
2	Cliff Richard	We Don't Talk Anymore
3	Ian Dury And The Blockheads	Reasons To Be Cheerful
4	Earth Wind & Fire	After The Love Has Gone
5	Abba	Angel Eyes / Voulez Vous
6	Sham 69	Hersham Boys
7	Police	Can't Stand Losing You
8	Dooleys	Wanted
9	Darts	Duke Of Earl
10	E.L.O.	The Diary Of Horace Wimp

The US Number One single: Chic – Good Times

The US Number One album: The Knack – Get The Knack

The UK Number One album: Various Artist Compilation – The Best Disco Album In The World

Also this week: Sebastian Coe sets the world record for the 1500 metres. (15th)

The UK Top 10 singles for the week ending August the 25th

1	Cliff Richard	We Don't Talk Anymore
2	Boomtown Rats	I Don't Like Mondays
3	B.A. Robertson	Bang Bang
4	Ian Dury And The Blockheads	Reasons To Be Cheerful
5	Earth Wind & Fire	After The Love Has Gone
6	Darts	Duke Of Earl
7	Sham 69	Hersham Boys
8	Specials	Gangsters
9	Abba	Angel Eyes / Voulez Vous
10	E.L.O.	The Diary Of Horace Wimp

The US Number One single: The Knack – My Sharona

The US Number One album: The Knack – Get The Knack

The UK Number One album: Various Artist Compilation – The Best Disco Album In The World

Also this week: Mass murderer Pol Pot is sentenced to death in absentia. (19th)

The song of the month for August 1979
I Can't Help It by Michael Jackson (album track)

Michael Jackson finally cut off the family umbilical cord to pursue his own musical path and made the best possible start with the Quincy Jones-produced 'Off The Wall'. This album would have been hailed as one of North America's finest long players were it not for the success of its successors, 'Thriller' and 'Bad'. Nevertheless 'Off The Wall' is overflowing with exquisite cuts. The title track and 'She's Out Of My Life' are two such musical wonders, but one of the great hidden jewels of planet pop is Jackson's attempt at Stevie Wonder's 'I Can't Help It'. Michael sings of "like a trip to Heaven" and when you hear the accompanying strings, you know precisely what he means. This is a truly beautiful song from a brilliant singer but odd individual.

The UK Top 10 singles for the week ending September the 1st

1 Cliff Richard | We Don't Talk Anymore
2 Boomtown Rats | I Don't Like Mondays
3 B.A. Robertson | Bang Bang
4 Roxy Music | Angel Eyes
5 Earth Wind & Fire | After The Love Has Gone
6 Specials | Gangsters
7 Darts | Duke Of Earl
8 Flying Lizards | Money
9 Ian Dury And The Blockheads | Reasons To Be Cheerful
10 Gibson Brothers | Ooh What A Life

The US Number One single: The Knack – My Sharona
The US Number One album: The Knack – Get The Knack
The UK Number One album: Various Artist Compilation – The Best Disco Album In The World
Also this week: Fifteen British soldiers are murdered in the Warrenpoint massacre. (27th)

The UK Top 10 singles for the week ending September the 8th

1 Cliff Richard | We Don't Talk Anymore
2 B.A. Robertson | Bang Bang
3 Gary Numan | Cars
4 Roxy Music | Angel Eyes
5 Flying Lizards | Money
6 Specials | Gangsters
7 Crusaders | Street Life
8 Boomtown Rats | I Don't Like Mondays
9 Randy Vanwarmer | Just When I Needed You Most
10 Earth Wind & Fire | After The Love Has Gone

The US Number One single: The Knack – My Sharona
The US Number One album: The Knack – Get The Knack
The UK Number One album: Led Zeppelin – In Through The Out Door
Also this week: IRA bomb victim Lord Mountbatten receives a state funeral. (5th)

The UK Top 10 singles for the week ending September the 15th

1	Cliff Richard	We Don't Talk Anymore
2	Gary Numan	Cars
3	B.A. Robertson	Bang Bang
4	E.L.O.	Don't Bring Me Down
5	Crusaders	Street Life
6	Roxy Music	Angel Eyes
7	Bellamy Brothers	If I Said You Had A Beautiful Body Would You Hold It Against Me
8	Randy Vanwarmer	Just When I Needed You Most
9	Dollar	Love's Gotta Hold On Me
10	Flying Lizards	Money

The US Number One single: The Knack – My Sharona
The US Number One album: Led Zeppelin – In Through The Out Door
The UK Number One album: Led Zeppelin – In Through The Out Door
Also this week: Hurricane Frederick creates havoc in Alabama and Florida. (12th)

The UK Top 10 singles for the week ending September the 22nd

1	Gary Numan	Cars
2	Cliff Richard	We Don't Talk Anymore
3	E.L.O.	Don't Bring Me Down
4	Bellamy Brothers	If I Said You Had A Beautiful Body Would You Hold It Against Me
5	Dollar	Love's Gotta Hold On Me
6	Crusaders	Street Life
7	B.A. Robertson	Bang Bang
8	Police	Message In A Bottle
9	Randy Vanwarmer	Just When I Needed You Most
10	Roxy Music	Angel Eyes

The US Number One single: The Knack – My Sharona
The US Number One album: Led Zeppelin – In Through The Out Door
The UK Number One album: Gary Numan – The Pleasure Principle
Also this week: Two families flee East Germany in a hot air balloon. (16th)

The UK Top 10 singles for the week ending September the 29th

1 Police   Message In A Bottle
2 Gary Numan   Cars
3 Bellamy Brothers   If I Said You Had A Beautiful Body
                             Would You Hold It Against Me
4 Dollar   Love's Gotta Hold On Me
5 E.L.O.   Don't Bring Me Down
6 Cliff Richard   We Don't Talk Anymore
7 Blondie   Dreaming
8 Commodores   Sail On
9 Crusaders   Street Life
10 Frantique   Strut Your Funky Stuff

The US Number One single: The Knack – My Sharona
The US Number One album: Led Zeppelin – In Through The Out Door
The UK Number One album: Boney M –Oceans Of Fantasy
Also this week: The Red Cross launches an aid operation for Cambodia. (26th)

The song of the month for September 1979
Video Killed The Radio Star by Buggles (peak chart position: No.1)

Island Records had been sponsors of a plethora of reggae, rock, and even punk artists who contributed many seminal performances to the charts, but it took the unusual source of Buggles to provide Chris Blackwell's company with their first British Number One. Blackwell was aghast when Trevor Horn explained that he had named his group after his dog. 'Video Killed The Radio Star' wasn't necessarily realised, but MTV cheekily used the video of this great pop song as its first-ever broadcast video. I was always keen on the group's follow-up, 'Plastic Age', but Trevor Horn would later find further fame as the producer of Frankie Goes To Hollywood.

The UK Top 10 singles for the week ending October the 6th

1 Police   Message In A Bottle
2 Blondie   Dreaming
3 Gary Numan   Cars
4 Status Quo   Whatever You Want
5 Bellamy Brothers   If I Said You Had A Beautiful Body
                          Would You Hold It Against Me
6 Buggles   Video Killed The Radio Star
7 Michael Jackson   Don't Stop 'Til You Get Enough
8 Rainbow   Since You've Been Gone
9 Dollar   Love's Gotta Hold On Me
10 E.L.O.   Don't Bring Me Down

The US Number One single: Robert John – Sad Eyes
The US Number One album: Led Zeppelin – In Through The Out Door
The UK Number One album: Gary Numan – The Pleasure Principle
Also this week: On Irish soil, the new Pope pleads for peace. (30th)

The UK Top 10 singles for the week ending October the 13th

1 Police   Message In A Bottle
2 Buggles   Video Killed The Radio Star
3 Blondie   Dreaming
4 Michael Jackson   Don't Stop 'Til You Get Enough
5 Status Quo   Whatever You Want
6 Rainbow   Since You've Been Gone
7 Gary Numan   Cars
8 Bellamy Brothers   If I Said You Had A Beautiful Body
                          Would You Hold It Against Me
9 Lena Martell   One Day At A Time
10 Kate Bush   Live On Stage

The US Number One single: Michael Jackson – Don't Stop 'Til You Get Enough
The US Number One album: Led Zeppelin – In Through The Out Door
The UK Number One album: Blondie – Eat To The Beat TIED WITH The Police –
Regatta De Blanc
Also this week: Jeremy Thorpe states he will not stand for Parliament again. (10th)

The UK Top 10 singles for the week ending October the 20th

1	Buggles	Video Killed The Radio Star
2	Police	Message In A Bottle
3	Michael Jackson	Don't Stop 'Til You Get Enough
4	Blondie	Dreaming
5	Lena Martell	One Day At A Time
6	Sad Cafe	Every Day Hurts
7	Rainbow	Since You've Been Gone
8	Status Quo	Whatever You Want
9	Dr. Hook	When You're In Love With A Beautiful Woman
10	Dooleys	Chosen Few

The US Number One single: Herb Alpert – Rise
The US Number One album: Led Zeppelin – In Through The Out Door
The UK Number One album: The Police – Regatta De Blanc
Also this week: Guerrilla leaders accept Britain's Rhodesian charter. (18th)

The UK Top 10 singles for the week ending October the 27th

1	Lena Martell	One Day At A Time
2	Buggles	Video Killed The Radio Star
3	Dr. Hook	When You're In Love With A Beautiful Woman
4	Michael Jackson	Don't Stop 'Til You Get Enough
5	Sad Cafe	Every Day Hurts
6	Abba	Gimme Gimme Gimme
7	Dooleys	Chosen Few
8	Police	Message In A Bottle
9	Fleetwood Mac	Tusk
10	Blondie	Dreaming

The US Number One single: Herb Alpert – Rise
The US Number One album: Led Zeppelin – In Through The Out Door
The UK Number One album: The Police – Regatta De Blanc
Also this week: South Korea's President Park Chung Hee is 'accidentally' shot dead. (26th)

The song of the month for October 1979

On My Radio by The Selecter (peak chart position: No.8)

The Selecter had enjoyed a previous outing when their self-titled instrumental comprised the flip side of the spongy ska of 'Gangsters' by their stable mates, the Specials. This time around the group released their own single, complete with Pauline Black's lead vocals. 'On My Radio' wailed about the same old songs on the airwaves, but here was a new treat for the youth generation to feast themselves on. The Selecter never really built on the success of this fine debut, and by 1981 they were going their separate ways.

The UK Top 10 singles for the week ending November the 3rd

1	Lena Martell	One Day At A Time
2	Dr. Hook	When You're In Love With A Beautiful Woman
3	Sad Cafe	Everyday Hurts
4	Abba	Gimme Gimme Gimme
5	Buggles	Video Killed The Radio Star
6	Michael Jackson	Don't Stop 'Til You Get Enough
7	Dooleys	Chosen Few
8	Fleetwood Mac	Tusk
9	Viola Wills	Gonna Get Along Without You Now
10	Queen	Crazy Little Thing Called Love

The US Number One single: M – Pop Muzik

The US Number One album: Eagles – The Long Run

The UK Number One album: The Police – Regatta De Blanc

Also this week: Chinese leader, Hua Kuo-feng, pays a visit to Britain. (28th)

The UK Top 10 singles for the week ending November the 10th

1	Lena Martell	One Day At A Time
2	Dr. Hook	When You're In Love With A Beautiful Woman
3	Abba	Gimme Gimme Gimme
4	Sad Cafe	Everyday Hurts
5	Queen	Crazy Little Thing Called Love
6	Fleetwood Mac	Tusk
7	Jam	Eton Rifles
8	Viola Wills	Gonna Get Along Without You Now
9	Selecter	On My Radio
10	Commodores	Still

The US Number One single: Eagles – Heartache Tonight
The US Number One album: Eagles – The Long Run
The UK Number One album: Fleetwood Mac – Tusk
Also this week: Hostages are seized from the American Embassy in Tehran. (4th)

The UK Top 10 singles for the week ending November the 17th

1	Dr. Hook	When You're In Love With A Beautiful Woman
2	Lena Martell	One Day At A Time
3	Queen	Crazy Little Thing Called Love
4	Jam	Eton Rifles
5	Commodores	Still
6	Abba	Gimme Gimme Gimme
7	Sad Cafe	Everyday Hurts
8	Selecter	On My Radio
9	Fleetwood Mac	Tusk
10	Specials	Message To You Rudy

The US Number One single: Commodores – Still
The US Number One album: Eagles – The Long Run
The UK Number One album: Abba – Greatest Hits, Volume 2
Also this week: Ayatollah Khomeini orders the release of all female hostages. (17th)

The UK Top 10 singles for the week ending November the 24th

1	Dr. Hook	When You're In Love With A Beautiful Woman
2	Queen	Crazy Little Thing Called Love
3	Jam	Eton Rifles
4	Commodores	Still
5	Lena Martell	One Day At A Time
6	Donna Summer & Barbra Streisand	No More Tears (Enough Is Enough)
7	Abba	Gimme Gimme Gimme
8	B.A. Robertson	Knocked It Off
9	Kool And The Gang	Ladies Night
10	Madness	One Step Beyond

The US Number One single: Donna Summer & Barbra Streisand – No More Tears (Enough Is Enough)

The US Number One album: Eagles – The Long Run

The UK Number One album: Abba – Greatest Hits, Volume 2

Also this week: A mob attempts to storm the American Embassy in Islamabad. (21st)

The song of the month for November 1979

One Step Beyond by Madness (peak chart position: No.7)

Madness had previously dipped their toes in the Top Twenty with 'The Prince' which was a tribute to the Jamaican ska legend, Prince Buster. This time around the crazy north Londoners thrilled all and sundry with their 'One Step Beyond' instrumental. The recording was dominated by the saxophone of Lee Thompson, while the accompanying video displays the choreography of the nutty dance. Carl Smyth (then called Chas Smash) introduces the song and its "heavy heavy monster sound." Here was a new group on the brink of fame.

The UK Top 10 singles for the week ending December the 1st

1	Dr. Hook	When You're In Love With A Beautiful Woman
2	Queen	Crazy Little Thing Called Love
3	Donna Summer & Barbra Streisand	No More Tears (Enough Is Enough)
4	Commodores	Still
5	Police	Walking On The Moon
6	Gary Numan	Complex
7	Madness	One Step Beyond
8	E.L.O.	Confusion/Last Train To London
9	Jam	Eton Rifles
10	B.A. Robertson	Knocked It Off

The US Number One single: Donna Summer & Barbra Streisand – No More Tears (Enough Is Enough)

The US Number One album: Eagles – The Long Run

The UK Number One album: Abba – Greatest Hits, Volume 2

Also this week: Mrs Thatcher demands a rebate at a European summit meeting. (30th)

The UK Top 10 singles for the week ending December the 8th

1	Police	Walking On The Moon
2	Pink Floyd	Another Brick In The Wall
3	Donna Summer & Barbra Streisand	No More Tears (Enough Is Enough)
4	Dr. Hook	When You're In Love With A Beautiful Woman
5	Gibson Brothers	Que Sera Mi Vida
6	Tourists	I Only Want To Be With You
7	Queen	Crazy Little Thing Called Love
8	Gary Numan	Complex
9	E.L.O.	Confusion/Last Train To London
10	Madness	One Step Beyond

The US Number One single: Styx – Babe

The US Number One album: Eagles – The Long Run

The UK Number One album: Rod Stewart – Rod Stewart – Greatest Hits, Vol.1

Also this week: Charles Haughey succeeds Jack Lynch as the new Irish Taoiseach. (7th)

The UK Top 10 singles for the week ending December the 15th

1 Pink Floyd   Another Brick In The Wall
2 Police   Walking On The Moon
3 Sugarhill Gang   Rappers Delight
4 Tourists   I Only Want To Be With You
5 Donna Summer &
   Barbra Streisand   No More Tears (Enough Is Enough)
6 Gibson Brothers   Que Sera Mi Vida
7 Michael Jackson   Off The Wall
8 Dr. Hook   When You're In Love With A Beautiful Woman
9 Madness   One Step Beyond
10 Three Degrees   My Simple Heart

The US Number One single: Styx – Babe
The US Number One album: Eagles – The Long Run
The UK Number One album: Rod Stewart – Rod Stewart – Greatest Hits, Vol.1
Also this week: Mother Teresa accepts the Nobel Peace Prize in Oslo. (10th)

The UK Top 10 singles for the week ending December the 22nd

1 Pink Floyd   Another Brick In The Wall
2 Abba   I Have A Dream
3 Police   Walking On The Moon
4 Fiddlers Dram   Day Trip To Bangor
5 Tourists   I Only Want To Be With You
6 Sugarhill Gang   Rappers Delight
7 Paul McCartney   Wonderful Christmas Time
8 Gibson Brothers   Que Sera Mi Vida
9 Three Degrees   My Simple Heart
10 Pretenders   Brass In Pocket

The US Number One single: Rupert Holmes – Escape (The Pina Colada Song)
The US Number One album: Eagles – The Long Run
The UK Number One album: Rod Stewart – Rod Stewart – Greatest Hits, Vol.1
Also this week: Australia defeat England in a (non-Ashes) Perth test match. (19th)

The UK Top 10 singles for the week ending December the 29th

1 Pink Floyd — Another Brick In The Wall
2 Abba — I Have A Dream
3 Police — Walking On The Moon
4 Fiddlers Dram — Day Trip To Bangor
5 Tourists — I Only Want To Be With You
6 Sugarhill Gang — Rappers Delight
7 Paul McCartney — Wonderful Christmas Time
8 Gibson Brothers — Que Sera Mi Vida
9 Three Degrees — My Simple Heart
10 Pretenders — Brass In Pocket

The US Number One single: Rupert Holmes – Escape (The Pina Colada Song)
The US Number One album: Eagles – The Long Run
The UK Number One album: Rod Stewart – Rod Stewart – Greatest Hits, Vol.1
Also this week: The Soviet Union begins an invasion of Afganistan. (24th)

The song of the month for December 1979
Sara by Fleetwood Mac (peak chart position: No.37)

Sara only just sneaked into the British Top 75 at the end of December but this was the highlight of Fleetwood Mac's latest LP, the ambitious double album, 'Tusk'. The great Stevie Nicks takes time out from her extra-curricular cocaine consumption to sing of "Drowning in the sea of love/Where everyone would love to drown." Gosh, drowning has never seemed so attractive. Mick Fleetwood weighs in with a tremendous rhythm while the backing harmonies only add to the majesty of this track. Here is one song that merits the word 'classic'.

Listed Below are the Top 10 Best Selling UK Singles of 1979

1	Bright Eyes	Art Garfunkel
2	Heart Of Glass	Blondie
3	We Don't Talk Anymore	Cliff Richard
4	I Don't Like Mondays	The Boomtown Rats
5	When You're In Love With A Beautiful Woman	Dr. Hook
6	I Will Survive	Gloria Gaynor
7	Are Friends Electric	Tubeway Army
8	Sunday Girl	Blondie
9	Dance Away	Roxy Music
10	One Day At A Time	Lena Martell

1979's CONCERTS OF THE YEAR

Led Zeppelin made their first UK appearance in four years when they performed at the Knebworth music festival in August. It would be the last outings of the original four on their native soil. Meanwhile, a new stable of artists from the west Midlands and London were instigating a new dance craze, as the Specials, the Selecter, the Beat, and Madness were prompting youngsters to get rather dizzy from the sounds of ska. Another new outfit, the Pretenders, took to the road, with another combo, entitled UB40, acting as their support. The Clash too were up close and personal with concert-goers throughout the UK. Then, at the end of December, as a turbulent decade drew to a close, the likes of the Clash, the Pretenders, and the Specials joined three Zeppelins for a series of concerts at the Hammersmith Odeon to raise funds for the people of war-torn Kampuchea. The performances were dominated by characteristically show-stopping efforts from the Who and Queen. Rockpile and Wings weighed in with their contributions, while Paul McCartney assembled a hugely impressive Rockestra, consisting of some of the best musicians in the business. The Rockestra concept was almost certainly Band Aid ahead of its time. It was a noble means of bringing the curtain down on the 1970s, though it would not be long before Macca was back in the news headlines, but for all the wrong reasons.

1979's ALBUM OF THE YEAR

Eat To The Beat by Blondie
(released in October; reached No.1 in the UK)

Side One:

1. Dreaming; 3:08
2. The Hardest Part; 3:42
3. Union City Blue; 3:21
4. Shayla; 3:57
5. Eat to the Beat; 2:40
6. Accidents Never Happen; 4:15

Side Two:

1. Die Young, Stay Pretty; 3:34
2. Slow Motion; 3:28
3. Atomic; 4:40
4. Sound-A-Sleep; 4:18
5. Victor; 3:19
6. Living in the Real World; 2:53

'Eat To The Beat' boasted the world's first accompanying video cassette. It also had the peculiar distinction of sharing the Number One position in the UK chart for one week with the Police. Above all, this was arguably Blondie's best record, better even than 'Parallel Lines'. The record ranged in style from the reggae of 'Die Young Stay Pretty' to the punk of 'Living In The Real World', from the mellow 'Sound Asleep' to the loud 'Victor'. The most recognisable tracks were the hugely popular 'Atomic' (a subsequent UK chart-topper) and 'Dreaming', as well as the excellent 'Union City Blue' which mysteriously failed to reach the British Top Ten. Also worthy of respect are 'Shayla', 'The Hardest Part', and the outstanding 'Slow Motion'. Any one of the latter three could have excelled itself in the singles listings. After this impressive offering, it is rather hard to believe that Deborah Harry and the gang would run out of gas two albums later.

SPORT IN 1979

English Division One football champions: Liverpool; runners-up: Nottingham Forest

English FA Cup final: Arsenal 3 Manchester United 2

English League Cup Final: Nottingham Forest 3 Southampton 2

Scottish Division One football champions: Glasgow Celtic; runners-up: Glasgow Rangers

Scottish FA Cup final: Glasgow Rangers 3 Hibernian 2 (in a replay)

Scottish League Cup final: Glasgow Rangers 2 Aberdeen 1

Irish League football champions: Linfield; Irish Cup final: Cliftonville 3 Portadown 2

League Of Ireland football champions: Dundalk; cup winners: Dundalk

European Cup final: Nottingham Forest 1 Malmo 0

European Cup-Winners' Cup final: Barcelona 4 Fortuna Dusseldorf 3 (after extra time)

UEFA Cup final: Borussia Moenchengladbach beat Red Star Belgrade 2–1 on aggregate

English county cricket champions: Essex

Five Nations' rugby union champions: Wales (six points); runners-up: France

Formula One world drivers' champion: Jody Scheckter (South Africa) in a Ferrari car

Gaelic football All-Ireland champions: Kerry; runners-up: Dublin

British Open golf champion: Severiano Ballesteros (at Royal Lytham & St Annes)

US Masters golf champion: Fuzzy Zoeller

US Open golf champion: Hale Irwin

USPGA golf champion: David Graham

Rugby league Challenge Cup final: Widnes 12 Wakefield Trinity 3

Wimbledon men's singles tennis final: B Borg beat R Tanner 6–7, 6–1, 3–6, 6–3, 6–4

Wimbledon ladies' singles tennis final: M Navratilova beat C Evert-Lloyd 6–4 6–4

World snooker final: Terry Griffiths (Wales) beat Dennis Taylor (Northern Ireland) 24–16

The Aintree Grand National steeplechase winner: Rubstic; price 25–1

The Epsom Derby winner: Troy; jockey – Willie Carson; price 6–1

The Ryder Cup golf contest: United States 17 Europe 11

1979's DEATHS

January 13th: Donny Hathaway (US singer), aged 33

January 26th: Nelson Rockefeller (ex-US Vice-President), aged 70

February 2nd: 'Sid Vicious' (British musician), aged 21

February 12th: Jean Renoir (French film director), aged 84

March 19th: Richard Beckinsale (Britsh actor), aged 31

March 30th: Airey Middleton Sheffield Neave (British politician), aged 63

April 4th: Zulfikar Ali Bhutto (ex-Pakistani Prime Minister), aged 51

April 24th: Clement Blair Peach (British political activist), aged 33

May 29th: Mary Pickford (Canadian actress), aged 86

June 11th: John Wayne (US actor), aged 72

June 29th: Lowell Thomas George (US musician), aged 34

July 6th: Van Allen Clinton McCoy (US musician), aged 39

July 12th: Minnie Julia Riperton (US singer), aged 31

July 29th: Herbert Marcuse (German philosopher), aged 81

August 16th: John George Diefenbaker (ex-Canadian Prime Minister), aged 83

August 27th: Earl Louis Mountbatten of Burma (British statesman), aged 79

September 8th: Jean Seberg (US actress), aged 40

September 27th: Dame Gracie Fields (British actress), aged 81

September 27th: Jimmy McCulloch (British musician), aged 26

October 30th: Sir Barnes Neville Wallis (British air engineer), aged 92

APPENDIX I
CRIMINALLY OVERLOOKED?

Here follows thirty 'seventies classic tunes which mysteriously fail to get enough recognition in this volume ... until now!

Kentucky Rain by Elvis Presley (1970)
Band Of Gold by Freda Payne (1970)
Woodstock by Matthews' Southern Comfort (1970)
What's Happening Brother by Marvin Gaye (1971)
Coz I Luv You by Slade (1971)
Black Dog by Led Zeppelin (1971)
Son Of My Father by Chicory Tip (1972)
Join Together by The Who (1972)
Automatically Sunshine by The Supremes (1972)
Also Sprach Zarathustra by Deodato (1973)
The Boston Rag by Steely Dan (1973)
Caroline by Status Quo (1973)
When Will I See You Again by The Three Degrees (1974)
Gonna Make You A Star by David Essex (1974)
You're The First, The Last, My Everything by Barry White (1974)
If by Telly Savalas (1975)
Pick Up The Pieces by The Average White Band (1975)
Hurt So Good by Susan Cadogan (1975)
December '63 (Oh What A Night) by The Four Seasons (1976)
Mississippi by Pussycat (1976)
Why Must I Cry by Peter Tosh (1976)
Show You The Way To Go by The Jacksons (1977)
Ma Baker by Boney M (1977)
Float On by The Floaters (1977)
What A Waste by Ian Dury And The Blockheads (1978)
Public Image by Public Image Limited (1978)
September by Earth, Wind And Fire (1978)
Living On The Front Line by Eddy Grant (1979)
Kid by The Pretenders (1979)
Reggae For It Now by Bill Lovelady (1979)

APPENDIX II
MORE CLASSIC ALBUMS

Here follows 25 more classic albums which are widely considered to be among the best LPs of the decade:

Bridge Over Troubled Water by Simon And Garfunkel (1970)
After The Goldrush by Neil Young (1970)
Let It Be by The Beatles (1970)
Four Symbols by Led Zeppelin (1971)
L.A. Woman by The Doors (1971)
Tapestry by Carole King (1971)
What's Going On? by Marvin Gaye (1971)
Exile On Main St. by The Rolling Stones (1972)
The Rise And Fall Of Ziggy Stardust And The Spiders From Mars by David Bowie (1972)
Transformer by Lou Reed (1972)
Band On The Run by Wings (1973)
Countdown To Ecstacy by Steely Dan (1973)
The Dark Side Of The Moon by Pink Floyd (1973)
Tubular Bells by Mike Oldfield (1973)
A Night At The Opera by Queen (1975)
Rastaman Vibration by Bob Marley And The Wailers (1976)
Bat Out Of Hell by Meat Loaf (1977)
Never Mind The Bollocks by The Sex Pistols (1977)
Oxygene by Jean-Michel Jarre (1977)
Plastic Letters by Blondie (1978)
London Calling by The Clash (1979)
Off The Wall by Michael Jackson (1979)
One Step Beyond by Madness (1979)
Specials by The Specials (1979)
Unknown Pleasures by Joy Division (1979)

APPENDIX III
THE OSCAR WINNERS IN THE 1970s

1970: BEST PICTURE – Patton (directed by Franklin Schaffner)

1970: BEST ACTOR – George C. Scott (Patton)

1970: BEST ACTRESS – Glenda Jackson (Women In Love)

1971: BEST PICTURE – The French Connection (directed by William Friedkin)

1971: BEST ACTOR – Gene Hackman (The French Connection)

1971: BEST ACTRESS – Jane Fonda (Klute)

1972: BEST PICTURE – The Godfather (directed by Francis Ford Coppola)

1972: BEST ACTOR – Marlon Brando (The Godfather)

1972: BEST ACTRESS – Liza Minnelli (Cabaret)

1973: BEST PICTURE – The Sting (directed by George Roy Hill)

1973: BEST ACTOR – Jack Lemmon (Save The Tiger)

1973: BEST ACTRESS – Glenda Jackson (A Touch Of Class)

1974: BEST PICTURE – The Godfather, Part II (directed by Francis Ford Coppola)

1974: BEST ACTOR – Art Carney (Harry And Tonto)

1974: BEST ACTRESS – Ellen Burstyn (Alice Doesn't Live Here Anymore)

1975: BEST PICTURE – One Flew Over The Cuckoo's Nest (directed by Milos Forman)

1975: BEST ACTOR – Jack Nicholson (One Flew Over The Cuckoo's Nest)

1975: BEST ACTRESS – Louise Fletcher (One Flew Over The Cuckoo's Nest)

1976: BEST PICTURE – Rocky (directed by John G. Avildsen)

1976: BEST ACTOR – Peter Finch (Network)

1976: BEST ACTRESS – Faye Dunaway (Network)

1977: BEST PICTURE – Annie Hall (directed by Woody Allen)

1977: BEST ACTOR – Richard Dreyfuss (The Goodbye Girl)

1977: BEST ACTRESS – Diane Keaton (Annie Hall)

1978: BEST PICTURE – The Deer Hunter (directed by Michael Cimino)

1978: BEST ACTOR – Jon Voight (Coming Home)

1978: BEST ACTRESS – Jane Fonda (Coming Home)

1979: BEST PICTURE – Kramer vs. Kramer (directed by Robert Benton)

1979: BEST ACTOR – Dustin Hoffman (Kramer vs. Kramer)

1979: BEST ACTRESS – Sally Field (Norma Rae)

APPENDIX IV – THE TOP 10 BEST SELLING UK SINGLES OF THE 1970s

No.	Year	SONG TITLE	ARTIST
1	1977	Mull Of Kintyre	Wings
2	1978	Rivers Of Babylon / Brown Girl In The Ring	Boney M
3	1978	You're The One That I Want	John Travolta & Olivia Newton John
4	1978	Mary's Boy Child – Oh My Lord	Boney M
5	1978	Summer Nights	John Travolta & Olivia Newton John
6	1978	Y.M.C.A	Village People
7	1975	Bohemian Rhapsody	Queen
8	1979	Heart Of Glass	Blondie
9	1976	Don't Give Up On Us	David Soul
10	1973	Merry Xmas Everybody	Slade

APPENDIX V – THE EUROVISION SONG CONTESTS OF THE 1970s

1970: Winner – Dana (of Ireland); runner-up – United Kingdom; venue – Amsterdam

1971: Winner – Severine (of Monaco); runner-up – Spain; venue – Dublin

1972: Winner – Vicky Leandros (of Luxembourg); runner-up – United Kingdom; venue – Edinburgh

1973: Winner – Anne-Marie David (of Luxembourg); runner-up – Spain; venue – Luxembourg

1974: Winner – Abba (of Sweden); runner-up – Italy; venue – Brighton

1975: Winner – Teach-in (of the Netherlands); runner-up – United Kingdom; venue – Stockholm

1976: Winner – Brotherhood Of Man (of United Kingdom); runner-up – France; venue – The Hague

1977: Winner – Marie Myriam (of France); runner-up – United Kingdom; venue – London

1978: Winner – Izhar Cohen & Alphabeta (of Israel); runner-up – Belgium; venue – Paris

1979: Winner – Gali Atari & Milk And Honey (of Israel); runner-up – Spain; venue – Jerusalem

APPENDIX VI: HERE FOLLOWS SEVERAL SEVENTIES' SUDOKUS!

1. ALBUMS OF THE 1970s

Can you solve the puzzle and name the performers of these classic albums?

Harvest; Imagine; Kaya; Lionheart; Low; Meddle; Rumours; Tapestry; Transformer

Low				Meddle				Kaya
			Low		Harvest			
Tapestry			Lionheart	Imagine	Kaya	Low		Rumours
	Meddle			Low			Imagine	
		Imagine		Harvest		Tapestry		
	Transformer			Rumours			Meddle	
Imagine		r	Harvest	Kaya	Tapestry			Meddle
			Rumours		Low			
Kaya				Lionheart				Tapestry

2. THE GREAT GIG IN THE SKY

The listed rock and pop performers all died in the 1970s. Where are they on the grid?

Allman; Bolan; Denny; Drake; Hendrix; Joplin; Morrison; Parsons; Presley

		Presley		Hendrix		Allman		
	Hendrix		Parsons		Allman		Bolan	
Morrison		Allman						Presley
	Drake		Morrison		Bolan		Parsons	
	Bolan		Hendrix		Presley		Drake	
Allman					Bolan			Denny
	Joplin		Allman		Drake		Presley	
		Parsons		Bolan		Drake		

3. FLEETWOOD MAC PERSONNEL

The following 9 members contributed to Fleetwood Mac's rock journey in the 1970s:
Buckingham; Fleetwood; Green; Kirwan; McVie; Nicks; Perfect; Spencer; Welch

Spencer		McVie						Buckingham
	Welch	Nicks	Buckingham		Green	Kirwan		
Buckingham			Perfect					McVie
				Spencer				Nicks
	Nicks			Welch				Fleetwood
		Kirwan	Green	Perfect				
						Perfect		
Welch	McVie	Perfect	Kirwan	Nicks				

4. POP AND ROCK GROUPS OF THE 1970s

Arrange the following pop and rock acts from the 1970s into the grid:
Ace; Boston; Buggles; Chic; Chicago; Genesis; Racey; Slik; Wizzard

	Ace						Chicago	
		Genesis				Chic		
Racey			Chicago		Chic			Boston
		Buggles			Chicago	Racey	Genesis	
Genesis			Buggles		Ace			Wizzard
	Wizzard	Ace	Genesis			Chicago		
Slik			Ace		Genesis			Buggles
		Chicago				Boston		
	Chic						Slik	

5. THE SPECIALS

Listed are the nine Specials who contributed to their debut album of 1979:
Dick; Horace; Jerry; John; Lynval; Neville; Rico; Roddy; Terry

Horace			John		Rico	Jerry		Lynval
		Jerry	Roddy	Dick		Neville	Horace	
Roddy				Jerry	Lynval			
						Dick		Rico
		Horace	Dick				Lynval	Neville
Rico	Jerry					Terry		
Terry				John				Jerry
	John	Roddy	Rico				Neville	
						John		

6. SONGS WITH A NAME AS THE TITLE

Don't just re-arrange the following song titles. Name the performers!
Angie; Ben; Clair; Daniel; Donna; Lucille; Sally; Sam; Sandy

Angie	Donna							Daniel
Sally	Sam			Angie		Sandy		Lucille
			Sally				Angie	Sam
Sam	Sandy	Sally	Daniel			Clair	Ben	
		Daniel						Sandy
				Ben	Sandy	Sally		
Sandy				Daniel				
	Lucille		Angie			Sam		
		Clair		Lucille				

7. US CHART-TOPPERS IN THE 1970s

Arrange the following Billboard Number One hit singles into the grid:
Babe; Dreams; Fame; Fire; Grease; Mandy; Rise; Still; Venus

Mandy	Rise					Venus		
Fame		Venus		Dreams	Grease	Mandy		
				Still		Grease		
Babe				Venus			Grease	Mandy
Rise			Still		Dreams		Fire	
		Dreams		Fire			Still	
			Dreams		Venus			
	Grease	Fame	Fire			Babe		
						Still	Mandy	

8. RADIO ONE DISC JOCKEYS OF THE 1970s

Can you sort the listed classic disc jockeys of bygone times into the grid?
Bates; Blackburn; Freeman; Jensen; Peel; Powell; Saville; Travis; Wright

	Jensen			Bates		Powell		
			Peel			Blackburn		Travis
	Powell	Travis			Wright	Saville	Freeman	
Powell	Wright			Freeman	Jensen	Peel		
	Blackburn	Freeman	Bates		Peel	Jensen		
Bates				Saville				
			Jensen	Peel	Freeman			
				Travis		Freeman		
	Saville				Bates		Powell	Jensen

9. THE UNLUCKY UK NUMBER 2 HIT SINGLES

Don't just re-arrange the song titles, but name the artists!
Albatross; Denis; Lola; Misty; Patches; Question; Rasputin; Substitute; Till

				Denis				
Misty	Rasputin			Till	Question		Lola	
		Till	Patches			Albatross	Misty	
	Albatross	Denis		Lola				
Till								
Patches	Lola						Till	
	Question	Misty						
Rasputin	Substitute			Albatross	Till	Denis	Question	
Denis		Albatross	Lola				Substitute	

10. MOVIES OF THE 'SEVENTIES

Can you sort the following films into their correct positions?
Carrie; Equus; Hedda; Jaws; Julia; Lenny; Shampoo; Sleuth; Tommy

				Shampoo				Julia
Equus								
Lenny		Sleuth		Julia		Tommy		Carrie
Tommy	Lenny		Equus				Jaws	Shampoo
		Hedda				Equus		
Carrie	Jaws				Shampoo		Sleuth	Lenny
Hedda		Shampoo		Jaws		Carrie		Equus
								Jaws
Julia				Hedda				

ALSO AVAILABLE (FOR YOUR PLEASURE)

A Concise Guide to Eighties' Music
by Karl Vorderman
(courtesy of Parkbench Publications)

This fact-filled well of information contains songs from such acts as Madonna/the Smiths/Michael Jackson/UB40/Madness/the Pet Shop Boys/Queen/ the Specials/George Michael/David Bowie/Debbie Harry/Duran Duran/the Housemartins/Cyndi Lauper/Bob Marley And The Wailers/New Order/the Pogues/the Pretenders/Public Image Limited/Roxy Music/the Stone Roses/the Stranglers/Paul Young, and lots more!

Also available: *The Song For Today* by Jimmie Oliver (£9.99), a unique reference book which features a different song for each day of the year.

Also available: *That Was The Decade That Was* by Arthur TS Jackson (£9.99), which covers all the major news stories throughout the 'swinging sixties'.

Finally, if you have got a book in you, then feel free to send a sample or your idea to Parkbench Publications, PO Box 1081, Belfast, BT1 9EP. Alternatively, email parkbench@fsmail.net